Voices in the Book of Mormon

Discovering Distinctive Witnesses of Jesus Christ

John Hilton III

**Religious Studies Center
Brigham Young University**

In loving memory of my grandfather John Levi Hilton,
a pioneer in the study of unique Book of Mormon voices,
and my Opa John.

Published by the Religious Studies Center, Brigham Young University, Provo, Utah, in cooperation with Deseret Book Company, Salt Lake City, Utah. Visit us at rsc.byu.edu.

DESERET BOOK is a registered trademark of Deseret Book Company. Visit us at DeseretBook.com.

Cover design and interior layout by Alex Socarras.

ISBN: 978-1-9503-0449-3

Library of Congress Cataloging-in-Publication Data

Names: Hilton, John, III, author.
Title: Voices in the Book of Mormon / John L. Hilton III.
Description: Provo, Utah : Religious Studies Center, Brigham Young
   University ; Salt Lake City, Utah : Deseret Book, [2024] | Includes
   index. | Summary: "In the Book of Mormon, we hear the voices of many
   individuals. Nephi speaks, Laman and Lemuel complain, Abinadi preaches,
   Korihor mocks, Alma exhorts, and Giddianhi threatens. Altogether, 150
   different individuals are portrayed as speaking in the Book of Mormon.
   These are real people with important lessons to teach. Identifying their
   voices can provide new perspectives on the Book of Mormon. This book
   explores the insights that can be gained from examining these
   distinctive voices. Studying these unique voices of the past can lend
   great meaning to our lives today"-- Provided by publisher.
Identifiers: LCCN 2023033877 | ISBN 9781950304493 (hardcover)
Subjects: LCSH: Church of Jesus Christ of Latter-day Saints--Doctrines. |
   Book of Mormon--Criticism, Textual. | Latter Day Saint
   churches--Doctrines.
Classification: LCC BX8627 .H526 2024 | DDC 230/.9332--dc23/eng/20230928
LC record available at https://lccn.loc.gov/2023033877

Contents

Acknowledgments vii

Introduction ix

Part 1: Unique Voices

1. Voices in the Book of Mormon 3

2. Jacob: Tender and Stern 25

3. Alma and the Plan of Redemption 41

4. Abinadi and Nephi$_2$: Two Contrasting Voices 63

5. The Savior's Voice in the Book of Mormon 83

Part 2: Voices in Harmony

6. Intertextuality in the Book of Mormon 105

7. Jacob's Textual Legacy 131

8. There Was More Than One:
    Abinadi's Influence on the Book of Mormon 151

9. Turning to Prophets: Similarities in the Words
    of Abinadi and Alma's Counsel to Corianton 171

10. Fathers and Sons: Textual Connections
    between 2 Nephi 2 and Alma 42 189

Contents

11. Samuel's Nephite Sources 205

12. "Expound[ing] All the Scriptures in One":
Christ's Use of Nephi's Words 227

Conclusion 247

Appendix A: Alphabetized List of Speakers 251

Appendix B: List of Speakers in Order of Appearance 255

Appendix C: Speakers Organized from the Greatest
to Least Amount of Words 259

Appendix D (Digital): Speaker Chronology 263

Index 265

About the Author 275

Acknowledgments

This book has been more than a decade in the making, and I'm grateful to everyone who has helped along the way. My wife, Lani, has offered insight into most aspects of this project, as have my parents, Lee and Shawna Hilton. My son Joseph, who made an important textual discovery at the age of eleven, also deserves credit for motivating me to move forward with this publication.

I'm deeply indebted to my colleagues who helped initiate and create the Voices in the Book of Mormon Database: Randal Wright, Shon Hopkin, Jennifer Brinkerhoff Platt, and Jana Johnson. Others, including Nicholas Frederick, Grant and Heather Hardy, Paul Hoskisson, Dave LeFevre, Benjamin McGuire, Noel Reynolds, Avram Shannon, Joseph Spencer, Jenny Webb, John Welch, and Lynne Wilson, have generously offered feedback on various parts of this manuscript. Special recognition is due to Michelle Wilson, who edited the entire book and offered many suggestions that significantly strengthened it. Several research assistants, including Alyssa Aramaki, Matthew Critchley, Sunny Hendry Hafen, Jaron Hansen, Dana Knudsen, Jaclyn Nielson, and Lily Skinner, have also made valuable contributions.

Acknowledgments

I'm very grateful to Monte Shelley, Jason Dzubak, and Jesse Vincent for their technical expertise with WordCruncher. Without their unique capabilities, this book would not exist.

Finally, I'm grateful for the capable people at Brigham Young University's Religious Studies Center who have made this book possible: Jared Ludlow, Leigh Ann Copas, Brent Nordgren, Julie Newman, Alex Socarras, Don Brugger, and Adi Marshall. I also appreciate the helpful suggestions of anonymous peer reviewers.

Introduction

In the Book of Mormon we hear the voices of many people. Nephi speaks, Laman and Lemuel complain, Jacob quotes Zenos, Korihor mocks, Alma exhorts, and Giddianhi threatens. Altogether, 149 different individuals or groups are portrayed as speaking in the Book of Mormon. These include the voices of God the Father and Jesus Christ, angels and prophets, wives and mothers, anti-Christs and missionaries, and many others.[1]

These are real people with important lessons to teach. Identifying their voices can provide new perspectives on the Book of Mormon. What insights might we gain from examining their distinctive voices? What meaning can studying unique voices of the past lend to our lives today?

I am excited to explore these questions with you. In this book we will carefully examine some of the unique voices in the Book of Mormon through two approaches: first, a study of select individual voices; and second, an analysis of how later Book of Mormon speakers draw on the voices of their predecessors.

---

1   See the appendixes for a detailed list of these voices.

Part 1: Unique Voices

Because the Book of Mormon contains writings from different people, unique writing styles should be found within its pages.[2] In part 1 I will highlight some of the distinctive voices that are heard throughout its pages. The first chapter provides an overview of identifying voices in the Book of Mormon and discusses how distinguishing between these voices can deepen our understanding of this sacred text. In the following four chapters, I discuss five individual voices: Jacob, Alma, Abinadi, Nephi$_2$ (the son of Helaman),[3] and Jesus Christ.[4] Examining their individual voices not only illustrates the complexity of the Book of Mormon but also illuminates spiritual insights uniquely emphasized by these speakers.

Part 2: Voices in Harmony

In part 2 I explore how later individuals in the Book of Mormon harmonize their voices with those of earlier Book of Mormon speakers by utilizing their unique words and phrases. After an overview of intertextuality in chapter 6, the following six chapters provide extended examples of textual connections within the Book of Mormon. I show how later Book of Mormon prophets use both Jacob's and Abinadi's words in their teachings, including the surprising connections between Abinadi and King Benjamin. We will see how Alma uses words from both Lehi and Abinadi as he counsels his son Corianton. Finally, we will discuss unique ways in which Samuel the

---

2   This assumes that unique voices can be detected after the processes of redaction and translation. This will be discussed further in chapter 1.

3   When possible, I avoid subscripts when naming Book of Mormon people to maintain simplicity. In this volume I use "Nephi" to refer to the son of Lehi, "Alma" to refer to the son of Alma$_1$ (Alma the Elder), and "Moroni" to refer to the son of Mormon. For clarity when introducing new figures whose names are shared by others, and in mixed contexts and tabular matter, I use subscripts.

4   Other key voices I could have examined include Nephi, Mormon, and Moroni. But since Grant Hardy has already extensively analyzed their unique voices, I have focused on other speakers in this volume. See Grant Hardy, *Understanding the Book of Mormon: A Reader's Guide* (New York: Oxford University Press, 2010).

Lamanite quotes from Nephite prophets in his sermon atop a wall and examine the Savior's use of Nephi's words.

Therefore, What?

Elder Jeffrey R. Holland remarked that President Boyd K. Packer would often say, after hearing a presentation, "Therefore, what?"[5] The implication was that while the presentation might introduce interesting details or facts, the questions "Why does this matter?" and "What should we do as a result?" remained.[6] Thus I want to pause now, and at the end of each chapter, to consider how this information might be relevant in our lives.

Collectively, the chapters in this book illustrate the textual complexity of the Book of Mormon, adding evidence that it was not the product of Joseph Smith. But perhaps more importantly, these chapters add another layer of insight into our understanding of who the speakers in the Book of Mormon were and what they can teach us. For example, what words did Jesus Christ emphasize, and how can this affect our lives today? What does Alma's use of Lehi's and Abinadi's words teach us about counseling those who are struggling? How can modern-day parents and teachers emulate the ways in which Samuel used the words of previous prophets?

Elder Neal A. Maxwell wrote, "The [B]ook [of Mormon] is like a vast mansion with gardens, towers, courtyards, and wings. There are rooms yet to be entered, with flaming fireplaces waiting to warm us. The rooms glimpsed so far contain further furnishings and rich

---

5   Jeffrey R. Holland, "Therefore, What?" (address given to religious educators at a symposium on the New Testament, Brigham Young University, August 8, 2000), 3.

6   President Dallin H. Oaks wrote, "A few years ago I showed one of my senior brethren a talk I had prepared for future delivery. He returned it with a stimulating two-word comment: 'Therefore, what?' The talk was incomplete because it omitted a vital element: what a listener should do. I had failed to follow the example of King Benjamin, who concluded an important message by saying, 'And now, if you believe all these things see that ye do them' (Mosiah 4:10)." Dallin H. Oaks, "Following the Pioneers," *Ensign*, November 1997, 72.

detail yet to be savored."[7] This book will provide a glimpse into one such room—a room focused on the voices heard within the pages of the Book of Mormon. Carefully studying these individual voices and hearing them harmonize has deepened my appreciation for the Book of Mormon and its doctrine. It has strengthened my testimony of scripture, God, and his choreography in our lives. I sincerely hope it does the same for you.

*** Author's Note ***

In this book I operate on the assumption that the Book of Mormon is a literal translation of ancient voices.[8] While Joseph Smith may have had some leeway in the translation process, the fact that unique voices appear throughout the Book of Mormon argues for some degree of "original voice" remaining throughout redaction and translation processes (discussed further in chapter 1).

Throughout this book I use the 2013 version of the Book of Mormon. I have compared textual details with Royal Skousen's *The Book of Mormon: The Earliest Text* and note significant differences when they occur.

---

7 Neal A. Maxwell, *Not My Will, but Thine* (Salt Lake City: Bookcraft, 1988), 33.

8 This is sometimes referred to as a "tight translation." See Royal Skousen, "How Joseph Smith Translated the Book of Mormon: Evidence from the Original Manuscript," *Journal of Book of Mormon Studies* 7, no. 1 (1997): 22–31. For a discussion on different translation possibilities, see Brant A. Gardner, *The Gift and Power: Translating the Book of Mormon* (Salt Lake City: Greg Kofford Books, 2011), or, more briefly, Nicholas J. Frederick and Joseph M. Spencer, "The Book of Mormon and the Academy," *Religious Educator* 21, no. 2 (2020): 173–75.

Part 1

Unique Voices

Chapter 1
Voices in the Book of Mormon

Our voices are more than the sound we make when we communicate. They are a complex mixture of our past experiences, our present purposes, and our future hopes. They reflect personal idiosyncrasies and passionate ideologies. We can learn much from a study of voices, especially when it comes to the narrative voices of prophets of old and particularly the Savior himself.

Identifying the distinctive voices in the Book of Mormon can be a useful lens to gain more spiritual insights from its pages. Doing so illuminates and emphasizes specific gospel teachings. It also helps answer questions regarding what themes specific figures in the Book of Mormon talk about most frequently and how the teachings of one Book of Mormon prophet differ from or complement the teachings of another. This can shed important light on the messages of the individual voices in the Book of Mormon.

In addition, the different voices in the Book of Mormon provide a type of evidence about the book's truthfulness. Consider the unique voices of some of your closest friends. Are there distinctive words or phrases they frequently use that could help you identify their voices? Because several different people write or are quoted in the Book of Mormon, their unique voices should be found within its pages. If there were no differences in voices, it could suggest that the Book of Mormon was authored by one person, but that is not what the text indicates. In fact, there are discernible differences in the voices present in the Book of Mormon. As a simple way of visualizing some of the distinctive voices in the Book of Mormon, compare the following three word clouds.[1]

Figure 1.1. Jacob's word cloud

Figure 1.2. Alma's word cloud

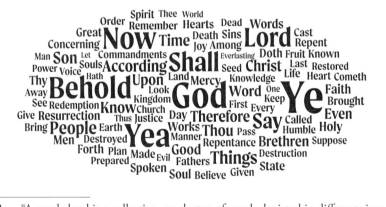

---

1   "A word cloud is a collection, or cluster, of words depicted in different sizes. The bigger and bolder the word appears, the more often it's mentioned within a given text." "Word Clouds and the Value of Simple Visualizations," Boost Labs, https://boostlabs.com/what-are-word-clouds-value-simple-visualizations/. In creating these word clouds, I eliminated commonly used words (such as *the, it, or,* and *and*) so that differences in more significant words could be more easily visualized.

Figure 1.3. Jesus Christ's word cloud

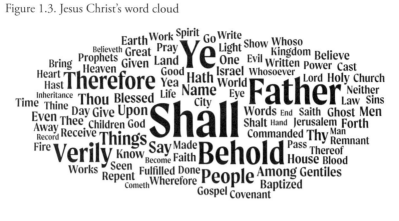

A cursory look at these three word clouds shows different words that are emphasized by each of these speakers. Jacob speaks of *brethren*, Alma says *now*, and Jesus honors the *Father* with distinctive frequencies. Each of these words (and many others) will be discussed in further chapters; I mention them here to illustrate that one can literally see differences in the words used by different speakers in the Book of Mormon.

A more refined approach scholars have used to explore Book of Mormon authorship is through stylometry, which is a statistical analysis of individual writing styles. One application of stylometry that has received attention in Book of Mormon scholarship is sometimes referred to as "wordprints." This branch of stylometry suggests that just as everyone has a unique fingerprint, authors likewise have a distinct voice and style. Contrasted with a subjective recognition that various authors have a similar theme or tone in their writing, stylometry uses quantifiable metrics and statistical techniques to inform the analysis. Stylometry, or wordprint analysis, has been used by scholars to determine the authorship of many disputed texts, including some of the *Federalist Papers*, writings purportedly authored by Shakespeare, *Wuthering Heights*, and several other works of literature.

I first heard about wordprints in my teen years; I learned about them in connection with the "Unabomber"—a twentieth-century terrorist who planted sixteen bombs that killed three people and injured nearly two dozen others.[2] From 1978 to 1995 the Unabomber was one of the most wanted criminals in the United States but managed to evade local and state police—even the FBI. In 1995 the Unabomber demanded that a paper he had written about the dangers of technology be published in major newspapers. The *New York Times* and the *Washington Post* agreed to publish it, hoping that somebody could identify his writing style, and that's exactly what happened. The Unabomber's brother recognized the style of prose and tipped off the FBI; on April 3, 1996, the Unabomber was arrested.

Just before the Unabomber's brother contacted the FBI, the FBI had begun working with a BYU statistics professor who specialized in wordprints. They wanted him to do a stylometric analysis on the Unabomber's essay and compare it with their list of suspects. The professor they contacted was John Hilton (the first)—my grandfather! I remember the excitement I felt when I learned that my grandfather's work was contributing to fighting crime.

As fascinated as I was with the work my grandfather did with the FBI, I was even more intrigued when I learned of the work he and others were doing on wordprints and the Book of Mormon. Their initial studies on wordprints in the Book of Mormon looked at sample sizes of at least five thousand words and examined "the use of the small function words, i.e., *the, and, but, of,* etc.," in an effort to determine whether "different authors did indeed write the various strands within the Book of Mormon."[3] The idea was that the ways speakers used these small words could indicate unique writing patterns. My grandfather and his colleagues found that "it is statistically

---

2   See "The Unabomber," Federal Bureau of Investigation, https://www.fbi.gov /history/famous-cases/unabomber.

3   Roger R. Keller, *Book of Mormon Authors: Their Words and Messages* (Provo, UT: Religious Studies Center, Brigham Young University, 1996), xii. See also Wayne A. Larsen and Alvin C. Rencher, "Who Wrote the Book of Mormon? An Analysis of Wordprints," in *Book of Mormon Authorship: New Light on Ancient Origins*, ed. Noel B. Reynolds, Religious Studies Monograph Series 7 (Provo, UT: Religious Studies Center, Brigham Young University, 1982), 157–88; and John L. Hilton, "On Verifying Book of Mormon Wordprint Studies: Book of Mormon Authorship," *BYU Studies Quarterly* 30, no. 3 (1990): 89–108.

indefensible to propose Joseph Smith or Oliver Cowdery or Solomon Spaulding"[4] as authoring text attributed to Nephi or Alma. Although two wordprint studies disputed these findings,[5] the most recently published study on Book of Mormon wordprints concluded that "the Book of Mormon displays multiple writing styles throughout the text consistent with the book's claim of multiple authors and that the evidence does not show the writing styles of alleged nineteenth-century authors to be similar to those in the Book of Mormon."[6]

If the Book of Mormon were proven to have only one author with no unique voices, that could potentially be problematic, although it could be argued that distinctive voices might disappear in the processes of redaction and translation. However, while a redactor certainly could eliminate original voices, Mormon often tells readers that he is using the direct words of another person (for example, Alma 35:16), and some authors are clearly speaking in their own voice without redaction (for example, Nephi and Jacob). This suggests that at least some individual voices should remain intact. Moreover, while academic research on the relationship between stylome-

---

4   Hilton, "On Verifying Book of MormonWordprint Studies," 101.

5   See David I. Holmes, "A Stylometric Analysis of Mormon Scripture and Related Texts," *Journal of the Royal Statistical Society, Series A (Statistics in Society)* 155, no. 1 (1992): 91–120; and Matthew L. Jockers, Daniela M. Witten, and Craig S. Criddle, "Reassessing Authorship of the *Book of Mormon* Using Delta and Nearest Shrunken Centroid Classification," *Literary and Linguistic Computing* 23, no. 4 (2008): 465–91. Multiple weaknesses in the Holmes study were identified by John B. Archer, John L. Hilton, and G. Bruce Schaalje, "Comparative Power of Three Author-Attribution Techniques for Differentiating Authors," *Journal of Book of Mormon Studies* 6, no. 1 (1997): 47–63. In response to the Jockers et al. article, researchers identified several flaws with its methodology. See Bruce G. Schaalje et al., "Extended Nearest Shrunken Centroid Classification: A New Method for Open-Set Authorship Attribution of Texts of Varying Sizes," *Literary and Linguistic Computing* 26, no. 1 (2011): 71–88.

6   Matthew Roper, Paul J. Fields, and G. Bruce Schaalje, "Stylometric Analyses of the Book of Mormon: A Short History," *Journal of Book of Mormon Studies* 21, no. 1 (2012): 43.

try and translation is ongoing, several studies suggest that individual voices can still be heard after the process of translation.[7]

Although multiple stylometric studies clearly show distinctive voices in the Book of Mormon, some might wonder, "Is it possible for a clever author to create distinctive voices within a text?" The answer is yes, it is possible. For example, when Dorota M. Dutsch examined Roman literature written by notable Roman playwrights Plautus and Terence, she found that the female characters of these authors had distinctive patterns of speech relative to male speakers.[8]

More recently, scholars Paul Fields, Larry Bassist, and Matt Roper used stylometry to show that famous nineteenth-century novelists were able to create a distinct voice for multiple fictional characters, including the narrators, in their stories.[9] However, these scholars also found that "the level of voice diversity among Book of Mormon characters surpassed the diversity among fictional characters created by the 19th-century novelists. The Book of Mormon's voice diversity value was more than *twice* that of the average for the 19th century novelists."[10]

This research suggests that while it is technically *possible* for sophisticated authors to create multiple voices for different characters, the distinctive voices in the Book of Mormon go beyond what would likely be created by one sophisticated author. This finding is

---

7   See, for example, Jan Rybicki, "The Great Mystery of the (Almost) Invisible Translator: Stylometry in Translation," in *Quantitative Methods in Corpus-Based Translation Studies*, ed. Michael P. Oakes and Meng Ji (Amsterdam: John Benjamins, 2012), 231–48; and Richard S. Forsyth and Phoenix W. Y. Lam, "Found in Translation: To What Extent Is Authorial Discriminability Preserved by Translators?," *Literary and Linguistic Computing* 29, no. 2 (2014): 199–217.

8   See Dorota M. Dutsch, *Feminine Discourse in Roman Comedy* (New York: Oxford University Press, 2008), 51.

9   These authors were Charles Dickens, Jane Austen, Samuel Clemens (Mark Twain), and James Fenimore Cooper. This research, which still has not been formally published, was reported at "Book of Mormon Evidence: Voice Diversity," updated November 22, 2021, Evidence Central, Charis Legacy Foundation, https://evidencecentral.org/recency/evidence/voice-diversity.

10   "Book of Mormon Evidence: Voice Diversity."

particularly striking when we acknowledge that Joseph Smith was twenty-three years old and had very little formal education at the time of the Book of Mormon translation. While I am certainly not advocating basing one's testimony of the Book of Mormon on wordprints, at a minimum, the different voices in the Book of Mormon demonstrate a level of complexity clearly beyond Joseph's capabilities.[11]

This textual intricacy is enhanced when we recognize that stylometry is not the only useful approach for examining different voices in the Book of Mormon. Roger Keller examined individual voices by studying "content words," or words that "are theologically, culturally, and historically significant."[12] He created related groups of words and analyzed them to determine whether there were statistically significant differences in how they were used. For example, Keller identified a group of 109 words related to the ancient Near East, such as *Babylon, Egypt, Jeremiah,* and *Moses.* Keller found that "the authors who are most distant in time from the Ancient Near East context use the words of this group the least, while those nearest in time [for example, Lehi, Nephi, and Jacob] use them the most."[13] This led Keller to argue that the Book of Mormon is in fact a multi-authored work, noting that "there are clear and recognizable differences in the content words used and the meanings attached to them by the authors within the Book of Mormon."[14]

Other studies have shown unique writing patterns of Book of Mormon authors by examining words or phrases they use in distinctive ways. For example, in his book *Understanding the Book of Mormon,* Grant Hardy shows that Mormon's narrative style is different

---

11 Among many other excellent books and articles illustrating the textual complexity of the Book of Mormon, the idea that Hebrew elements remained a key part of the book even through translation can be found in Donald W. Parry, *Preserved in Translation: Hebrew and Other Ancient Literary Forms in the Book of Mormon* (Provo, UT: Religious Studies Center, Brigham Young University; Salt Lake City: Deseret Book, 2020).

12 Keller, *Book of Mormon Authors*, 4.

13 Keller, *Book of Mormon Authors*, 8. Keller also notes two exceptions to this general pattern—namely, Nephi$_2$ and Mormon in his sermonic materials.

14 Keller, *Book of Mormon Authors*, xiii.

from Nephi's: "[Mormon] does not offer much scriptural exegesis, and he has little interest in House of Israel connections or messiah theology—the word *messiah* occurs twenty-three times in Nephi's writings but only twice in Mormon's work."[15]

John W. Welch has focused on the different names for Jesus Christ used by Book of Mormon authors. He wrote, "The many personal testimonies of Jesus Christ . . . differ in their emphasis and style. Most interestingly, the attributes of Jesus Christ emphasized by the various prophets are often the attributes with which each prophet especially identified because of his own spiritual experiences, callings, and individual circumstances. . . . *Each Book of Mormon prophet related to and testified of Jesus in his own individual way.*"[16] Collectively, these and similar studies suggest that, based on unique words, phrases, and emphases, the Book of Mormon was in fact written by multiple authors—just as it claims.

The Origin of This Book

I first began an in-depth exploration of the voices in the Book of Mormon in 2011. I was a brand-new assistant professor in ancient scripture at Brigham Young University; I had been hired at the same time as Shon Hopkin and Jennifer Brinkerhoff Platt. The three of us had a mutual friend in Randal Wright, an institute teacher in Texas who suggested we all work together on a project to identify the different voices in the Book of Mormon. We hired an extremely capable BYU student named Jana Johnson as a research assistant and began the process of determining who was speaking in any given Book of Mormon passage.

---

15 Grant Hardy, *Understanding the Book of Mormon: A Reader's Guide* (New York: Oxford University Press, 2010), 91. Hardy also notes that Moroni's writing style is distinctive from both Nephi's and Mormon's. Because Hardy primarily focused on Nephi, Mormon, and Moroni in his book, in the present volume I focus on the distinctive characteristics of other major Book of Mormon speakers.

16 John W. Welch, "Ten Testimonies of Jesus Christ from the Book of Mormon," in *A Book of Mormon Treasury: Gospel Insights from General Authorities and Religious Educators* (Provo, UT: Religious Studies Center, Brigham Young University, 2003), 316; emphasis added.

The five of us first independently read the Book of Mormon, noting who was speaking in each verse. We then reviewed our individual findings and examined more closely passages in which we disagreed on who was speaking. After creating an integrated version of the Book of Mormon parsed out by the person speaking, we compared our work to other scholars who had made similar efforts, and in some cases we adjusted our original speaker designations.[17]

It was often straightforward to identify which Book of Mormon figure was speaking. For example, Nephi begins his record saying, "I, Nephi, having been born of goodly parents . . . ," making it clear who the first speaker is (1 Nephi 1:1). Nephi goes on to introduce his father's story, and in verses 12–13, Nephi writes, "As he [Lehi] read, he was filled with the Spirit of the Lord. And he [Lehi] read, saying: ['] Wo, wo, unto Jerusalem, for I have seen thine abominations!['] Yea, and many things did my father read concerning Jerusalem."

However, in some instances, discerning the differences between the various voices could be tricky. As Latter-day Saint historian Richard Bushman commented, Mormon "quotes other prophets

---

17   We compared our work with Robert Smith's critical text, which was based on John L. Hilton and Kenneth D. Jenkins, "A Full Listing of Book of Mormon References by Author and Literary Form," FARMS Preliminary Report (Provo, UT: FARMS, 1983). However, they identified only major speakers and called minor speakers "Misc." My colleagues and I identified (where possible) every speaker. In addition, we examined Alvin C. Rencher's speaker divisions, which were the basis of Larsen and Rencher, "Analysis of Wordprints," 157–88. We also consulted the use of quotation marks in Grant Hardy's *The Book of Mormon: A Reader's Edition* (Urbana: University of Illinois Press, 2003) to identify how he chose where to begin or end quotes. For Isaiah passages we consulted John D. W. Watts, *Isaiah 1–33*, Word Biblical Commentary 24 (Waco, TX: Word Books, 1985); and Watts, *Isaiah 34–66*, Word Biblical Commentary 25 (Waco, TX: Word Books, 1987). Separately, I want to highlight two people who had been making efforts to split apart the text like my colleagues and I were doing. We did not compare our work to theirs, as theirs was unpublished at the time. However, in 2016 they published their work as *A New Approach to Studying the Book of Mormon*. Those interested in a printed copy of the Book of Mormon separated by voices could consult this study edition of the Book of Mormon. See Lynn A. Rosenvall and David L. Rosenvall, *A New Approach to Studying the Book of Mormon* (Olive Leaf Foundation, 2016).

and sometimes quotes them quoting still others. Moroni injects a letter from his father, and Nephi inserts lengthy passages from previous scriptures. Mormon moves in and out of the narrative. . . . Almost always two minds are present, and sometimes three, all kept account of in the flow of words."[18]

The Book of Mormon's "editorially complex narrative structure"[19] and constant change of speaker made it difficult, at times, to determine precisely who was speaking in any given passage. This isn't surprising when the person that is speaking changes more than seventeen hundred times! An example from Jacob 5 illustrates the layers of quotations that can be more closely examined through a study of individual voices. In the following passage, notice how Jacob quotes Zenos, who in turn quotes the Lord (who portrays the voice of the master of the vineyard):

Jacob

1 Behold, my brethren, do ye not remember to have read the words of the prophet Zenos, which he spake unto the house of Israel, saying:

Zenos

2 Hearken, O ye house of Israel, and hear the words of me, a prophet of the Lord.

3 For behold, thus saith the Lord,

The Lord

I will liken thee, O house of Israel, like unto a tame olive-tree, which a man took and nourished in his vineyard; and it grew, and waxed old, and began to decay.

4 And it came to pass that the master of the vineyard went forth, and he saw that his olive-tree began to decay; and he said:

The Master of the Vineyard

I will prune it, and dig about it, and nourish it, that perhaps it may shoot forth young and tender branches, and it perish not.

---

18 Richard L. Bushman, *Joseph Smith and the Beginnings of Mormonism* (Chicago: University of Illinois Press, 1984), 119.

19 Terryl L. Givens, *By the Hand of Mormon* (New York: Oxford University Press, 2002), 156.

In assigning specific voices to individual passages, especially in the more complicated sections, my colleagues and I made a critical methodological assumption—we chose to take the Book of Mormon authors at face value. For example, when Nephi writes, "Laman said unto Lemuel and also unto the sons of Ishmael: *Behold, let us slay our father, and also our brother Nephi, who has taken it upon him to be our ruler and our teacher, who are his elder brethren*" (1 Nephi 16:37), we assigned the italicized portion of this verse to Laman.

This assumption certainly imposes limitations. The possibility (indeed likelihood) exists that since Nephi was writing some thirty years after the event occurred, he was paraphrasing Laman's words rather than providing a word-for-word account of what Laman actually said. Nephi is not the only historian who faced such challenges. Thucydides, a Greek historian living in approximately 400 BC, wrote of the difficulties of maintaining an accurate history, saying, "With reference to the speeches in this history, some were delivered before the war began, others while it was going on; some I heard myself, others I got from various quarters; it was in all cases difficult to carry them word for word in one's memory, so my habit has been to make the speakers say what was in my opinion demanded of them by the various occasions, of course adhering as closely as possible to the general sense of what they really said."[20]

As I will discuss later in this chapter, there clearly are times in the Book of Mormon when a narrator is likely creating dialogue as Thucydides did—that is, with the intent of adhering to the general sense of what was being said but not necessarily providing a direct quote. However, in other instances, it appears that words may have been recorded with more precision. For example, at the beginning of Alma 5, Mormon records, "These are the words which [Alma] spake to the people in the church which was established in the city of Zarahemla, according to his own record," and then proceeds to include Alma's first-person voice (Alma 5:2; see Mosiah 2:8; 17:4;

---

20 Thucydides, *The History of the Peloponnesian War*, trans. Richard Crawley, book 1, chap. 1, https://www.gutenberg.org/files/7142/7142-h/7142-h.htm. I thank Ben Spackman for pointing this out to me.

Alma 35:16). Thus in many cases we can be confident that the words we are reading belong to the person reported to have said them.

Who Speaks in the Book of Mormon?

Although 149 different voices are present in the Book of Mormon, many of these are people who speak only a few words, including people from Amnor to Zeram.[21] The fifteen people who each account for at least 1 percent of the Book of Mormon are listed in table 1.1 (see the appendixes for a list of all the voices in the Book of Mormon). Collectively, these fifteen voices account for 87 percent of the words spoken in the Book of Mormon. Throughout this book I will refer to these fifteen figures as "major speakers" in the Book of Mormon.

Table 1.1. Book of Mormon speakers attributed with more than 1 percent of the text[22]

Rank	Speaker	Words spoken	Words as a percentage of text
1	Mormon	97,591	36.4%
2	Nephi	28,166	10.5%
3	Alma	20,051	7.5%
4	Moroni$_2$	19,513	7.3%
5	Jesus Christ*	14,161	5.3%
6	The Lord*	11,971	4.5%
7	Jacob	8,486	3.2%

---

21 Amnor and Zeram are quoted as speaking together, along with Manti and Limher, in Alma 2:24–25.

22 Additional speakers who account for at least 1,000 words include the lord (master) of the vineyard (2,428 words, 0.9% of the text); Ammon, the son of Mosiah (2,280 words, 0.85% of the text); Nephi, the son of Nephi (2,213 words, 0.8% of the text); an angel speaking to Nephi (1,973 words, 0.7% of the text); Zeniff (1,815 words, 0.7% of the text); the Father (1,501 words, 0.6% of the text); Limhi (1,383 words, 0.5% of the text); and King Mosiah$_2$ (1,178 words, 0.4% of the text). All other speakers account for fewer than 1,000 words.

8	Isaiah	8,118	3.0%
9	Helaman$_2$	5,042	1.9%
10	Lehi$_1$	4,662	1.7%
11	King Benjamin	4,201	1.6%
12	Amulek	3,162	1.2%
13	Samuel the Lamanite	3,054	1.1%
14	Moroni$_1$	3,050	1.1%
15	Abinadi	2,786	1.0%

* Reasons for separating these speakers will be discussed in the following section.

The number of words spoken by some of these speakers is in many cases no surprise. For instance, because of their key roles as primary Book of Mormon narrators, Mormon and Nephi obviously have the top two positions. Some may not have realized, however, that Alma's voice is heard more than that of Nephi's brother Jacob or Mormon's son Moroni. Certain individuals speak more (or less) than might be expected. For example, because of Helaman's[23] lengthy epistle in Alma 56–58, we hear his voice more than Lehi's, the prophet who taught in Jerusalem and traveled to the promised land.

Once we identified the different voices in the Book of Mormon, we worked with the developers of the software program Word-Cruncher[24] to develop a database we called "Voices in the Book of Mormon."[25] This database can be used to determine who spoke

---

23 Three individuals named Helaman appear in the Book of Mormon. The first is a brother of Mosiah (see Mosiah 1:2); he does not speak in the Book of Mormon. The second is the son of Alma, and the third is Helaman, the son of Helaman, who speaks in Helaman 5:6–12. The only Helaman who speaks with sufficient frequency to examine his words is Helaman, the son of Alma. For simplicity in the present volume, I will refer to him simply as Helaman.

24 This software is available at http://wordcruncher.com.

25 More details on this database, including instructions for downloading and using it, can be found at https://johnhiltoniii.com/voices-in-the-book-of -mormon/.

a particular word or phrase in the Book of Mormon. Traditional electronic database searches show *where* a specific word appears in the Book of Mormon. For example, using a traditional database to search for occurrences of the word *Gentiles* provides the results listed in table 1.2.

Table 1.2. Occurrences of the word *Gentiles* organized by book

Book	Number of occurrences of *Gentiles*
1 Nephi	56
2 Nephi	31
Jacob	0
Enos	0
Jarom	0
Omni	0
Words of Mormon	0
Mosiah	0
Alma	0
Helaman	0
3 Nephi	35
4 Nephi	0
Mormon	0
Ether	10
Moroni	11

While this is interesting information, it is not immediately clear which individuals most frequently talk about Gentiles. Thus, a database that can identify not only *where* passages appear but *who* says them can be a useful tool in analyzing the text of the Book of Mormon. The Voices in the Book of Mormon Database makes this explicit, as demonstrated in table 1.3.

Table 1.3. Occurrences of the word *Gentiles* attributed to major speakers[26]

Speaker	Times used per 1,000 words spoken	Times used	Percent of total uses of *Gentiles* in the Book of Mormon	Percent of total words in the Book of Mormon attributed to speaker
Jesus Christ	2.7	38	26.0%	5.3%
Nephi	1.5	43	29.5%	10.5%
The Lord	0.8	9	6.2%	4.5%
Moroni$_2$	0.6	11	7.5%	7.3%
Jacob	0.4	2	1.4%	3.2%
Isaiah	0.2	1	0.7%	3.0%
Mormon	0.2	16	11.0%	36.4%

While table 1.2 indicates that *Gentiles* is used fifty-six times in 1 Nephi and thirty-five times in 3 Nephi, it may be more interesting to discover that Jesus Christ is represented as using the word thirty-eight times, while the primary author of the Book of Mormon, Mormon, uses it only sixteen times. When one accounts for the total number of words spoken, Jesus Christ proportionally uses the word *Gentiles* nearly twice as often as any other major speaker.[27]

The idea of "proportionally using" a word will be used throughout this book. This is an important concept because if words in the Book of Mormon were randomly distributed, we would expect Jesus, who speaks 5 percent of the text, to account for 5 percent of the usage of a specific word. When we see that he accounts for 26 percent of *Gentiles*, or 30 percent of *baptize* (see chapter 5), it suggests an unusual speech pattern that bears further investigation. In this book I will often use the measurement of the number of times a word appears

---

26 Other speakers who use *Gentiles* include the angel speaking to Nephi (eighteen times), the Father (seven times), and Nephi's brethren (one time).

27 See John Hilton III et al., "Gentiles in the Book of Mormon," *Interpreter: A Journal of Latter-day Saint Faith and Scholarship* 33 (2019): 267–88.

per one thousand words a person speaks. This provides a proportional measurement that accounts for the different number of words spoken by the various figures in the Book of Mormon.

The findings we have discussed thus far depend on the accuracy with which my colleagues and I identified the voices in the Book of Mormon. Because this is such a crucial point, I next briefly discuss the methodology we used when assigning voices to passages in situations when the speaker wasn't completely clear.

Difficult Choices in Assigning the Voice

As I previously mentioned, for much of the text, identifying the speakers in the Book of Mormon was straightforward. Some areas, however, were quite difficult. These included labeling the voices of Deity, discerning between real and hypothetical quotations, dealing with potential allusions, and handling statements that may not have been said.

The Lord, the Father, and Jesus Christ

One challenge we faced was how to attribute the various titles given to God when he speaks. For example, "the Lord" speaks in 1 Nephi 17:53, "the Lord God almighty" speaks in 2 Nephi 28:15, and "the Lord of Hosts" speaks in Jacob 2:29. Five quotations (all by Jacob) are attributed to "God."[28] In some cases these terms appear to be used interchangeably. For example, in 2 Nephi 28:32 we read, "Wo be unto the Gentiles, *saith the Lord God of Hosts*! For notwithstanding I shall lengthen out mine arm unto them from day to day, they will deny me; nevertheless, I will be merciful unto them, *saith the Lord God*, if they will repent and come unto me; for mine arm is lengthened out all the day long, *saith the Lord God of Hosts*." Although quotations in this verse are attributed to "the Lord God" and "the Lord God of Hosts," it seems most probable that they refer to the same being. Thus, we grouped all nonspecific quotations by Deity as being attributable to the Lord.

The titles for Deity described above stand in contrast to the very specific designations of the Father and Jesus Christ. At times the Father or Jesus is explicitly quoted as speaking. For example, in 2 Nephi 31:10–13 Nephi writes:

---

28 See 2 Nephi 10:8–19.

Nephi
Can we follow Jesus save we shall be willing to keep the commandments of the Father? And the Father said:

> **The Father**
> Repent ye, repent ye, and be baptized in the name of my Beloved Son.

Nephi
And also, the voice of the Son came unto me, saying:

> **The Son (Jesus Christ)**
> He that is baptized in my name, to him will the Father give the Holy Ghost, like unto me; wherefore, follow me, and do the things which ye have seen me do.

Nephi
Wherefore, my beloved brethren, I know that if ye shall follow the Son . . .

In this passage, Nephi clearly delineates the voice of the Father and the voice of Jesus Christ. Several other passages give similar explicit identifications of either the Father or Jesus Christ as the speaker. While good arguments could be made for combining the voices of Jesus Christ, the Father, and the Lord into one voice, my colleagues and I determined that if a statement was specifically attributed to the Father or Jesus Christ, or if context made it very clear that they were speaking (for example, 3 Nephi 11:7), we categorized that statement as coming from them. Generic references to Deity (for example, "Lord" or "God") were assigned to the Lord.

When we analyzed the text based on these conventions, we found that the voice of Jesus Christ has distinguishing characteristics, indicating there are real textual differences in words explicitly attributed to Jesus Christ. Many of the insights we can gain from this identification are described in chapter 5.

Hypothetical statements

In some instances, people in the Book of Mormon appear to make statements attributed to the hypothetical phrases of others. For example, Samuel the Lamanite prophesies of a curse that will come upon the wicked, stating, "Yea, in that day, ye shall say: *O that we had remembered the Lord our God in the day that he gave us our riches*" (Helaman 13:33). To whom should the italicized words be attributed?

In instances like this one, we determined that while it is certainly possible that future individuals would in fact speak these exact words, it was more likely that the prophet was speaking hypothetically, as in "These are the kinds of words that will be spoken in a future day." Thus in these situations we attributed the words being spoken to the original speaker (in this case Samuel), *not* a future hypothetical speaker.[29]

Potential allusions

At times speakers in the Book of Mormon appear to allude to what others had previously said. For example, Alma, when speaking to Corianton, says, "And behold, again *it hath been spoken*, that there is a first resurrection, a resurrection of all those who have been, or who are, or who shall be, down to the resurrection of Christ from the dead" (Alma 40:16). In this case, Alma acknowledges that he is drawing on a previous source, although he does not identify who this person is. Because of the difficulty in correctly attributing allusions, we did so only in cases when the speaker explicitly cited another individual as the source of the statement. Thus, in this case, we counted the words as coming from Alma, even though they could be reasonably attributed to Abinadi.[30]

Statements that may not have actually been said

Although we chose to take every statement ascribed to an individual as actually having been stated by that person, this was problematic in some cases. For example, it sometimes appears unlikely that the source authors would have had access to the actual conversation that took place. One instance of this is when Mormon reports on the five who run to the judgment seat to verify Nephi's prophecy of the death of the chief judge. We read that

---

29 For additional examples, see Alma 5:16 and 3 Nephi 14:22.

30 It appears that Alma is using Abinadi's words (see Mosiah 15:21). This is discussed further in chapter 9.

when Nephi had spoken these words, certain men who were among them ran to the judgment-seat; yea, even there were five who went, and they said among themselves, as they went: ["]Behold, now we will know of a surety whether this man be a prophet and God hath commanded him to prophesy such marvelous things unto us. Behold, we do not believe that he hath; yea, we do not believe that he is a prophet; nevertheless, if this thing which he has said concerning the chief judge be true, that he be dead, then will we believe that the other words which he has spoken are true.["] (Helaman 9:1–2)

Book of Mormon scholar Brant Gardner points out:

> The fact that five messengers went to investigate was no doubt part of Nephi's record, but it seems unlikely that Nephi would also have recorded the conversation, since it occurred "among themselves, as they went." Even if they reconstructed this conversation later, possibly in reporting it to Nephi, it was not a word-for-word report. While oral cultures demonstrate a proficient memory for certain types of practiced texts, that does not translate into remembering conversations that they had not expected to need to know.[31]

Another example of this kind of difficulty concerns Alma and Amulek's speech to the people in Ammonihah. Did someone acting in the function of "court reporter" transcribe the conversations that took place, or did Alma write a retrospective account? If Alma recorded what transpired at Ammonihah six months after it occurred, how literally should we take the words he attributes to himself, Amulek, Zeezrom, or Antionah?

Because there is no way to arrive at conclusive answers to these questions, we retained our convention of assigning voices to the

---

31 Brant A. Gardner, *Second Witness: Analytical and Contextual Commentary on the Book of Mormon*, vol. 5, *Helaman through 3 Nephi* (Salt Lake City: Greg Kofford Books, 2007), 137. It could be argued that this line of reasoning diminishes the value of this study since many instances of what I term "voices" in the Book of Mormon could have been invented dialogue. However, the insights described throughout this book lead me to believe there is significant merit in distinguishing the various speakers in the text, particularly those individuals whose words account for 1 percent or more of the Book of Mormon text.

person attributed in the text. Thus, the identification of 149 voices does not necessarily indicate a belief that the final editor of the ancient text (usually Mormon) was always quoting the original speakers' words verbatim. Nevertheless, for many of the major writers of the Book of Mormon, we have enough of their words to make the case that we can hear their distinctive voices.

Therefore, What?

The Book of Mormon is a rich text that bears close exploration. Hugh Nibley observed, "The Book of Mormon is tough. It thrives on investigation. You may kick it around like a football, as many have done; and I promise you it will wear you out long before you ever make a dent in it."[32] Examining the Book of Mormon by the person who is speaking provides new ways to investigate the fulness of what the Book of Mormon offers.

In this chapter, we have seen an overview of the diverse speakers in the Book of Mormon. Although there are some limitations, most of the time we can clearly identify individual speakers. Carefully analyzing individual Book of Mormon voices has helped me better understand the unique viewpoints, speaking patterns, and personalities of those who speak in the Book Mormon. This has led to spiritual insights that I would have otherwise missed, bringing a greater appreciation for this sacred record.

In addition, annotating the text of the Book of Mormon with names of the individuals who speak makes it easier to see its intricacy. This complexity strongly suggests that the Book of Mormon is a multiauthored work and that Joseph Smith did *not* write it. While not required for deep spiritual conviction, this type of intellectual evidence can strengthen our faith. As Austin Farrer wrote, "Though argument does not create conviction, the lack of it destroys belief. What seems to be proved may not be embraced; but what no one shows the ability to defend is quickly abandoned. Rational argument

---

32 "A Twilight World," in *The Collected Works of Hugh Nibley*, vol. 5, *Lehi in the Desert / The World of the Jaredites / There Were Jaredites* (Provo, UT: FARMS; Salt Lake City: Deseret Book, 1988), 149.

does not create belief, but it maintains a climate in which belief may flourish."[33]

Before his call to the Quorum of the Twelve, David A. Bednar was a university professor. While working as a professor, he and a colleague wrote a textbook together. On one occasion he shared how writing this book deepened his understanding of how Joseph Smith could not have written the Book of Mormon:

> One of the books I authored with a colleague . . . [is] 650 pages long, . . . contains 17 chapters, and . . . took us two years to write. The colleague with whom I wrote this book also has a Ph.D., which means that we . . . [have] more than 16 years of formal higher education between the two of us. It is a remarkable experience to receive a box of these brand-new books from the publisher. . . . I opened up the box and thumbed through one of the books. As I did so, I looked out the window of my office and asked myself the question, "Why did you write this book?" When you really think about it, investing so much time and effort in a project that so quickly becomes obsolete is rather foolish. As I . . . was pondering [that question], the thought came to me, "Because now you know by experience that Joseph Smith could not have written the Book of Mormon. . . .
>
> With eight years of university training, with two years of very dedicated work, with an editorial staff, with personal computers, with spell checkers and thesauruses on-line, with the Internet and the other resources that are so readily available, when I picked up the book that I had written and opened it up, I still found mistakes. And within a matter of twelve months, this book upon which I had worked so hard and so long was obsolete and had to be revised. . . .
>
> . . . Intellectually I know the Book of Mormon is true; and I know it through personal experience as an author. And that type of knowledge is nice. But what is most important is the witness of the Spirit. And I know by the witness of the Spirit, I know intellectually,

---

33 Austin Farrer, "Grete Clerk," in *Light on C. S. Lewis*, comp. Jocelyn Gibb (New York: Harcourt and Brace, 1965), 26; cited in Neal A. Maxwell, "Discipleship and Scholarship," *BYU Studies Quarterly* 32, no. 3 (1992): 5.

and I know as an author and by personal experience that Joseph Smith could not and did not write the Book of Mormon.[34]

My hope is that this chapter has strengthened your interest in and testimony of the Book of Mormon, the good people that grace its pages, and the validity of this book of scripture. I also hope the following chapters will offer you additional understanding—not only in seeing the Book of Mormon's complexity but also in identifying life-changing doctrines taught by specific individuals with unique voices. This will be seen in the following chapters, beginning with analysis of Jacob's distinctive voice.[35]

---

34 David A. Bednar, "Come unto Christ," BYU—Idaho devotional, January 29, 2000, https://www.byui.edu/devotionals/president-david-a-bednar-devotional-winter-2000.

35 As noted previously, Grant Hardy has extensively analyzed Nephi's voice, so I begin with Jacob. See Hardy, *Understanding the Book of Mormon*, 12–86.

Chapter 2
Jacob: Tender and Stern

Jacob's life was filled with deep sorrows and tender mercies, similar to his elder brother Nephi's.[1] And yet there were some differences that likely shaped who he was and the voice he had. Jacob never experienced the comfortable life in Jerusalem. Born in a desert to a mother who lived off raw meat and God's grace, Jacob experienced challenging formative years. His initial social circle consisted of only his at-times troubled nuclear and extended family.

At a young age he sailed across the ocean; on this voyage he witnessed his parents "brought down . . . near to be cast with sorrow into a watery grave" and was "grieved because of the afflictions of [his] mother" (1 Nephi 18:18–19). In his "childhood [he] suffered afflictions and much sorrow, because of the rudeness of [his brothers]" (2 Nephi 2:1). At the same time, Jacob knew "the greatness of God" and "beheld in [his] youth" the glory of Jesus Christ (2 Nephi 2:2, 4).

---

1   This chapter is a revised version of John Hilton III, "Jacob: A Distinctive Book of Mormon Author," in *Jacob: Faith and Great Anxiety*, ed. Avram R. Shannon and George A. Pierce (Provo, UT: Religious Studies Center, Brigham Young University; Salt Lake City: Deseret Book, 2024), 1–18. Used with permission.

Toward the end of his life, he reflected that his years had "passed away like as it were . . . a dream, [his people] being a lonesome and solemn people, wanderers, cast out from Jerusalem, born in tribulation, in a wilderness, and hated of [their] brethren, which caused wars and contentions" (Jacob 7:26). On the other hand, he reverently acknowledged God's greatness and mercy (see Jacob 4:8; 6:4), knew of Christ, and had hope of his coming (see Jacob 4:4). Whether the duality of his experience and faith informed Jacob's tender and thoughtful spirit or the other way around, it's clear that Jacob was coming from a complicated place of hardship, empathy, faith, and love.

Jacob's varied experiences may connect with a duality in his voice, which is stern yet tender, boldly rebuking while lovingly testifying and inviting. Jacob records some 8,500 of his own words, placing him as the seventh most frequently heard voice in the Book of Mormon.[2] However, he is sometimes underappreciated among Book of Mormon prophets. C. Terry Warner writes, "This is partly because his story is scattered over 125 pages of the Book of Mormon, and partly because he wrote little about himself. Nevertheless, from what we do know, a picture emerges of a shepherd of his people who also loved us, the Saints of future years, and who by that love calls forth our love for him."[3]

Even though readers tend to focus more on major narrators such as Nephi or Mormon than they do on Jacob, several scholars have written about Jacob's contributions and distinctive voice. Deidre Nicole Green began her 2020 book *Jacob: A Brief Theological Introduction* by writing, "Jacob has a unique voice in the Book of Mormon."[4] Writing some thirty years earlier, John Tanner noted, "Jacob's style is unique among Book of Mormon authors. He simply sounds differ-

---

2   In this chapter, when I use word counts of Jacob's writings, I'm specifically referring to words directly attributed to Jacob in the text. Words that could be attributed to Zenos or the lord of the vineyard in Jacob 5 were *not* counted as belonging to Jacob.

3   C. Terry Warner, "Jacob," *Ensign*, October 1976, 25.

4   Deidre Nicole Green, *Jacob: A Brief Theological Introduction* (Provo, UT: Neal A. Maxwell Institute for Religious Scholarship, Brigham Young University, 2020), 2.

ent. He used a more personal vocabulary than most and took a more intimate approach to his audience."[5]

Marilyn Arnold similarly points to the tender nature of Jacob's writing, suggesting that his words stand in contrast to those of others. She writes, "Although Jacob is gifted in language and solid in his testimony, to me he seems unusually tender, even a bit fragile, in his emotional makeup."[6]

Tanner highlighted specific words that are predominantly used by Jacob in the Book of Mormon. For example, Tanner pointed out that half of the eight references to *anxiety* in the Book of Mormon occur in Jacob's words. In fact, Jacob is the only speaker in the Book of Mormon to use this word more than once. At the outset of his discourse beginning in 2 Nephi 6, Jacob states, "I am desirous for the welfare of your souls. Yea, mine *anxiety* is great for you; and ye yourselves know that it ever has been" (verse 3). At the start of another significant sermon, given several years later, Jacob said, "I this day am weighed down with much more desire and *anxiety* for the welfare of your souls than I have hitherto been" (Jacob 2:3).[7] Thus not only does Jacob most frequently use the word *anxiety*, he also has a distinctive way of using it by describing his feelings before beginning important discourses.

Furthermore, Tanner writes that half of the occurrences of *shame* come from Jacob and notes that "he is the only person to have used *delicate*, *contempt*, and *lonesome*. Likewise, he is the only Book of Mormon author to have employed *wound* in reference to emotions; and he never used it, as everyone else did, to describe a physical injury. Similarly, Jacob used *pierce* or its variants frequently (four of the ten instances in the Book of Mormon), and he used it exclusively in

---

5   John S. Tanner, "Jacob and His Descendants as Authors," in *Rediscovering the Book of Mormon*, ed. John L. Sorenson and Melvin J. Thorne (Salt Lake City: Deseret Book; Provo, UT: FARMS, 1991), 58.

6   Marilyn Arnold, "Unlocking the Sacred Text," *Journal of Book of Mormon Studies* 8, no. 1 (1999): 52.

7   Note that Jacob connects *desire* with *anxiety* in both passages. These words collocate four times in the Book of Mormon: twice in Jacob's words, once in Lehi's (see 2 Nephi 1:16), and once in Mormon's (see Mosiah 28:12).

a spiritual sense. Such evidence suggests an author who lived close to his emotions and who knew how to express those emotions."[8]

Part of Tanner's overall thesis is that individual Book of Mormon authors, such as Jacob, have distinctive writing styles. He writes, "I do not believe that God's co-authorship normally eradicates an individual's voice, since the Lord speaks through his servants 'in their weakness, after the manner of their language' (Doctrine and Covenants 1:24)."[9] The purpose of this chapter is to deepen our understanding of Jacob, the person and prophet, by further examining distinctive aspects of his words.

In this chapter I will identify and briefly discuss several phrases that collectively illustrate Jacob's unique voice. As we will see, Jacob has distinctive ways he speaks of Deity. He also emphasizes harsh words and phrases such as "angels to a devil," "monster," "fire and brimstone," and "awful guilt" (2 Nephi 9:9, 10, 16, 46). At the same time, he tenderly focuses on the power of Christ's Atonement in unique ways as he teaches of the Lord's "great condescensions," "the power of the resurrection," "the pleasing word of God," and Christ's ability to raise us from death and bring us "into the eternal kingdom of God" (Jacob 4:7; 2 Nephi 9:12; Jacob 2:8; 2 Nephi 10:25).

I first identify the specific passages where we hear Jacob's voice. Next, I discuss Jacob's references to Deity, followed by distinctive phrases from Jacob found in both 2 Nephi and Jacob. Finally, I examine selected phrases that are unique to Jacob but used in only one of the pericopes—that is to say, sections of text—in which he speaks.

Jacob's Words in the Book of Mormon

There are two sections in the Book of Mormon where we hear Jacob's voice in first person. The first is found in a sermon Jacob gives at Ne-

---

8   Tanner, "Jacob and His Descendants as Authors," 59.

9   Tanner, "Jacob and His Descendants as Authors," 58. John Tvedtnes points out that Jacob's literary style may have been influenced by Lehi. He states, "An examination of Jacob's two sermons and his treatise show that he was clearly influenced by the admonitions addressed to him by his father Lehi in 2 Nephi 2." John A. Tvedtnes, "The Influence of Lehi's Admonitions on the Teachings of His Son Jacob," *Journal of Book of Mormon Studies* 3, no. 2 (1994): 35.

phi's behest in 2 Nephi 6, 9–10.[10] Although Jacob quotes from others in these chapters, most of the words belong to him.[11] The second pericope is the book of Jacob, which, other than a large quotation from Zenos, is nearly entirely written in Jacob's voice.[12] When all of Jacob's words are collected, they account for approximately 3 percent of the text of the Book of Mormon.

It is particularly noteworthy when patterns for Jacob's words hold across his speech in 2 Nephi 6, 9–10 and the book that bears his name. Because nearly forty pages of text separate 2 Nephi 10 from Jacob 1, we might expect the text from 2 Nephi 6, 9–10 to be closer to Nephi's voice in 2 Nephi 4–5, 11 than to the book of Jacob. However, in several instances Jacob's distinctive voice can be heard in both pericopes, suggesting that in fact Jacob was indeed a separate author from Nephi.

Jacob's References to Deity

John W. Welch has pointed out some unique aspects of Jacob's descriptions of Deity, noting that Jacob uses the word *Creator* more than any other author (four out of ten total Book of Mormon references), and he accounts for two of the six Book of Mormon uses of the word *Maker*.[13] Jacob is the only author to refer to Jesus as the "great Creator," and he does so three times (2 Nephi 9:5, 6; Jacob 3:7). Jacob both numerically and proportionally uses the title "the

---

10 2 Nephi 7 and 8 are quotations from Isaiah.

11 In 2 Nephi 6–10, Jacob quotes several sources, including Jesus Christ (textually identified as such), the Lord (textually identified as such), Isaiah, and an angel. For the purposes of analyzing Jacob's words in the present study, I examine only the words specifically attributed to him.

12 In the book of Jacob, Jacob quotes from the Lord, Zenos, and Sherem. Again, herein I examine only words specifically attributed to Jacob.

13 *Maker* appears six times in the Book of Mormon; it is used twice by Jacob, twice by the Lord, and once each by Enos and Mormon. For more information on distinctive titles for Christ used by different Book of Mormon authors, see John W. Welch, "Ten Testimonies of Jesus Christ from the Book of Mormon," *A Book of Mormon Treasury: Gospel Insights from General Authorities and Religious Educators* (Provo, UT: Religious Studies Center, Brigham Young University, 2003), 316–42.

Holy One of Israel" more than any other author.[14] All of these distinguishing characteristics appear both in 2 Nephi 6, 9–10 and in the book of Jacob, adding credibility to the thesis that Jacob is the unique author of both pericopes.

An easy-to-overlook yet fascinating aspect of Jacob's references to Deity was pointed out to me by my son Joseph when he was eleven years old. Joseph had been inspired by President Russell M. Nelson's invitation to find every reference to Jesus Christ in the Book of Mormon.[15] While doing so, Joseph created a spreadsheet of each title and where it occurred. He discovered that Nephi was much more likely than Jacob to use the word *Lord* but that Jacob was much more likely than Nephi to use the word *God*. Using the Voices in the Book of Mormon Database, I verified this finding by counting the number of times that Nephi and Jacob each used the words *Lord* and *God*. The results are summarized in table 2.1.

Table 2.1. Comparing Nephi's and Jacob's uses of the words *Lord* and *God*

Speaker	Total uses of *Lord*	Uses of *Lord* per 1,000 words	Total uses of *God*	Uses of *God* per 1,000 words
Nephi	271	9.6	203	7.2
Jacob	50	5.9	107	12.6

---

14 This title appears forty times in the Book of Mormon and is used seventeen times by Jacob; ten times by Nephi; six times by Isaiah; two times each by Zenos, Amaleki, and Lehi; and once by the Lord. Welch notes that Nephi and Lehi use it most frequently after Jacob and points out that "after the time of the small plates, this title drops out of Nephite usage—perhaps because the temple service declined in prominence as people knew that its sacrifice merely typified the only meaningful sacrifice—Christ's—or perhaps because the Nephites, over time, became less inclined to identify personally with a remote and by then unfamiliar land of Israel." Welch, "Ten Testimonies," 325–26.

15 See Russell M. Nelson, "Sisters' Participation in the Gathering of Israel," *Ensign*, November 2018, 69–70. Joseph's insight was a significant inspiration for writing this chapter, which was in fact a catalyst for bringing this book to fruition.

These data clearly show different frequency patterns in the ways Nephi and Jacob use the words *Lord* and *God*. Nephi is much more likely to use the word *Lord* than Jacob is, whereas Jacob is more likely to use the word *God*.[16]

Jacob's distinctive use of the word *God* holds true both in 2 Nephi 6, 9–10 and in the book of Jacob, again emphasizing that Jacob's distinctive voice remains intact in the chapters attributed to his voice. Although many modern readers might consider the words *Lord* and *God* synonymous, Nephi and Jacob use the word *God* with distinctively different frequencies that are statistically measurable.[17] One commonly accepted measure of statistical significance in corpus linguistics is log-likelihood (LL). The higher the LL, the less likely that differences in word use between two texts are due to chance.[18]

---

16 Nephi uses the phrase "Lord God" 39 times (1.4 times per 1,000 words spoken), while Jacob uses it 13 times (1.5 times per 1,000 words spoken). Although they use "Lord God" with essentially the same frequency, this is not the case with the titles "Lord" and "God."

17 While Nephi and Jacob use the words *Lord* and *God* distinctively, it is not clear whether Nephi and Jacob saw these words as having different meanings or simply preferred one word over the other. For an overview of the meanings of various names for God in the Old Testament, see Dana M. Pike, "The Name and Titles of God in the Old Testament," *Religious Educator* 11, no. 1 (2010): 17–32.

18 Daniel Allington provides additional background to this statistical technique: "In corpus analysis, it is customary to compare word frequencies within the language corpus under analysis with word frequencies within a 'reference corpus' considered typical of language use more generally, with log-likelihood generally being considered the best measure of statistical significance. The log-likelihood of a lexical item is referred to as its 'keyness,' which is customarily treated as a measure of the item's overuse or underuse relative to its expected frequency of occurrence in the corpus under analysis, taking its frequency within the reference corpus as the assumed norm. Thus, while a log-likelihood of 6.63 is sufficient to indicate significance at the level of $p < 0.01$, log-likelihood is also conventionally used to compare the relative importance of items within a corpus: the higher the log-likelihood, the more 'key' an item's presence or absence is assumed to be." Daniel Allington, "'It Actually Painted a Picture of the Village and the Sea and the Bottom of the Sea': Reading Groups, Cultural Legitimacy, and Description in Narrative (with Particular Reference to John Steinbeck's *The Pearl*),"

An LL score of 6.63 is equivalent to a p value < .01, indicating statistical significance. When comparing Jacob's words to Nephi's, the LL values for *God* and *Lord* are respectively 20.5 and 11.0, making it extremely unlikely that their distinctive usages of these words occur by chance. It is also interesting to note that the word *God*, which Jacob has a penchant for using, does not appear in Jacob 5. This chapter, the longest in the book of Jacob, is almost entirely a quotation from a different voice—that of Zenos.

Distinctive Phrases in Both 2 Nephi and Jacob

In addition to his descriptions of Deity, there are other phrases that are distinctively used by Jacob across his words in 2 Nephi and the book of Jacob. In this section, I briefly identify and discuss these phrases; my purpose is not to exhaustively analyze each case but rather to broadly illustrate the distinctive phrases used by Jacob.

Fire and brimstone and endless torment

The phrase "fire and brimstone" appears ten times in the Book of Mormon, six of which are in the words of Jacob.[19] The first time it occurs in the Book of Mormon is in 2 Nephi 9, where it appears three times. In this stern discourse Jacob warns of the torment that awaits those who are filthy. Jacob specifically identifies the filthy as "the devil and his angels" and says their torment "is as a lake of *fire and brimstone*, whose flame ascendeth up forever and ever and has no end" (2 Nephi 9:16). He also twice highlights a merciful Savior who "delivereth his saints from . . . that lake of *fire and brimstone*, which is endless torment" (2 Nephi 9:19; compare verse 26).

As in 2 Nephi 9:16, the next time Jacob uses the phrase "fire and brimstone," it is connected with the devil's angels. In Jacob 3:11 he exhorts, "Arouse the faculties of your souls; shake yourselves that ye

---

Language and Literature 20, no. 4 (2011): 320. I note that most of the distinctive phrases I discuss in this book do not occur with sufficient frequency to merit statistical analysis. In this chapter, one other phrase, discussed below, will be statistically analyzed.

19 The other four uses are by Nephi, Alma, the chief judge of Ammonihah, and the Lord (all one time each).

may awake from the slumber of death; and loose yourselves from the pains of hell that ye may not become angels to the devil, to be cast into that lake of *fire and brimstone* which is the second death."

Jacob's final two uses of the phrase "fire and brimstone" occur in Jacob 6:10, where he writes that those who reject the words of Christ "must go away into that lake of *fire and brimstone,* whose flames are unquenchable, and whose smoke ascendeth up forever and ever, which lake of *fire and brimstone* is endless torment." This highlights another distinctive Jacob phrase. In both 2 Nephi 9:19 and 2 Nephi 9:26, Jacob defines the "lake of fire and brimstone" as "endless torment," something he reiterates in Jacob 6:10. The phrase "endless torment" appears six times in the Book of Mormon (Jacob accounts for half of those usages). The only other speaker who connects "fire and brimstone" with "endless torment" is Nephi (see 2 Nephi 28:23).[20]

Angels to the devil

There are six instances in the Book of Mormon that specifically refer to the devil's angels, and half of them come from Jacob (see 2 Nephi 9:9, 16; Jacob 3:11).[21] In addition to the passages described in the previous section, Jacob teaches that without God's mercy and grace, we would "become devils, *angels to a devil,* to be shut out from the presence of our God" (2 Nephi 9:9). Jacob is the only author on the small plates to talk about the devil's angels.[22] He is also the only Book of Mormon author to connect the devil's angels with fire and brimstone.[23]

---

20 The phrase "fire and brimstone" collocates with the word *torment(s)* in Mosiah 3:27 and Alma 12:17.

21 The other three occur in the words of Jesus Christ (see Mosiah 26:27; 3 Nephi 9:2) and Mormon (Moroni 7:17).

22 Lehi and Jacob refer to the devil as an angel (see 2 Nephi 2:17; 9:8). Korihor speaks of the devil appearing "in the form of an angel" (Alma 30:53).

23 In Mosiah 26:27, Jesus Christ says that those who never knew him "shall depart into everlasting fire prepared for the devil and his angels." This is the only other Book of Mormon reference outside of Jacob's words that collocates *fire, devil,* and *angels.*

Awful guilt

The word *awful* and its derivatives appear forty-nine times in the Book of Mormon; thirteen of these occurrences (27 percent) come from Jacob. Jacob speaks of the "awful" state of the wicked (2 Nephi 9:27), the "awfulness of yielding to the enticings" of the devil (verse 39), and the "awful consequences" of "every kind of sin" (Jacob 3:12). Jacob's use of "awful monster" (discussed in a later section of this chapter) is unique to his sermon in 2 Nephi; his use of the phrase "awful guilt" is also unique to Jacob and appears in both pericopes where he speaks.

In 2 Nephi 9:46 Jacob says, "Prepare your souls for that glorious day when justice shall be administered unto the righteous, even the day of judgment, that ye may not shrink with awful fear; that ye may not remember your *awful guilt* in perfectness, and be constrained to exclaim: Holy, holy are thy judgments, O Lord God Almighty—but I know my guilt; I transgressed thy law, and my transgressions are mine; and the devil hath obtained me, that I am a prey to his awful misery." For Jacob, "awful guilt" connects to the day of judgment when, in front of God, we acknowledge our sins.

This same structure appears in Jacob's other use of this phrase. As he draws to the conclusion of his book, Jacob tells those who reject prophetic words that "the power of the redemption and the resurrection, which is in Christ, will bring you to stand with shame and *awful guilt* before the bar of God" (Jacob 6:9).

To modern ears, sermons on "fire and brimstone," "endless torment," becoming "angels to a devil," and "awful guilt" sound extremely severe. In the following generation, Jacob's son Enos tells readers, "There was nothing save it was exceeding harshness, preaching and prophesying of wars, and contentions, and destructions, and continually reminding them of death, and the duration of eternity, and the judgments and the power of God, and all these things—stirring them up continually to keep them in the fear of the Lord. . . . Nothing short of these things . . . would keep [the people] from going down speedily to destruction" (Enos 1:23). In light of Enos's words, we can see that Jacob likely used such intense phrases to "stir up" the people to repentance.

The power of the resurrection

The phrase "power of [. . .] resurrection" occurs seven times in the Book of Mormon, and five of these instances come from Jacob.[24] Jacob consistently focuses on Jesus Christ as the source of the power of resurrection. Jacob speaks of "*the power of the resurrection* of the Holy One of Israel" (2 Nephi 9:12) and twice refers to "*the power of the resurrection* which is in Christ" (Jacob 4:11; see 6:9). Although Jacob emphasizes the centrality of the "power of the resurrection" in overcoming death, he also points out that for those who have rejected God's word, "*the power of the redemption and the resurrection, which is in Christ, will bring you to stand with shame and awful guilt before the bar of God*" (Jacob 6:9).

Beloved brethren

The phrase "beloved brethren" appears seventy-two times in the Book of Mormon, and nobody uses it more than Jacob. Jacob is the first person to use this phrase; he does so by beginning his speech in 2 Nephi 6 with the statement "Behold, my *beloved brethren*" (verse 2). After completing a lengthy quotation from Isaiah, he resumes speaking by stating, "And now, my *beloved brethren* . . ." (2 Nephi 9:1). After taking a break for the evening, Jacob again begins speaking by saying, "And now I, Jacob, speak unto you again, my *beloved brethren*" (2 Nephi 10:1). Similarly, as Jacob begins his later discourse to the Nephites, the first words he says are "Now, my *beloved brethren*" (Jacob 2:2).

Jacob uses the phrase "beloved brethren" twenty times, more than 25 percent of the total occurrences in the Book of Mormon. The only speaker to come close to Jacob's usage is Nephi, who uses the phrase sixteen times. Given that Nephi speaks more than three

---

24 The other two are in 2 Nephi 2:8 and Moroni 7:41. Four additional verses that speak of Christ's "power" in terms of the "resurrection" (without using the specific phrase "power of [. . .] resurrection") are Mosiah 15:20; 18:2; Alma 4:14; 41:2.

times as many words as Jacob, we see a statistically significant difference in the frequency with which Jacob and Nephi use this phrase.[25]

Shame and cross

The words *shame* and *cross* collocate (appear together) two times in the Book of Mormon,[26] both in the words of Jacob. In 2 Nephi 9:18, Jacob says that "they who have endured the *crosses* of the world, and despised the *shame* of it" will "inherit the kingdom of God, . . . and their joy shall be full forever." Later Jacob writes of his deep desire to persuade all people to "believe in Christ, and view his death, and suffer his *cross* and bear the *shame* of the world" (Jacob 1:8). Deidre Green notes, "Jacob is the only Book of Mormon figure besides Christ himself to explicitly call on followers of Christ to suffer Christ's cross and thereby to make suffering with Christ a required task of discipleship."[27]

God's great condescensions

The word *condescension* and its variants appear only five times in the Book of Mormon. The angel guiding Nephi twice speaks of "the condescension of God" (1 Nephi 11:16, 26), and Nephi speaks of the Lord's "condescension unto the children of men" (2 Nephi 4:26). Jacob uniquely uses the adjective *great* to describe God's condescensions on two separate occasions. In 2 Nephi 9:53 he says, "Behold how great the covenants of the Lord, and how *great his condescensions unto the children of men.*" Similarly, he later writes that it is by the Lord's "grace, and *his great condescensions unto the children of men*" that he has power to perform miracles (Jacob 4:7).

Counseling with God

The ideas of counseling with God and receiving/rejecting counsel from God's hand are not unique to Jacob; however, no Book of Mor-

---

25 The LL for "beloved brethren" between Nephi and Jacob is 17.49. Between Jacob and the Book of Mormon as a whole, the LL for this phrase is 60.8. Speaking probabilistically, this means it is extremely unlikely that Jacob's heavy use of this phrase is due to chance.

26 These words also collocate in Hebrews 12:2.

27 Green, *Jacob*, 21.

mon author speaks of these topics more frequently than he does.[28] In both 2 Nephi 9 and Jacob 4, Jacob urges his audience to receive counsel from the Lord. He warns that those who "hearken not unto the counsel of God . . . shall perish" (2 Nephi 9:28), at the same time stating that "to be learned is good if [one] hearken[s] unto the counsels of God" (2 Nephi 9:29). Similarly, in Jacob 4:10 he urges, "Seek not to counsel the Lord, but to take counsel from his hand. For behold, ye yourselves know that he counseleth in wisdom, and in justice, and in great mercy, over all his works." Thus in both pericopes where he speaks, Jacob emphasizes the importance of receiving guidance from God.

Jacob's Unique Phrases

In addition to the distinctive phrases that Jacob used in both 2 Nephi and the book of Jacob, he authored many unique phrases that do not appear elsewhere in the Book of Mormon. In this section, I briefly identify and discuss two of these phrases, although many more could be added.[29]

Hell and the awful monster

The word *hell* appears fifty-nine times in the Book of Mormon, and ten of those occurrences are in the words of Jacob. Thus Jacob,

---

28 See 1 Nephi 19:7; 2 Nephi 9:28–29; 28:30; Jacob 4:10; Alma 29:8; 37:12, 37; and Helaman 12:5–6. It is possible that Alma was influenced by Jacob's words regarding "counsel[ing] in wisdom" (Jacob 4:10; compare Alma 29:8; 37:12). For additional information on how later Book of Mormon authors use Jacob's words, see chapter 7 herein.

29 Additional words or phrases unique to Jacob in the Book of Mormon but not discussed herein include the following: "merciful plan" (2 Nephi 9:6), "father of lies" (2 Nephi 9:9), "angel of light" (2 Nephi 9:9), "captive spirits" and "captive bodies" (2 Nephi 9:12), "delivereth his saints" (2 Nephi 9:19), "not [. . .] shaken" (2 Nephi 9:40; Jacob 7:5), "hearken diligently" (2 Nephi 9:51), "hang down" (2 Nephi 10:20), "cheer up" (2 Nephi 10:23), "grace divine" (2 Nephi 10:25), "responsibility" (Jacob 1:19; 2:2), "labor in sin" (Jacob 2:5), "wounded soul" (Jacob 2:8), "piercing eye" (Jacob 2:10), "hand of Providence" (Jacob 2:13), "be familiar with all" (Jacob 2:17), "sobbings" (Jacob 2:35), "slumber of death" (Jacob 3:11), "thankful hearts" (Jacob 4:3), "beyond the mark" (Jacob 4:14), and "power of justice" (Jacob 6:10).

writing just 3 percent of the total words in the Book of Mormon, disproportionately accounts for 17 percent of the instances of *hell*. Jacob uses the word *hell* more than any other author in the Book of Mormon.

Jacob not only speaks of hell frequently, he also talks about it in unique ways. More than any other author, Jacob collocates *death* and *hell* in his descriptions of what happens to the wicked. He is also the only scriptural author to collocate *monster* with *hell* and the only scriptural author to use the phrase "awful monster," which he does three times in 2 Nephi 9.[30] In verse 10, Jacob refers to "death and hell" as an "awful monster," which he calls "the death of the body, and also the death of the spirit."[31] On two additional occasions in this discourse, Jacob speaks similarly, praising the Holy One of Israel who "delivereth his saints from that *awful monster* the devil, and death, and hell" (verse 19), and explaining that those who do not receive the law "are delivered from that *awful monster*, death and hell" (verse 26).

As a point of contrast in how the word *hell* is used by Book of Mormon authors, Alma (who proportionally speaking is the second-highest user of *hell*) frequently refers to the "chains of hell," whereas Jacob never uses this phrase.[32] Jacob uses the phrase "death and hell" four times, and he refers to hell as an "awful monster" three times, but these phrases are never used by Alma.[33]

---

30 For more details on Jacob's use of the word *monster*, see Daniel Belnap, "'I Will Contend with Them That Contendeth with Thee': The Divine Warrior in Jacob's Speech of 2 Nephi 6–10," *Journal of the Book of Mormon and Restoration Scripture* 17, nos. 1–2 (2008): 20–39.

31 Two verses later, Jacob explains that "spiritual death is hell" (2 Nephi 9:12). Jacob is the only scriptural author to explicitly equate "spiritual death" with "hell."

32 The phrase "chains of hell" appears six times in the Book of Mormon and is nearly unique to Alma (see Alma 5:7, 9–10; 12:11; 13:30). Ammon uses it one time in Alma 26:14.

33 The phrase "death and hell" appears six times in the 2013 edition of the Book of Mormon—four times in Jacob's words and twice in Nephi's (see 2 Nephi 28:23, where the phrase comes twice in quick succession). Royal Skousen suggests that one of the phrases attributed to Nephi is a duplicate

The pleasing word of God

The word *pleasing* occurs twelve times in the Book of Mormon; half of these occurrences come from Jacob's words. As Jacob draws his book to a close, he writes, "I bid you farewell, until I shall meet you before the pleasing bar of God" (Jacob 6:13). It appears that Moroni uses this phrase from Jacob in his final words, writing, "I bid unto all, farewell. . . . [I will] meet you before the pleasing bar of the great Jehovah" (Moroni 10:34).[34]

Jacob uses the phrase "the pleasing word of God" three times and is the only author to use this phrase (see Jacob 2:8, 9; 3:2).[35] He uses it during his speech to Nephite men in Jacob 2–3. He tells the Nephites that the "*pleasing word of God* . . . healeth the wounded soul" (Jacob 2:8). Jacob also encourages listeners to "receive the *pleasing word of God*, and feast upon his love" (Jacob 3:2). As with other Jacobean sayings discussed throughout this chapter, this distinctive phrase indicates his unique authorial voice.

Therefore, What?

Jacob is a key figure in the Book of Mormon, and his words had a lasting impact—not only in their original form but also in how later Book of Mormon prophets echoed his words (see chapter 7). In this chapter, I have focused on Jacob's distinctive words and phrases,

---

and was not present in the earliest text. See Royal Skousen, "Some Textual Changes for a Scholarly Study of the Book of Mormon," *BYU Studies Quarterly* 51, no. 4 (2012): 99–117. If Skousen is correct, this makes Jacob's use of this phrase even more unique. Given that Nephi's writings in 2 Nephi 28 take place after Jacob's sermon in 2 Nephi 9, it is possible that Nephi is drawing on Jacob's words.

34 Royal Skousen suggests that both Jacob 6:13 and Moroni 10:34 should read "pleading bar." But given Jacob's unusual penchant for using the word *pleasing* and the fact that he never uses the word *pleading*, it is certainly possible that "pleasing bar" is in fact the correct reading and that Moroni was alluding to Jacob's words. For further discussion, see Royal Skousen, *Analysis of Textual Variants of the Book of Mormon: Part Two; 2 Nephi 11–Mosiah 16* (Provo, UT: FARMS, 2005), 1047–52.

35 The shorter phrase "pleasing word" appears only in these same three verses as part of the phrase "the pleasing word of God."

such as "God," "fire and brimstone," "endless torment," "angels to a devil," "awful guilt," "power of resurrection," and "beloved brethren." These words and phrases are disproportionately used by Jacob and appear in his words in both 2 Nephi and the book of Jacob. While these phrases do not provide definitive evidence that Jacob is a separate author from Nephi, the fact that several phrases appear to be uniquely used by Jacob certainly suggests two distinct voices.

Ultimately, the power of identifying Jacob's distinctive voice may not be in its apologetic value but rather in its portrait of a faithful prophet. He knew both agony and abuse. As a child, Jacob "suffered afflictions and much sorrow, because of the rudeness of [his] brethren" (2 Nephi 2:1), and yet he taught that the "pleasing word of God . . . healeth the wounded soul" (Jacob 2:8). Although Jacob was concerned he would "stumble because of [his] over anxiety" (Jacob 4:18), he taught that through the Lord's "grace, and his great condescensions unto the children of men," weaknesses can be overcome (Jacob 4:7). He knew what it was like to hurt, to pray, to work, and to heal. He knew, in part, what many of us experience today. Jacob's voice speaks to those who have suffered and points to the Savior as the source of healing.

Jacob's distinctive phrases also provide rich doctrinal insights that reach beyond empathy and understanding to the power that can change lives. Although some of his words could be seen as severe or strict—like his teachings regarding an "awful monster," "death and hell," and "a lake of fire and brimstone"[36]—Jacob also offers tender words of hope that God will "raise [us] from death by the power of the resurrection, and also from everlasting death by the power of the atonement, that [we] may be received into the eternal kingdom of God" (2 Nephi 10:25). The undercurrent of Jacob's words is one of hope and empowerment: God will keep his promises to his children, and it is within our power to keep our promises to him and live (see 2 Nephi 10:2, 17; Jacob 6:5–6).

---

36 On a personal note, my first encounter with Jacob's words came when I was ten years old. While I was certainly not wicked, I could be quite mischievous at times. One Monday night we had a home evening and read from 2 Nephi chapter 9. Jacob's teachings regarding fire, brimstone, and hell motivated me to make some changes. I am not suggesting I was an evil ten-year-old, nor that the best reason to be righteous is fear; I am simply illustrating in a personal way the influence Jacob's words can have.

Chapter 3
Alma and the Plan of Redemption

Approximately five hundred years after Jacob's stern yet tender preaching, another powerful prophet emerged. Alma the Younger was a rabble-rouser turned high priest and chief judge whose voice testified with authority and love.[1] We hear the voice of Alma the Younger (herein simply referred to as "Alma") more than any other, with the exceptions of Mormon and Nephi. Alma speaks some twenty thousand words in the Book of Mormon, accounting for approximately 7.5 percent of the entire text. His words occur more than the combined total of those of Lehi, King Benjamin, Amulek, Samuel the Lamanite, and Abinadi.

We know relatively little of Alma's youth. His father was converted by the teachings of Abinadi and became the leader of the Church in Zarahemla. In Alma's younger years, Alma and the sons

---

1   S. Kent Brown writes, "The sermons of Alma deserve at least a fraction of the centuries-long attention that the epistles of the Apostle Paul have received. Alma's recorded sermons, whether formal or spontaneous, weave a tapestry of complex and variegated colors, of rich imagery, and yet of a bold and simple unity which holds in tight focus the unspeakable blessings of accepting the atonement of Jesus Christ." S. Kent Brown, "Alma's Conversion: Reminiscences in His Sermons," in *The Book of Mormon: Alma, the Testimony of the Word*, ed. Monte S. Nyman and Charles D. Tate Jr. (Provo, UT: Religious Studies Center, Brigham Young University, 1992), 141.

of Mosiah went about "seeking to destroy the church, and to lead astray the people of the Lord" (Mosiah 27:10). Mormon describes Alma as a "very wicked and an idolatrous man[,] . . . a man of many words, [who] did speak much flattery to the people; therefore he led many of the people to do after the manner of his iniquities" (Mosiah 27:8). In this earliest description of Alma, we are told that he has particularly strong powers of speech; these powers are evident in his later discourses.

On one occasion, when Alma was traveling with some friends with the specific purpose "to destroy the church of God," an angel appeared and spoke "with a voice of thunder" (Mosiah 27:10–11). Alma and his friends were so astonished that they "fell to the earth" (verse 12). The angel then said, "Alma, arise and stand forth, for why persecutest thou the church of God? For the Lord hath said: This is my church, and I will establish it; and nothing shall overthrow it, save it is the transgression of my people" (verse 13).

Alma was so astonished that he lost his ability to both speak and move, and his friends carried him to his father. After two days and two nights, Alma's strength returned; Alma declared, "I have repented of my sins, and have been redeemed of the Lord; behold I am born of the Spirit" (verse 24). From this point forward, Alma dedicated his life to testifying of Jesus Christ and played multiple important roles in Nephite society. At one point he was the chief judge (the highest political office) and the high priest (the highest ecclesiastical office). In about 83 BC, after juggling both roles for approximately five years, Alma gave up the judgment seat to focus on "bearing down in pure testimony" to the people (Alma 4:19). Alma would spend the last decade of his life preaching to all who would hear.

Near the end of his reign, King Mosiah$_2$ transferred to Alma the sacred records in his possession. When Alma received the plates, he was instructed to "keep a record" (Mosiah 28:20), a commandment that he clearly kept. Mormon begins the book of Alma specifically acknowledging that he is drawing on Alma's record and also notes that his abridgment of the mission of the sons of Mosiah to the Lamanites comes from Alma's record (see the heading to the book of Alma and the heading just before Alma 17).

Most of the words we hear Alma speak come from his sermons to the people of Zarahemla (Alma 5), Gideon (Alma 7), Ammonihah (Alma 9, 12–13), and Antionum (Alma 32–33), as well as his words of counsel to Helaman, Shiblon, and Corianton (Alma 36–42). With only one exception, prefacing each of these messages is a statement from Mormon that the words have come from Alma's own record.[2]

For example, just before Alma 7, Alma's message to the people of Gideon, Mormon writes, "The words of Alma which he delivered to the people in Gideon, *according to his own record.*" Before recording Alma's words to his three sons, Mormon notes, "[Alma] caused that his sons should be gathered together, that he might give unto them every one his charge, separately, concerning the things pertaining unto righteousness. And *we have an account of his commandments, which he gave unto them according to his own record*" (Alma 35:16).

In Mormon's multiple and specific notations of Alma's records, we see evidence that Mormon is preserving Alma's actual words. In this chapter we will explore Alma's unique voice through three different approaches. We will first examine two seemingly insignificant words that Alma uses with unusual frequency. We will then look at four theologically significant words that Alma disproportionately uses. Finally, we will briefly explore Alma's propensity to ask questions.

Insignificant Words

There are at least two seemingly insignificant words that Alma disproportionately uses: *now* and *yea*. There does not seem to be anything theologically significant about Alma's use of these words; rather, he frequently uses them as a discourse marker. For example, in Alma 7:17 Alma says, "And *now* my beloved brethren, do you believe these things? Behold, I say unto you, *yea*, I know that ye believe them; and the way that I know that ye believe them is by the manifestation of the Spirit which is in me. And *now* because your faith is strong concerning that, *yea*, concerning the things which I have

---

2   There is no such statement before Alma's message to the people of Antionum (the Zoramites).

spoken, great is my joy." In Alma 32:23 Alma declares, "And *now*, he imparteth his word by angels unto men, *yea*, not only men but women also. *Now* this is not all. . . ."

The words *now* and *yea* are common in the Book of Mormon. Each of these words appears more than one thousand times throughout the text and in the voices of more than fifty people (both are used by speakers ranging from Aaron to Zeniff). Although these are commonly used words, Alma uses them with unusual frequency that is statistically measurable.[3] Table 3.1 provides an overview of Alma's use of these two words relative to other Book of Mormon speakers.

Table 3.1. Comparing major speakers' uses of *now* and *yea*

Speaker	Times *now* is used per 1,000 words spoken	Times *yea* is used per 1,000 words spoken
Mormon	6.2	4.1
Nephi	2.7	4.3
Alma	8.9	9.0
Moroni$_2$	2.8	2.3
Jesus Christ	1.1	2.1
The Lord	1.0	4.3
Jacob	3.5	2.0
Isaiah	0.2	1.8
Helaman	7.9	6.3
Lehi$_1$	2.6	4.1

---

3   As noted previously, a commonly accepted measure of statistical significance in corpus linguistics is log-likelihood (LL). The higher the LL, the less likely that differences in word use between two texts are due to chance. An LL score of 6.63 is equivalent to a p value < .01, indicating statistical significance. When comparing Alma's voice to all other Book of Mormon speakers, the LL values for *now* and *yea* are respectively 71.2 and 70, making it extremely unlikely that Alma's frequent use of these words occurs by chance.

King Benjamin	3.8	0.2
Amulek	7.0	9.5
Samuel the Lamanite	2.0	12.4
Moroni$_1$	7.5	16.1
Abinadi	4.3	10.1

Speaking proportionally, no major speaker uses the word *now* as frequently as Alma does. When considering the eleven most frequent speakers in the Book of Mormon, the same is true of *yea*, although Amulek, Samuel the Lamanite, Chief Captain Moroni, and Abinadi use *yea* more frequently than Alma does. When contrasted with the top ten speakers, Alma's use of the common discourse markers *now* and *yea* highlights his distinctive voice.[4]

These words—*now* and *yea*—might be insignificant in and of themselves, but Alma may use them in a way that is significant. Alma appears to use *now* as a rhetorical device to help his audience apply what he is teaching. For example, in preaching to the Nephites, Alma reminds them of their fathers' deliverance from the Lamanites, then asks, "And *now* behold, I say unto you, my brethren, you that belong to this church, have you sufficiently retained in remembrance the captivity of your fathers?" (Alma 5:6). On multiple occasions Alma follows the word *now* with a question meant to cause self-analysis and reflection.[5] He wanted his people to not only understand and believe the doctrine of salvation but also apply it in their lives.

---

4   When comparing Nephi and Alma, one might argue that a substantial portion of Nephi's words in the Book of Mormon are narrative while Alma's are primarily sermonic. But when only Alma's words in Alma 36–42 and Nephi's in 2 Nephi 25–33 (both written versions of sermons given to others) are compared, Alma uses *now* 10 times per 1,000 words spoken, compared to 2.9 times for Nephi (LL = 36.8). Alma uses *yea* 8.1 times per 1,000 words spoken, compared to 3.7 times for Nephi (LL = 14.5). Even more disparate results are found between the voices of Alma and Jesus Christ (LL for *now* = 108.9; LL for *yea* = 73).

5   See Alma 5:8, 10, 14, 22, 26, 39, 53, 58; 7:17; 30:40; 32:18, 29, 30, 31, 34, 35; 33:14; 37:15; 41:12; 42:17, 19.

Alma's use of *yea* seems to be one of calling for listeners' attention or reinforcing the words he is speaking. To the people of Zarahemla Alma says,

> *Yea*, can ye lay aside these things, and trample the Holy One under your feet; *yea*, can ye be puffed up in the pride of your hearts; *yea*, will ye still persist in the wearing of costly apparel and setting your hearts upon the vain things of the world, upon your riches?
>
> *Yea*, will ye persist in supposing that ye are better one than another; *yea*, will ye persist in the persecution of your brethren. . . .
>
> *Yea*, and will you persist in turning your backs upon the poor, and the needy, and in withholding your substance from them? (Alma 5:53–55)

In Alma's frequent use of *yea*, we hear the urgency he feels for people to act on his words.

Significant Words

Clearly the ways in which speakers in the Book of Mormon use specific words can indicate distinctive voices. In Alma's case, words like *now* and *yea* seem to signal a unique speaking pattern. With theologically significant words, which appear much less frequently, it is difficult to determine whether individual speakers use any given word in a unique way. As Philip Allred writes, "Even though an author's use of a word might potentially qualify for statistical significance, any statistical model that could be employed to determine such significance would necessarily assume normal or similar topic distribution within the Book of Mormon. Because the different writers treated diverse subjects, . . . it is nearly impossible to prove *objectively* that an author's word usage is statistically significant on the basis of word frequency alone."[6]

Nevertheless, Allred provides a cogent example of distinctive voices by explaining Alma's use of the word *state* (meaning "condition"). He points out that "all but two of the eleven writers who used *state* did so infrequently and sporadically. In contrast, the recorded

---

6   Philip A. Allred, "Alma's Use of *State* in the Book of Mormon: Evidence of Multiple Authorship," *Journal of Book of Mormon Studies* 5, no. 1 (1996): 141.

writings of Alma, and in one case, Lehi, contain passages that display unusual concentrations of the word *state*.[7] Allred goes on to demonstrate that Alma not only uses the word *state* more frequently than other speakers in the Book of Mormon but also uses it differently than others do, further establishing his distinctive patterns of speech.

Allred writes, "Alma certainly stands distinct from the other authors in the Book of Mormon when his use of *state* is analyzed. Alma's unique concentration of *state*, his tendency to reword with *state*, and his distinctive treatment of a shared topic involving *state* all point to him as a unique writer within the Book of Mormon. This is perfectly consistent with Joseph's claims about the Book of Mormon."[8] *State* is one example of a word that Alma uniquely uses. Let us now examine the following significant words Alma uses in distinctive ways: *soul(s)*, *plan*, *resurrection*, and *remembering captivity*.

Souls(s)

The words *soul* and *souls* collectively appear 251 times in the Book of Mormon, and 60 of these (24 percent) come from Alma. Alma uses these words not only proportionally more than anybody else but also numerically more. His frequent use of these words relative to other Book of Mormon voices is statistically significant.[9] Table 3.2 summarizes the frequency with which major speakers use these words.

Table 3.2. Comparing major speakers' use of *souls(s)*

Speaker	Times *soul(s)* is used per 1,000 words spoken	Times *soul(s)* is used	Percent of total uses of *soul(s)* in the Book of Mormon	Percent of total words in the Book of Mormon attributed to speaker
Alma	3.0	60	23.9%	7.5%
Jacob	2.0	17	6.8%	3.2%

---

7   Allred, "Alma's Use of *State* in the Book of Mormon," 141.

8   Allred, "Alma's Use of *State* in the Book of Mormon," 146.

9   Comparing Alma's words with words from all other Book of Mormon speakers provides an LL value of 43.4.

Lehi₁	1.5	7	2.8%	1.7%
Helaman	1.4	7	2.8%	1.9%
Nephi	1.2	35	13.9%	10.5%
King Benjamin	1.2	5	2.0%	1.6%
Samuel the Lamanite	0.7	2	0.8%	1.1%
Abinadi	0.7	2	0.8%	1.0%
Mormon	0.6	56	22.3%	36.4%
Isaiah	0.6	5	2.0%	3.0%
Moroni₂	0.5	10	4.0%	7.3%
Jesus Christ	0.4	6	2.4%	5.3%
The Lord	0.3	3	1.2%	4.5%
Amulek	0.3	1	0.4%	1.2%
Moroni₁	0	0	0.0%	1.1%

The word *soul* or *souls* appears in every major message Alma gives. For example, to the people of Zarahemla, Alma asks, "Can ye imagine yourselves brought before the tribunal of God with your *souls* filled with guilt and remorse?" (Alma 5:18). In the land of Gideon, Alma says, "My *soul* doth exceedingly rejoice, because of the exceeding diligence and heed which ye have given unto my word" (Alma 7:26). Alma declares to the people of Ammonihah, "The time is at hand that all men shall reap a reward of their works, according to that which they have been—if they have been righteous they shall reap the salvation of their *souls*, according to the power and deliverance of Jesus Christ; and if they have been evil they shall reap the damnation of their *souls*" (Alma 9:28).

In addition to using the word *soul* in each of his major messages, Alma also employs it in many of his shorter statements. For example, the first time we hear Alma's voice is when he regained strength after his angelic visitation. Alma said, "My *soul* hath been redeemed from the gall of bitterness and bonds of iniquity. I was in the darkest abyss; but now I behold the marvelous light of God. My *soul* was racked with eternal torment; but I am snatched, and my *soul* is pained no more" (Mosiah 27:29). As he later said of his conversion, "My *soul* was harrowed up to the greatest degree" (Alma 36:12); "God did wrack my *soul* with inexpressible horror" (verse 14); and "For three days and for three nights was I racked, even with the pains of a damned *soul*" (verse 16). Alma knew, in a very real and personal way, the awful state of a damned soul and the joyful state of a saved one.

Several years after his first angelic encounter, Alma expressed his joy in sharing the gospel with others by exclaiming, "This is my glory, that perhaps I may be an instrument in the hands of God to bring some *soul* to repentance; and this is my joy. And behold, when I see many of my brethren truly penitent, and coming to the Lord their God, then is my *soul* filled with joy" (Alma 29:9–10).

While Alma experienced joy with those who came to God, Korihor's actions pained Alma. Alma told Korihor, "I am grieved because of the hardness of your heart, yea, that ye will still resist the spirit of the truth, that thy *soul* may be destroyed. But behold, it is better that thy *soul* should be lost than that thou shouldst be the means of bringing many *souls* down to destruction, by thy lying and by thy flattering words" (Alma 30:46–47).

In his prayer just before preaching to the Zoramites, Alma implored, "I am infirm, and such wickedness among this people doth pain my *soul*. O Lord, my heart is exceedingly sorrowful; wilt thou comfort my *soul* in Christ. . . . O Lord, wilt thou comfort my *soul*, and give unto me success, and also my fellow laborers who are with me—yea, . . . even all these wilt thou comfort, O Lord. Yea, wilt thou comfort their *souls* in Christ" (Alma 31:30–32).

Not only does Alma use *souls(s)* more frequently than other speakers, but he also uses these words differently than other speakers do. This can be seen both in Alma's distinctive use of *soul* (discussed below) and in ways he *does not* use it. For example, five Book of Mormon speakers on seven occasions speak of the *welfare* of another's *soul*, but Alma never does so.[10] Eleven different times in four different chapters, Nephi uses the phrase "My soul delighteth." Not only does Alma not use that phrase, but nobody else in the Book of Mormon does, highlighting a phrase that is unique to Nephi.

Alma has his own distinctive uses of *soul*. For example, the phrase "state of . . . the soul" appears six times in the Book of Mormon; four of those come from Alma.[11] The words *soul* and *body* appear together in the same verse eighteen times in the Book of Mormon; half of those come from Alma. Three times Alma prays for his or others' *souls* to be *comforted* (see Alma 31:31–32), but nobody else in the Book of Mormon prays for this. Moreover, in scripture there are only five references to a *soul* being *racked* with extreme pain, and four of these come from Alma (see Mosiah 27:29; Alma 36:12, 14, 16).[12]

Alma's most concentrated use of *soul(s)* occurs in Alma 40. A key issue that Alma "inquired diligently of the Lord" to learn more about was "the state of the *soul* between death and the resurrection" (Alma 40:9, 11). Although latter-day revelation defines the "soul" as being "the spirit and the body" (Doctrine and Covenants 88:15), it's clear that Alma uses the word *soul* interchangeably with *spirit* in this pericope. For example, in Alma 40:13, Alma speaks of "the *spirits* of the wicked" and then, in verse 14, referring to the same group of people, calls them "the *souls* of the wicked." He also speaks of "the spirit, or the soul" (Alma 40:15). When Alma talks to Corianton about the Resurrection, he primarily describes it in terms of the *soul* and the *body*. Consider these examples:

- "[The First Resurrection] meaneth *the reuniting of the soul with the body*" (Alma 40:18).
- "Whether *the souls and the bodies* of those of whom has been spoken shall all be reunited at once, the wicked as well as the righteous, I do not say" (Alma 40:19).

---

10 These speakers are Jacob (2 Nephi 6:3; Jacob 2:3), Lehi (2 Nephi 2:30), Mormon (Mosiah 25:11; Alma 6:6), Moroni₂ (Moroni 6:5), and Nephi (2 Nephi 32:9).

11 The other two come from a conversation between Nephi and his brothers (see 1 Nephi 15:31, 35).

12 The other instance comes from Moroni₂ (see Mormon 9:3).

- "I give it as my opinion, that the *souls* and the *bodies* are reunited, of the righteous, at the resurrection of Christ" (Alma 40:20).

- "The dead shall come forth, and be reunited, both *soul* and *body*" (Alma 40:21).

- "The *soul* shall be restored to the *body*, and the *body* to the *soul*" (Alma 40:23).

- "It is requisite and just, according to the power and *resurrection* of Christ, that the *soul* of man should be restored to its *body*" (Alma 41:2).

Alma is the only Book of Mormon speaker to collocate the words *body*, *soul*, and *resurrection*. Moreover, Alma never describes the Resurrection in terms of *the spirit* and *the body*; he always uses the word *soul*. In contrast, Jacob, who is proportionally the second most frequent user of *soul*, never uses *soul* in connection with the Resurrection; he instead uses the word *spirit*:

> Death and hell must deliver up their dead, and hell must deliver up its captive *spirits*, and the grave must deliver up its captive *bodies*, and the bodies and the spirits of men will be restored one to the other; and it is by the power of the *resurrection* of the Holy One of Israel.
>
> O how great the plan of our God! For on the other hand, the paradise of God must deliver up the *spirits* of the righteous, and the grave deliver up the *body* of the righteous; and the *spirit* and the *body* is restored to itself again. (2 Nephi 9:12–13)

Plan

Alma uses the word *plan* numerically more than any other speaker and proportionally more than any major speaker except Amulek.[13] Some speakers, including Alma, use the word *plan* to refer to evil plans such as secret combinations. More significant, however, is the use of the word *plan* in terms of the plan of redemption or plan of salvation. This usage of *plan* is outlined in table 3.3.

---

13 Comparing Alma's use of *plan* to that of all other Book of Mormon speakers provides an LL value of 54.

Table 3.3. Use of *plan* in terms of God's plan of redemption/salvation by major Book of Mormon speakers[14]

Speaker	Times used per 1,000 words spoken	Times used	Percent of total uses of *plan* in terms of God's plan of redemption/ salvation	Percent of total words in the Book of Mormon attributed to speaker
Amulek	0.95	3	10.7%	1.2%
Alma	0.9	18	64.3%	7.5%
Jacob	0.4	3	10.7%	3.2%
Lehi₁	0.2	1	3.6%	1.7%
Nephi₁	0.04	1	3.6%	10.5%
Mormon	0.02	2	7.1%	36.4%

When speaking of God's plan for his children, Alma uses the word *plan* more than all other speakers combined (eighteen times for Alma versus twelve times for the remaining speakers). He also uses more unique phrases related to God's plan than any other author. In the Book of Mormon, nine titles for God's plan appear:

1. "The merciful plan of the great Creator" (2 Nephi 9:6, unique to Jacob)
2. "The plan of our God" (2 Nephi 9:13, unique to Jacob)
3. "The great and eternal plan of deliverance from death" (2 Nephi 11:5, unique to Nephi)
4. The "plan of redemption" (first used by Jacob, then used eleven times by Alma, three times by Mormon, and twice by Amulek)
5. "The plan of salvation" (first used by Jarom, then once by Alma and once by King Anti-Nephi-Lehi)
6. "The great plan of the Eternal God" (Alma 34:9, unique to Amulek)

14 The word *plan* is used in reference to the nefarious plans of men or the devil eleven times by Mormon, five times by Alma, four times by Moroni₂, and once each by Amulek, the daughter of Jared, Helaman₂, Jacob, and Nephi₂. Jarom and King Anti-Nephi-Lehi are the only minor Book of Mormon speakers to use the word *plan* in terms of "plan of salvation" (one time each).

7. "The plan of restoration" (Alma 41:2, unique to Alma)

8. "The plan of happiness" (Alma 42:8, 16, unique to Alma)

9. "The plan of mercy" (Alma 42:15, 31, occurring three times, all in Alma's voice)

Of these nine titles, Alma uses five of them, and three of these are unique to Alma. Across the thirty times that "plan of _____"[15] appears in the Book of Mormon, "the plan of redemption" is the most popular, occurring seventeen times, eleven of which are in Alma's voice.

Although Alma frequently talks about "the plan," he actually does so only in three pericopes. In Alma 29:1–2, he briefly mentions it, saying, "O that I were an angel, and could have the wish of mine heart, that I might go forth and . . . declare unto every soul, as with the voice of thunder, repentance and *the plan of redemption*, that they should repent and come unto our God."

In contrast, Alma refers to God's plan seven times in Alma 12 while preaching to the people of Ammonihah and ten times in Alma 39–42 while speaking to his son Corianton. Alma told the people of Ammonihah that because of Adam's Fall, "*all mankind became a lost and fallen people*," but "this life became *a probationary state; a time to prepare to meet God*" (Alma 12:22, 24). Alma further explained, "Now, *if it had not been for the plan of redemption*, which was laid from the foundation of the world, there could have been no resurrection of the dead" (Alma 12:25).

Alma similarly told Corianton that because of the Fall, "*man* became *lost* forever, yea, they *became fallen man*," although "there was *a time* granted unto man to repent, yea, *a probationary time, a time to repent and serve God*" (Alma 42:4, 6). As he specified to the people of Ammonihah, so he said to Corianton, "And now remember, my son, *if it were not for the plan of redemption*, (laying it aside) as soon as they were dead their souls were miserable, being cut off from the presence of the Lord" (verse 11). Observing Alma's consistent ways of speaking

---

15 This excludes seven additional times when the phrase "plan of _____" is used to refer to evil plans (e.g., Ether 13:15).

to the people of Ammonihah and his son Corianton suggests that Alma used a similar approach when discussing specific topics.[16]

Alma's three unique titles for God's plan all come as he counsels Corianton. It is noteworthy that these titles connect with Corianton's specific concerns. For example, Corianton was "worried . . . concerning the restoration" (Alma 41:1). In response, Alma taught about "the plan of restoration" (Alma 41:2). Corianton was also concerned about "the justice of God in the punishment of the sinner"; he felt it was "injustice that the sinner should be consigned to a state of misery" (Alma 42:1). In response to Corianton's concern about misery, Alma spoke of "the great plan of happiness" (Alma 42:8). He also taught Corianton that while justice is required, "God himself atoneth for the sins of the world, to bring about *the plan of mercy*, to appease the demands of justice, that God might be a perfect, just God, and a merciful God also" (Alma 42:15). Thus, as Alma taught Corianton, he tailored his phraseology regarding God's plan to meet Corianton's specific needs.

Resurrection

As outlined in table 3.4, Alma uses the word *resurrection* numerically more than any other speaker and proportionally more than any speaker except Abinadi.[17]

---

16 This is part of a broader set of connections between Alma's words to the people of Ammonihah and Corianton. See Grant Hardy, "Nurturing Faith: Literary Patterning in the Book of Alma," in *Give Ear to My Words*, ed. Kerry Hull, Nicholas J. Frederick, and Hank R. Smith (Provo, UT: Religious Studies Center, Brigham Young University; Salt Lake City: Deseret Book, 2019), 369–88.

17 Comparing Alma's use of *resurrection* to that of all other Book of Mormon speakers provides an LL value of 73.5. However, as Allred cautioned regarding the word *state*, statistical tools (such as LL) become less useful when examining words that appear with less frequency and are less likely to be randomly distributed.

Table 3.4. Use of *resurrection* by major Book of Mormon speakers[18]

Speaker	Times used per 1,000 words spoken	Times used	Percent of total uses of *resurrection* in the Book of Mormon	Percent of total words in the Book of Mormon attributed to speaker
Abinadi	5.7	16	19.6%	1.0%
Alma	1.7	34	42%	7.5%
Jacob	1.1	9	11.1%	3.2%
Samuel the Lamanite	1.0	3	3.7%	1.1%
Amulek	0.3	1	1.2%	1.2%
Lehi	0.21	1	1.2%	1.7%
Mormon	0.13	13	16%	36.4%
Moroni$_2$	0.05	1	1.2%	7.3%
Nephi	0.03	1	1.2%	10.5%

It's interesting to note the lineal descent in the use of *resurrection* between Abinadi, Alma the Elder, and his son Alma. As discussed further in chapter 9, Alma appears to draw on Abinadi's words when he teaches about the Resurrection. For example, Abinadi is the first speaker in the Book of Mormon to teach about the First Resurrection, a phrase used only by Abinadi, Alma the Elder, and his son Alma. Alma the Elder was obviously touched by Abinadi's words and recorded them (see Mosiah 17:4), and his son Alma "remembered [hearing his] father prophesy unto the people concerning the coming of one Jesus Christ" (Alma 36:17). Thus it is perhaps not surprising that together Alma and Abinadi account for more than half of the instances of *resurrection* in the Book of Mormon.

---

18 Two minor speakers, Alma$_1$ (Mosiah 18:9) and Zeezrom (Alma 12:8), also use the word resurrection.

Alma's uses of *resurrection* appear in just three passages. He uses it three times while preaching in Ammonihah (see Alma 12:24–25), once while preaching to the Zoramites (see Alma 33:22), and thirty times while talking to Corianton (twenty-seven times in Alma 40 alone). This concentrated usage in Alma 40 is explained by the fact that Corianton's "mind [was] worried concerning the resurrection of the dead" (Alma 40:1), and Alma worked to resolve this concern.

Alma distinctively collocates specific words with *resurrection*. Of the nine verses in which *resurrection* and *body* appear together in the Book of Mormon, seven of them are stated by Alma. Alma is the only Book of Mormon author to use *resurrection* and *time* together, which he does in six different verses.[19] In addition, the phrase "resurrection of Christ" appears nine times in the Book of Mormon, six times in Alma's voice.

Remembering captivity

When reading the Book of Mormon sequentially, a reader first encounters Alma when Mormon tells us that Alma, along with the sons of Mosiah, was "going about to destroy the church of God" (Mosiah 27:10). An angel stopped them along the way and delivered a message that said in part, "Go, and *remember the captivity* of thy fathers in the land of Helam, and in the land of Nephi; and *remember* how great things he has done for them; for they were in *bondage*, and he has *delivered* them" (Mosiah 27:16). This injunction to remember the captivity of his fathers had a significant impact on Alma.

But before discussing this impact, let us briefly review what the angel meant by "the captivity of thy fathers in the land of Helam." Alma's father, Alma the Elder, had been a priest in King Noah's court, living a life of iniquity. But Alma the Elder believed in the words of Abinadi and began teaching people who would listen to his message. Eventually Alma the Elder and a small group of believers settled in a land called Helam, where they peaceably lived for several years. Their tranquility was interrupted when some Lamanites discovered them and placed them in bondage. The Lamanites appointed Amulon, an-

---

19 On one occasion, Alma the Elder uses the words *times* and *resurrection* in the same verse (see Mosiah 18:9).

other former priest of King Noah and one who despised Alma the Elder, to rule over Alma the Elder's people. Mormon records that "Amulon began to exercise authority over Alma [the Elder] and his brethren, and began to persecute him, and cause that his children should persecute their children. . . . He [also] exercised authority over them, and put tasks upon them, and put task-masters over them" (Mosiah 24:8–9).

Despite these great afflictions, Alma the Elder and his people remained faithful. Eventually the Lord caused a miracle to occur: Alma the Elder and his people gathered their possessions and fled in the night, and the next morning their taskmasters overslept, allowing sufficient time for the escape. After they were safely away from the land of Helam, Alma the Elder and his people "poured out their thanks to God because he had been merciful unto them, and eased their burdens, and had *delivered* them out of *bondage*; for they were in *bondage*, and none could *deliver* them except it were the Lord their God" (Mosiah 24:21). Eventually they safely arrived in the land of Zarahemla.

One would think that with a miraculous heritage such as this, Alma would have been a diligent missionary rather than one seeking to destroy the church of God. Yet apparently, although this story was a part of his family history, he hadn't deeply integrated it into his heart. But once the angel told him to *remember* his fathers' *captivity*, *bondage*, and *deliverance*, Alma took this message seriously.

In his first recorded discourse to the Nephites, he declared, "Have you sufficiently retained in *remembrance* the *captivity* of your fathers? Yea, and have you sufficiently retained in *remembrance* his mercy and long-suffering towards them? And moreover, have ye sufficiently retained in *remembrance* that he has *delivered* their souls from hell?" (Alma 5:6).[20]

Later, after a reunion with the sons of Mosiah, Alma said, "I also *remember* the *captivity* of my fathers; for I surely do know that the Lord did *deliver* them out of *bondage* . . . ; yea, the Lord God . . . did *deliver* them out of *bondage*. Yea, I have *always remembered* the *captivity* of my

---

20 In this passage Alma seems to be referring to the spiritual bondage of his fathers, perhaps in addition to the temporal bondage they experienced in Helam.

fathers; and that same God who *delivered* them out of the hands of the Egyptians did *deliver* them out of *bondage*" (Alma 29:11–12).

Finally, Alma twice emphasized this concept in his conversation with his son Helaman, saying, "I would that ye should do as I have done, in *remembering* the *captivity* of our fathers; for they were in *bondage*, and none could *deliver* them except it was the God of Abraham . . . ; and he surely did *deliver* them in their afflictions. . . . I have *always retained in remembrance their captivity*; yea, and ye also ought to *retain in remembrance*, as I have done, their *captivity*" (Alma 36:2, 29).

Significantly, Alma and the angel who spoke to him are the only figures in the Book of Mormon to speak of remembering captivity. This suggests a real encounter between an angel and Alma, one that had a textually evident impact on Alma's life and ministry.

Alma's Pattern of Asking Questions

In addition to the words Alma disproportionately uses, we find as part of his unique voice a propensity to ask questions. With its current punctuation,[21] the Book of Mormon contains 543 questions, which are asked by a total of 61 people. Alma asks 102 questions, or 19 percent of all the questions in the Book of Mormon, more questions than any other speaker. Even if Alma 5, the chapter containing the most questions, were not included in the Book of Mormon, Alma would still ask more questions than any other speaker. Table 3.5 summarizes the number of questions asked by major Book of Mormon speakers.

---

21 Naturally, question marks were not a part of the original manuscript dictated by Joseph Smith. For the most part, punctuation was added by John Gilbert during the typesetting phase of the publishing process. Comparing the questions asked in the current (2013) edition of the Book of Mormon with Royal Skousen's *The Book of Mormon: The Earliest Text* (New Haven, CT: Yale University Press, 2009) shows some differences in punctuation. Of the 543 questions asked in the 2013 edition, 27 are not phrased as questions in *The Earliest Text*. Because the differences between the 2013 edition and *The Earliest Text* do not affect Alma's overall distinctive voice in terms of asking questions, for simplicity I have used the 2013 text herein.

Table 3.5. Comparing major speakers' use of questions

Speaker	Total times questions are asked per 1,000 words spoken	Total questions asked	Percent of total questions in the Book of Mormon	Percent of total words in the Book of Mormon attributed to speaker
Abinadi	8.7	24	4.4%	1.0%
Alma	5.1	102	18.8%	7.5%
Moroni₁	4.3	13	2.4%	1.1%
Amulek	2.8	9	1.7%	1.2%
Isaiah	2.7	22	5.2%	3.0%
Jesus Christ	2.5	35	6.4%	5.3%
Jacob	2.4	20	3.7%	3.2%
The Lord	2.2	25	4.6%	4.5%
King Benjamin	1.9	8	1.5%	1.6%
Nephi	1.5	42	7.7%	10.5%
Samuel the Lamanite	1.3	4	0.7%	1.1%
Moroni₂	1.2	25	4.6%	7.3%
Mormon	0.2	17	3.1%	36.4%
Helaman	0.2	1	0.2%	1.9%
Lehi₁	0	0	0.0%	1.7%

Although the most distinctive aspect of Alma's use of questions is the sheer volume he asks, there are at least two unique patterns in the type of questions Alma poses. The first pattern is asking people about their beliefs. On twenty different occasions in the Book of Mormon, a speaker asks a direct question about a person's or people's beliefs. Eight of these (40 percent) come from Alma.[22] He asks Zeezrom, "*Believest* thou in the power of Christ unto salvation?" (Alma 15:6), says to Korihor, "*Believest* thou that there is a God?" (Alma 30:37), and asks the Zoramites, "*Do ye believe* those scriptures which have been written by them of old?" (Alma 33:12). Perhaps this style of directly asking individuals and groups about their beliefs was part of Alma's rhetorical strategy.

A second pattern in Alma's questions is his use of the phrase "Can ye . . . ?" This occurs seventeen times in the Book of Mormon, eight of which are in Alma's voice.[23] He asks, "*Can ye* imagine yourselves brought before the tribunal of God?" (Alma 5:18) and "*Can ye* look up to God at that day" of judgment? (Alma 5:19). Alma also asks his audience if they have felt the "song of redeeming love" and if so, "*Can ye* feel so now?" (Alma 5:26). Later, when speaking to the Zoramites, he asks, "How *can ye* disbelieve on the Son of God?" (Alma 33:14). This pattern suggests that another part of Alma's rhetorical strategy is asking introspective questions to help his listeners reflect on what they are thinking and feeling.

Therefore, What?

Thanks to Alma's dutiful and detailed recordkeeping, we can clearly hear his distinct voice centuries later and glean beneficial lessons from his life and teachings. One of these lessons is the value of keeping a record. As discussed above, Mormon frequently mentions Alma's records, assuring us that we get to hear Alma's own voice. In contrast, note how relatively little we hear the voice of Alma's son Helaman. Other than a few words recorded in a conversation between Alma and Helaman and a lengthy letter Helaman writes to Chief Captain Moroni, we never hear his voice. Grant Hardy suggests that perhaps

---

22 Of the remaining twelve, four come from Ammon, three from Aaron, and one each from Nephi, the Spirit speaking to Nephi, Jacob, Amulek, and Jesus Christ.

23 The only other speaker in the Book of Mormon who uses "Can ye . . . ?" more than one time in a question is the angel who speaks to Alma. This angel says, "Can ye dispute the power of God? For behold, doth not my voice shake the earth? And can ye not also behold me before you?" (Mosiah 27:15).

Helaman "never got around to finishing his portion of the Large Plates of Nephi[, which would explain] why, contrary to convention in the Book of Mormon, Alma 45–62 was not made into a separate literary unit called 'the First Book of Helaman'—it seems that the underlying source had been too meager and incomplete to stand on its own."[24]

Without being overly critical of Helaman, we can celebrate Alma's efforts in recordkeeping. When I think about which of my ancestors I know the most about, they are the ancestors that kept the best records. Considering their examples, as well as Alma's, motivates me to keep a better record of my life and the "things of my soul" (2 Nephi 4:15). Perhaps some of us can do better in following Alma's exhortation: "I . . . command you that ye keep a record" (Alma 37:2).

A second lesson may be found in pondering Alma's frequent use of "plan of redemption" in contrast to his less frequent use of "plan of salvation." In modern Church discourse, "the plan of salvation" is the more common title. Between 1970 and 2022 the phrase "plan of redemption" was used 117 times in general conference, compared to 446 times for "plan of salvation." The difference between these phrases may be an unimportant semantic one—but what benefit might we gain from spending more time thinking about a plan of *redemption*?

Noah Webster's 1828 dictionary defines *redemption* as "repurchase of captured goods or prisoners; the act of procuring the deliverance of persons or things from the possession and power of captors by the payment of an equivalent; ransom; release; as the *redemption* of prisoners taken in war; the *redemption* of a ship and cargo. . . . In theology, the purchase of God's favor by the death and sufferings of Christ; the ransom or deliverance of sinners from the bondage

---

24   Grant Hardy, *Understanding the Book of Mormon: A Reader's Guide* (New York: Oxford University Press, 2010), 143. In this same volume, Hardy also notes, "Usually, a clear transition of record-keepers merits independent status as a separate book. We can see a deliberately demarcated transition at Alma 44:24, but Helaman$_2$'s actual contributions were probably minimal or fragmentary, like those of the record-keepers in the book of Omni" (305).

of sin and the penalties of God's violated law by the atonement of Christ."[25]

If this definition is in my mind when I think of God's plan of redemption, it helps me focus on Jesus Christ in an important way. Perhaps more frequently using the phrase "plan of redemption" could be a small change that reminds us that both *salvation* and *redemption* in God's great plan come through his son Jesus Christ.

In my study of Alma's voice, one final lesson that has struck me is Alma's intentionality in following through on promptings received by an angel. He was told to remember the captivity of his fathers and God's power in delivering them; Alma clearly obeyed this message throughout his life. Alma's example of giving diligent heed to heavenly promptings can also be seen in the life of his father. At one point, Alma the Elder faced a perplexing problem and turned to the Lord for guidance. The Lord responded with clear counsel, and "Alma . . . wrote down [the words of the Lord] *that he might have them*" (Mosiah 26:33), then followed through on the guidance he had been given. We may not receive angelic promptings or directly hear words from God, but we can follow the examples of Alma and his father by heeding President Russell M. Nelson's counsel to "record the thoughts that come to you as you pray" and to "follow through diligently" on the spiritual promptings we receive.[26]

---

25 Noah Webster, *An American Dictionary of the English Language* (New York: S. Converse, 1828), s.v. "redemption," https://webstersdictionary1828 .com/Dictionary/redemption.

26 Russell M. Nelson, "Overcome the World and Find Rest," *Liahona*, November 2022, 98.

Chapter 4
Abinadi and Nephi$_2$: Two Contrasting Voices

Among the many voices in the Book of Mormon, two relatively minor yet powerful ones are those of Abinadi and Nephi, the son of Helaman (herein referred to as Nephi$_2$).[1] In some respects, these speakers are similar. Both are Nephite prophets, and both preach to hostile audiences. Both appear to be well versed in scripture, and both make multiple attempts to preach as commanded by the Lord. Although both of their words come mediated through Mormon, there are still distinct differences between their voices as recorded in the Book of Mormon. The purpose of this chapter is to examine these differences and, in so doing, help readers better come to know Abinadi and Nephi$_2$ as individuals and better understand their messages.

In approximately 150 BC Abinadi was called to preach to a group of Nephites who had been led into wickedness by King Noah and his corrupt priests in the land of Nephi. We do not know anything of Abinadi's lineage, family situation, or even age (contrary to popular paintings depicting him as an old man). But we do know that when he was called by God to preach, he answered the call.

---

1   Some of the analysis of the material presented in this chapter was done by Matthew Critchley, a research assistant at Brigham Young University. I acknowledge his work and insights and consider him a coauthor of this chapter.

Abinadi prophesied to the Nephites that they would be placed in bondage if they did not repent. The people tried to kill Abinadi, "but the Lord delivered him out of their hands" (Mosiah 11:26). Two years later, Abinadi again came among the people—this time in disguise—and told them that now bondage would certainly come and if they did not repent they would perish. As with his first sermon, this call to repentance was not received well by the Nephites or their king. King Noah ordered Abinadi to be brought before him, where Noah's priests tried to entrap Abinadi. Abinadi, however, employed the words of Moses and Isaiah to confound Noah and his priests.

So far as we have recorded, Abinadi's words touched only one person, a priest named Alma (the Elder), who attempted to defend Abinadi before being forced to flee for his life. Abinadi was sentenced to death by fire, and as the flames scorched his skin, he raised a voice of powerful prophecy and warning. He then sealed his testimony of Jesus Christ by becoming the first recorded martyr in the Book of Mormon. Though death quieted Abinadi's voice, it did not have the power to silence his prophetic legacy (see chapter 8).

Approximately one hundred years after Abinadi's death, a man named $Nephi_2$, the great-great-grandson of Alma the Elder, began his prophetic ministry. In 39 BC $Nephi_2$ became chief judge of his people and reigned for nine years. In about 30 BC, upon seeing a concerning trend of wickedness among the local Lamanites and Nephites and understanding the power of the word, $Nephi_2$ gave up his position as chief judge to preach the gospel. He had great success among the Lamanites; however, this was countered by his failure to persuade the Nephites to repent. $Nephi_2$'s primary appearance in the Book of Mormon occurs as he prays on his garden tower, mourning for the wickedness of the people. While doing so, he attracts the attention of a great multitude, to which he directs an important discourse, including a prophetic declaration of the death of their chief judge. The final time his voice is heard in the Book of Mormon comes when he pleads with the Lord to intervene on behalf of the Nephites.[2]

---

2   In Helaman 10:14 $Nephi_2$ preaches to the people, but the only words we have him recorded as saying are "thus saith the Lord," followed by a quotation from the Lord.

I chose to compare the voices of Abinadi and Nephi₂ because they are both minor (but significant) voices in the Book of Mormon text who speak about the same number of words (2,788 words attributed to Abinadi, and 2,213 to Nephi₂).[3] Both of them experienced similar circumstances; Abinadi faced an unrighteous court of priests while Nephi₂ confronted members of a scheming secret combination. Both men stepped away from their personal lives to preach to unresponsive audiences. However, despite their similar overall message of crying repentance, Abinadi and Nephi₂ speak differently from each other. In this chapter we will explore these differences by examining both their significant and seemingly insignificant words, as well as their use of quotations.

Significant Words

One clear manifestation of Abinadi's and Nephi₂'s distinctive speaking styles is found in how they use theologically significant words. Table 4.1 illustrates some of these words and their different usages by Abinadi and Nephi₂.[4]

Table 4.1. Abinadi's and Nephi₂'s uses of theologically significant words

Word	Times used by Abinadi per 1,000 words spoken	Total times used by Abinadi	Times used by Nephi₂ per 1,000 words spoken	Total times used by Nephi₂
Abraham	0	0	2.26	5
Christ	2.87	8	0.45	1

---

3   In both cases their words come to us through the mediation of others. Alma the Elder records the words of Abinadi, and Mormon eventually includes (and likely abridges) Alma the Elder's record. Likewise, the words we attribute to Nephi₂ come through Mormon's editing.

4   Because of the relatively small number of words spoken by Abinadi and Nephi₂, I have not attempted to calculate statistical significance; nevertheless, the stark differences between these speakers clearly indicate different voices.

Commanded/ commandments	4.3	12	0.45	1
Death	4.66	13	0.45	1
Destroy/ destruction	0.72	2	6.33	14
Except	0.36	1	4.52	10
Father	2.87	8	0.9	2
First	2.51	7	0.45	1
God	12.55	35	7.68	17
Law	6.1	17	0	0
Lord	10.76	30	8.59	19
Moses	3.95	11	1.36	3
Redeem/ redemption	6.82	19	0.9	2
Repent	1.08	3	5.42	12
Resurrection	5.74	16	0	0
Salvation	3.95	10	0	0
Teach	3.95	11	0	0
Testify	0	0	4.07	9
Understand	2.51	7	0	0
Wo	0.36	1	2.26	5

Abinadi's significant words

Many of Abinadi's significant words relate to Christ and his Atonement. While both prophets preach for the purpose of bringing people to Christ, Abinadi focuses much more on teaching about the Savior's Atonement and Resurrection than Nephi$_2$ does. This is manifest in their respective usage counts for words such as *resurrection*, *salvation*, *redemption*, and *death*.

Abinadi says *resurrection* sixteen times, more frequently than any other speaker in the Book of Mormon.[5] He speaks about a first resurrection[6] and a resurrection of endless life or of endless damnation.[7] He specifically talks about Christ's role in resurrection and refers to other prophets' teachings, saying that Christ "should bring to pass the *resurrection* of the dead, and that he, himself, should be oppressed and afflicted" (Mosiah 13:35). He also explains that Christ "bringeth to pass the *resurrection*" (Mosiah 15:20) and that "the sting of death is swallowed up in Christ" (Mosiah 16:8).

Abinadi says *salvation* eleven times, more than any other speaker, emphasizing that salvation does not come from the law of Moses alone (see Mosiah 13:27–28) but from the Savior. On four occasions he associates *salvation* with the Lord; for example, "the time shall come that the *salvation of the Lord* shall be declared to every nation, kindred, tongue, and people" (Mosiah 15:28; see also Mosiah 15:18; 16:1; and 17:15). The word *law* appears a total of seventeen times in Abinadi's words. Nine of Abinadi's uses are part of the exact phrase "law of Moses,"[8] and the other eight refer to the law of Moses, as Abinadi focuses on the importance of Christ in addition to the law for people's salvation (see Mosiah 13:27–28). In contrast to Abinadi, Nephi₂ never uses the words *resurrection*, *salvation*, or *law*.

---

5   Although Alma says *resurrection* more times than Abinadi does, proportionally speaking, Alma uses this word less frequently than Abinadi does. Abinadi says *resurrection* 6.5 times per 1,000 words, while Alma (with 34 uses) says it 1.7 times per 1,000 words.

6   The only other speakers who use the phrase "first resurrection" are Alma the Elder (Mosiah 18:9) and Alma (Alma 40:15–17).

7   Abinadi is the only one to say *endless* and *life* together with *resurrection*. While Alma does refer to an "endless state" after the Resurrection (Alma 12:24), Abinadi is also the only one to use the phrase "endless damnation," though many others use similar phrases, such as "endless torment."

8   With the exception of Mormon, Abinadi employs this phrase more times than any other speaker in the Book of Mormon, and proportionally speaking, Abinadi uses this phrase more frequently than anyone else.

Abinadi also employs *redeem* and *redemption* a total of nineteen times, proportionally more frequently than any other speaker.[9] Nearly all Abinadi's uses of *redeem* refer to Christ redeeming people. For example, Abinadi says, "I would that ye should understand that God himself shall come down among the children of men, and shall *redeem* his people" (Mosiah 15:1); "these are they whose sins he has borne; these are they for whom he has died, to *redeem* them from their transgressions" (Mosiah 15:12); "they are raised to dwell with God who has *redeemed* them" (Mosiah 15:23); and "*redemption* cometh through Christ the Lord" (Mosiah 16:15). Abinadi's purpose is to show that it is Christ who redeems us, not the commandments themselves.

Abinadi also says *death* thirteen times, compared to Nephi₂'s one instance.[10] As with the words previously discussed, Abinadi specifically connects *death* with Christ and his role in the plan of salvation.[11] Abinadi teaches that death no longer has power over people, because "they have eternal life through Christ, who has broken the bands of *death*" (Mosiah 15:23; see also Mosiah 15:8, 9, 20; 16:7). He also states that "the sting of *death* is swallowed up in Christ" (Mosiah 16:8) and that "there can be no more *death*" (Mosiah 16:9). Nephi₂'s one use of *death* is completely different since he speaks of the murderer of the chief judge, who will "tremble, and shall look pale, even as if *death* had come upon him" (Helaman 9:33).

Nephi₂'s significant words

Although both Abinadi and Nephi₂ speak to antagonistic audiences, Nephi₂ focuses much more explicitly on repentance than Abinadi does.[12] Nephi₂ says *repent* fourteen times, while Abinadi says it only three times. Nephi₂ frequently uses *except* and *repent* together

---

9   Although Alma says these words more times than Abinadi (30 times), he says them only 1.3 times per 1,000 words spoken, as opposed to Abinadi's 6.5 times per 1,000 words spoken.

10 Proportionally speaking, nobody in the Book of Mormon uses the word *death* more frequently than Abinadi does.

11 In addition, Abinadi speaks of his own death three times.

12 Even when he prays, Nephi₂ focuses on the repentance of the people. See Helaman 11:4, 10, and 15.

in some form of the phrase "except ye repent," which he says eight times, typically associated with strong warnings. For example, he says, "And behold, instead of gathering you, *except ye will repent*, behold, he shall scatter you forth that ye shall become meat for dogs and wild beasts" (Helaman 7:19) and "O ye ought to begin to howl and mourn, because of the great destruction which at this time doth await you, *except ye shall repent*" (Helaman 9:22). Proportionally speaking, Nephi₂ uses the words *except* and *repent* together more times than any speaker.[13] Abinadi uses the word *except* only one time, and it is not in connection with repenting (see Mosiah 13:32).

Nephi₂ also focuses on destruction; *destroy* and *destruction* appear a total of fourteen times in his words. He employs these words consistently where his voice is heard in the Book of Mormon. Nephi₂'s preaching from his garden tower in Helaman 7 and 8 is focused on warning the people of destruction if they do not repent (Helaman 7:24, 28; 8:20, 21). In Helaman 9 he speaks of the efforts of the people to destroy him (Nephi₂ himself; see Helaman 9:24–25). Similarly, as he prays in Helaman 11, he twice speaks of people being destroyed (verses 4, 11). Conversely, Abinadi employs *destroy* or *destruction* only twice—both referring to himself being destroyed (Mosiah 13:3; 17:19). Although Abinadi warns King Noah and his people of the severe consequences of their actions, he uses words other than *destroy* and *destruction* to convey his message, such as *afflicted* or *smitten* (see Mosiah 12:31; 17:16–18).

Nephi₂ also uses *wo* in connection with the people's sins, using the word five times (compared with Abinadi's one time). One of these is in a question: "Yea, how could you have given way to the enticing of him who is seeking to hurl away your souls down to everlasting misery and endless *wo*?" (Helaman 7:16). The other four are in proximity to reasons why *wo* will come unto the people, including having their hearts set on riches, being prideful, uniting with secret combinations, and being wicked in general (Helaman 7: 21, 25, 26, 27).

---

13 The Lord collocates these words twelve times, more than Nephi₂. However, Nephi₂ does so 3.6 times per 1,000 words spoken while the Lord does it only 1 time per 1,000 words spoken.

Nephi$_2$ uses the word *testify* nine times, and most of the occurrences refer to prophets who *testified* of Christ (Helaman 8:16, 19, 22). Moreover, each use of *testify* refers to a prophet testifying of something he knows through revelation. Abinadi never employs this word, although he boldly testifies to Noah and his priests.[14]

References to Deity

Another way that Abinadi and Nephi$_2$ use significant words differently is in their references to Deity. Table 4.2 illustrates different ways in which Abinadi and Nephi$_2$ refer to Deity and how many times each does so.

Table 4.2. Abinadi's and Nephi$_2$'s references to Deity[15]

Name/title	Times used by Abinadi per 1,000 words spoken	Total times used by Abinadi	Times used by Nephi$_2$ per 1,000 words spoken	Total times used by Nephi$_2$
God	11.48	32	4.52	10
Lord	9.68	27	6.78	15
Lord God	0	0	0.45	1
Lord your God	0.72	2	1.36	3
Son of God	0.36	1	1.36	3
Son	2.51	7	0.45	1
Good Shepherd	0	0	0.45	1
Messiah	0.36	1	0.45	1
Christ	2.51	7	0.45	1
Christ the Lord	0.36	1	0	0

14 Abinadi does not use *testify*, but he does use *teach* while Nephi$_2$ does not. Refer to table 4.1.

15 In this table, phrases like "Lord God" and "Son of God" were counted separately from the words *Lord* or *God*.

Father	2.15	6	0	0
Eternal Father	0.72	2	0	0
Spirit	0.36	1	0	0
Total	30.85	86	16.27	36

Abinadi refers to Deity fifty more times than Nephi₂ does, with a ratio of 2.39 to 1.[16] This comparison is even starker when we exclusively focus on the public speeches delivered by Abinadi and Nephi₂. Given that eleven of Nephi₂'s references to Deity are when he is addressing the Lord in prayer (in contrast to only one for Abinadi), the references to Deity in public speeches are 85 (Abinadi) to 25 (Nephi₂), a ratio of 3.4 to 1. Part of this could be explained by the fact that Abinadi speaks more regarding the nature of God in Mosiah 15:1–5, but even when those sections are excluded, he still refers to Deity overwhelmingly more often than Nephi₂ does.[17]

In addition to referring to Deity more times than Nephi₂, Abinadi also uses specific titles that Nephi₂ does not. The most notable is the term *Father*, which Abinadi uses six times, in addition to twice using the title *Eternal Father*. Nephi₂ does not use the word *Father*.

The most unique name for Deity that Nephi₂ uses, which Abinadi does not, is *Good Shepherd*. Nephi₂ asks the people why they do not "hearken unto the voice of the *good shepherd*" (Helaman 7:18). This is a rare term for Deity in the Book of Mormon; the only other speaker to use it is Alma.[18]

Names

Another way in which Abinadi and Nephi₂ differ in their use of significant words is in how they reference people's names. Although Abinadi is much more prone than Nephi₂ to say names of Deity, Nephi₂ refers to mortals more frequently than Abinadi does. Nephi₂

---

16 Abinadi speaks 1.26 words for each word Nephi₂ says; thus we would expect him to utilize any given word slightly more than Nephi₂.

17 In Mosiah 15:1–5, Abinadi uses names of Deity sixteen times in quick succession as he describes the nature of God.

18 See Alma 5:38–39, 41, 57, 60. See also John 10:11, 14.

mentions Abraham, Moses, Isaiah, Lehi, Nephi, Jeremiah, Zenock, Zenos, Ezias, Mulek, Zedekiah, Gadianton, Seantum, Seezoram, and Nephi₂ himself. While some of these names are also commonly used by other people in the Book of Mormon (for example, Abraham, Moses, and Isaiah), Nephi₂ seems to have a special propensity for utilizing names. For instance, Lehi speaks more than twice as many words as Nephi₂ and was closer in time to the writings of the brass plates, yet he never mentions Abraham, Moses, or Isaiah by name.

Many of the names Nephi₂ uses are to show people how all prophets have testified of Christ. Referring to Moses, Nephi₂ says, "Did he not bear record that the Son of God should come?" (Helaman 8:14). Then he cites Abraham: "Abraham saw of his coming, and was filled with gladness and did rejoice" (verse 17). After invoking these two great prophets, Nephi₂ lists many more individuals, endeavoring to prove to the people that prophecy—specifically of Jesus Christ—is valid.

Nephi₂ mentions both Zenock and Zenos, stating that they testified of Christ. Mormon, Alma, Nephi, and Amulek are the only other speakers to mention both Zenock and Zenos. Similarly, Jeremiah's name is used relatively sparingly in the Book of Mormon, especially considering he was a contemporary of Lehi. Of the six times *Jeremiah* appears in the Book of Mormon, three come from Nephi₂'s words (Helaman 8:20).[19] Nephi₂ also mentions Ezias, another prophet who testified of Christ, and is the only person in the scriptures who speaks of this prophet.[20]

Nephi₂ is one of only four Book of Mormon speakers to say the name Zedekiah and is the only one among them who does not have a historical or clerical reason to refer to him. Most speakers in the Book of Mormon speak of Zedekiah in terms of marking time (for

19   The other two people who use Jeremiah's name are Mormon and Nephi (see 1 Nephi 5:13; 7:14; 3 Nephi 19:4).

20   The name Ezias appears in the Apocrypha once (see 1 Esdras 8:2). See Thomas Wayment, "Joseph Smith's Developing Relationship with the Apocrypha," in *Approaching Antiquity: Joseph Smith and the Ancient World*, ed. Lincoln H. Blumell, Matthew J. Grey, and Andrew H. Hedges (Provo, UT: Religious Studies Center, Brigham Young University; Salt Lake City: Deseret Book, 2015), 339.

example, 1 Nephi 5:12–13; 3 Nephi, heading). In contrast, Nephi$_2$ uses the fact that the seed of Zedekiah are among them as proof that Jeremiah's prophecy was fulfilled concerning the destruction of Jerusalem. Nephi$_2$ says, "Now we know that Jerusalem was destroyed according to the words of Jeremiah. . . . And now will you dispute that Jerusalem was destroyed? Will ye say that the sons of Zedekiah were not slain, all except it were Mulek? Yea, and do ye not behold that the seed of Zedekiah are with us, and they were driven out of the land of Jerusalem?" (Helaman 8:20–21).[21]

In Nephi$_2$'s frequent appeals to previous prophets, we perhaps see Nephi$_2$ looking to the past to establish his credibility. He may also have been seeking escape from the tribulations of his time by taking comfort from what he perceived to be better positions of his predecessors, or perhaps he was mourning a lost sense of community found among saints. When grieving about the wickedness of the people, he referred to the past, saying, "Oh, that I could have had my days in the days when my father Nephi first came out of the land of Jerusalem, that I could have joyed with him in the promised land; then were his people easy to be entreated, firm to keep the commandments of God, and slow to be led to do iniquity; and they were quick to hearken unto the words of the Lord—yea, if my days could have been in those days, then would my soul have had joy in the righteousness of my brethren" (Helaman 7:7–8). It may be that in quoting and citing ancient prophets, Nephi$_2$ felt a respite from his current conditions by metaphorically surrounding himself with previous prophets.

The remainder of the names Nephi$_2$ uses are of people living during his lifetime. These people, such as Gadianton, Seezoram, and Seantum, are integral to the central drama of Helaman 8–9. Nephi$_2$ also refers to himself by name twice. In contrast, Abinadi never mentions himself or any of his contemporaries by name. Considering that he is addressing King Noah, it is odd that he never directly says his name, especially since King Noah calls Abinadi by name three times.[22]

---

21 Here Nephi$_2$ mentions the only surviving son of Zedekiah, Mulek, making Nephi$_2$ the only individual other than Mormon to do so.

22 Abinadi does quote the Lord as rebuking Noah, as well as the Lord commanding Abinadi by name.

The only two names Abinadi employs are Moses and Isaiah. He says "Moses" eleven times (only Mormon and Nephi say it more); however, nine of those times are part of the phrase "law of Moses." In contrast, Nephi₂ talks about Moses three times but never says "law of Moses"; rather, he speaks of Moses's witness of Christ. Abinadi says Isaiah's name twice only: both times occur when he is beginning to quote from Isaiah. The fact that Nephi₂ mentions fifteen names compared to Abinadi's two suggests a possible difference in how these two prophets seek to establish credibility for their words.

Insignificant Words

As noted in the previous chapter, analyzing distinct voices in the Book of Mormon is made more difficult—and less objective—by the topics addressed by different speakers. While Abinadi uses *resurrection* sixteen times and Nephi₂ never says it, it is difficult to determine how much of this difference is influenced by the topics they address. However, an interesting phenomenon appears when one closely compares Abinadi's and Nephi₂'s use of seemingly insignificant words.

For example, consider the word *behold*. This is a commonly used word in the Book of Mormon (appearing 1,636 times). Abinadi employs this word in only six instances, while Nephi₂ utilizes it thirty-six times. There is no clear indication why Nephi₂ employs the word so frequently; it appears to be a nuance of his individual voice. Table 4.3 illustrates several of these insignificant words and their relative uses by Abinadi and Nephi₂.

Table 4.3. Use of insignificant words

Word	Times used by Abinadi per 1,000 words spoken	Total times used by Abinadi	Times used by Nephi₂ per 1,000 words spoken	Total times used by Nephi₂
A	7.89	22	3.62	8
Again	1.79	5	0.45	1
Away	0	0	3.16	7
Because	3.59	10	10.39	23

Behold	2.15	6	16.27	36
Being[23]	2.87	8	0.45	1
Great	0.36	1	4.52	10
Hath	3.95	11	1.36	3
I	18.65	52	12.65	28
Know	2.15	6	6.33	14
Me	6.46	18	2.71	6
Might	0	0	2.26	5
No	3.23	9	1.36	3
Not	16.14	45	8.13	18
O	1.08	3	6.78	15
Or	2.51	7	0	0
Pass	1.79	5	0	0
Thus	4.30	12	0.90	2
Turn	0	0	2.71	6
Ye	19.38	54	31.18	69

In the following sections I provide details on specific patterns concerning some of these seemingly insignificant words.

Connecting clauses

Abinadi and Nephi₂ use different connecting phrases. Abinadi often uses the word *thus* to connect phrases or ideas[24]—for example, he says, "They are raised to dwell with God who has redeemed them; *thus* they have eternal life through Christ, who has broken the bands of death" (Mosiah 15:23; see 15:3, 5, 23, 24; 16:4; 17:19). Nephi₂ never uses *thus* in this way.[25]

---

23 *Being* is always used as a verb by these speakers.

24 Abinadi also uses *thus* in the phrase "thus saith the Lord" (Mosiah 11:20, 25).

25 Nephi₂ uses the word *thus* only as part of the phrase "thus saith the Lord" (Helaman 7:23; 10:14).

Another way that Abinadi connects ideas is with the phrase "and again." He uses "and again . . ." to restate a point in a different way or to introduce a quote or paraphrase; these uses account for four out of his five uses of *again*. Consider two examples:

- Restating his own words: "Because I have told you the truth ye are angry with me. *And again*, because I have spoken the word of God ye have judged me that I am mad" (Mosiah 13:4).

- Quoting the law of Moses: "Thou shalt not make unto thee any graven image, or any likeness of things which are in heaven above, or which are in the earth beneath, or which are in the water under the earth. *And again*: Thou shalt not bow down thyself unto them, nor serve them" (Mosiah 13:12–13).

Nephi₂ never employs the phrase "and again"; in fact, he uses the word *again* on only one occasion, when he asks the Lord to see if his people will again serve him (see Helaman 11:16).

Clarifying clauses

Abinadi uses the word *or* to clarify his message, meaning "or, in other words." For example, he says, "These are his seed, *or* they are the heirs of the kingdom of God" (Mosiah 15:11); "All those that have believed in [the prophets'] words, *or* all those that have kept the commandments of God, shall come forth in the first resurrection" (Mosiah 15:22); and "If Christ had not risen from the dead, *or* have broken the bands of death that the grave should have no victory, and that death should have no sting, there could have been no resurrection" (Mosiah 16:7). While Abinadi shows a consistent pattern of using the word *or* to clarify an idea he has just set forth, Nephi₂ never utilizes this word.

Great

Nephi₂ utilizes the word *great* much more frequently than Abinadi does. He tends to use it as a modifier, speaking about the people's "great need" to marvel because of the "great hold" Satan has on their hearts (Helaman 7:15), and he refers to their "great city" and "great cities" (Helaman 7:22). He also speaks of "great knowledge" (Helaman 7:24), and he calls Gadianton's band a "great abomination"

(Helaman 7:25). Nephi₂ explains that "great riches" have corrupted the people (Helaman 7:26), teaches that Moses was given "great power" to part the Red Sea (Helaman 8:13), testifies that people knew of Christ a "great many thousand years" before his coming (Helaman 8:18), and prophesies that "great destruction" awaits the people if they don't repent (Helaman 9:22). In contrast, Abinadi's single use of *great* is found in Mosiah 12:29, which deals with the "great evil" he is accused of prophesying concerning the people. In this instance, Abinadi is echoing the words of the people who captured him and brought him to King Noah (see Mosiah 12:9–10, 13).

O

The word *O* is sometimes used to begin an exclamation or to address the Lord. Abinadi uses *O* three times: two instances of "O how beautiful . . ." in reference to Isaiah's words (Mosiah 15:15, 18), and one when he says "O God, receive my soul" as he dies (Mosiah 17:19). In comparison, Nephi₂ uses *O* fifteen times. Ten of these uses are part of the phrase "O Lord" that Nephi₂ says in prayer (Helaman 11:4, 10–16). However, Nephi₂ also employs the word *O* in other ways, such as "O repent ye" (Helaman 7:17), "O, how could you" (Helaman 7:20), "O then why not" (Helaman 8:20), "O ye fools" (Helaman 9:21), and "O ye ought to" (Helaman 9:22). From his consistent usage of *O*, both in prayer and public speaking, we see Nephi₂ putting passion and emphasis into his words. Of those who speak more than one thousand words in the Book of Mormon, proportionally speaking, nobody uses the word *O* more frequently than Nephi₂ does.[26]

Negatives

Abinadi uses negative words more frequently than Nephi₂ does. Abinadi says words such as *nay*, *not*, and *no* sixty-two times, almost three times as many as Nephi₂, whose negative word count totals

---

26 The brother of Jared uses this phrase twelve times. Because his words appear so infrequently in the Book of Mormon, proportionally speaking, he uses the word *O* more frequently than Nephi₂ does.

twenty-three.[27] For example, Abinadi uses the word *no* to emphasize what would have happened if there had been no Atonement: "If Christ had not come into the world, . . . there could have been *no* redemption" (Mosiah 16:6) and "[Without Christ] there could have been *no* resurrection" (Mosiah 16:7). Nephi₂ does not demonstrate any patterns in how he uses *no*.

Abinadi also uses the word *not* to describe what would have happened in the absence of Christ. Abinadi states, "For *were it not* for the redemption which he hath made for his people, . . . all mankind must have perished" (Mosiah 15:19; see also Mosiah 13:28; 16:4). Abinadi also uses this phrase to describe hypothetical conditions, stating, "*If Christ had not* come into the world, . . . there could have been no redemption. And *if Christ had not* risen from the dead, or have broken the bands of death that the grave should have no victory, and that death should have no sting, there could have been no resurrection" (Mosiah 16:6–7). Nephi₂ never utilizes the word *not* in this way.

Quotation Patterns

A final contrast between Abinadi and Nephi₂ is in their differing tendencies to use quotations. While Nephi₂ never explicitly quotes from mortals, on nine different occasions Abinadi specifically references the words of another prophet,[28] primarily referring to Moses and Isaiah. For example, Abinadi states, "I know if ye keep the commandments of God ye shall be saved; yea, if ye keep the commandments which the Lord delivered unto Moses in the mount of Sinai, saying: I am the Lord thy God . . ." (Mosiah 12:33–34). Abinadi goes on to quote the Ten Commandments. On another occasion, Abinadi prefaces a quote, saying, "Yea, even doth not Isaiah say: Who hath believed our report, and to whom is the arm of the Lord revealed?" (Mosiah 14:1), and then quotes Isaiah 53.

---

27 Abinadi uses *nay* four times, *not* forty-five times, *cannot* two times, *no* nine times, and *neither* two times. Nephi₂ uses *nay* one time, *not* eighteen times, *cannot* one time, *no* three times, and *neither* zero times.

28 Nephi₂ does quote the Lord. See Helaman 7:23 and 10:14.

In addition to quoting from mortals, Abinadi frequently quotes from the Lord. In total, his quotations of the Lord number 918 words.[29] Both of Abinadi's initial speeches to the people involve lengthy quotations from the Lord. For example, in Mosiah 11:20 we read:

Mormon
And it came to pass that there was a man among them whose name was Abinadi; and he went forth among them, and began to prophesy, saying:

> **Abinadi**
> Behold, thus saith the Lord, and thus hath he commanded me, saying,

>> **The Lord**
>> Go forth, and say unto this people, thus saith the Lord, Wo be unto this people, for I have seen their abominations, and their wickedness, and their whoredoms; and except they repent I will visit them in mine anger.

This quote continues for five verses. Two years later the same pattern takes place as recorded in Mosiah 12:1:

Mormon
And it came to pass that after the space of two years that Abinadi came among them in disguise, that they knew him not, and began to prophesy among them, saying:

> **Abinadi**
> Thus has the Lord commanded me, saying—

>> **The Lord**
>> Abinadi, go and prophesy unto this my people, for they have hardened their hearts against my words; they have repented not of their evil doings; therefore, I will visit them in my anger, yea, in my fierce anger will I visit them in their iniquities and abominations.

This quote continues for seven verses. Abinadi continues to quote from the Lord throughout his message to the priests. In contrast, throughout all his words, Nephi₂ quotes from the Lord on only two occasions, for a total of forty-one words.

---

29   These words are not included in Abinadi's total, nor are any explicit quotes.

Therefore, What?

The clear differences between the voices of Abinadi and Nephi₂ suggest that dissimilarities in voices can shine through the processes of abridgment and translation. This may tell us something about Mormon's efforts to maintain individual voices in the source texts he had access to. As we've seen elsewhere in this book, two prophets preaching the same gospel in different ways is another testament to unique authorship in the Book of Mormon. In addition, their distinct voices testify of who these men were as people as well.

Observing the specific ways in which Abinadi and Nephi₂ taught has helped me feel more connected to them as individuals and has provided a deeper feeling of the reality of their words. Abinadi and Nephi₂ are not just people on a page, they are real individuals in real-life situations. Abinadi preached to a people who claimed to follow the law of Moses. They asked him to interpret Isaiah, and in response, Abinadi used specific language to address this specific context. He showed how the law of Moses is fulfilled in Christ and explained that Isaiah's words centered on the Savior. In response to King Noah's question "Who is the Lord?" (Mosiah 11:27), Abinadi extensively quoted the Lord.

Nephi₂'s situation, while similar, was not identical. He faced corrupt judges who argued that his prophecy could not come to pass (see Helaman 8:6). Nephi₂'s patterns of speaking addressed such an audience, particularly as he provided a series of examples of how prophecies had come to pass. In my mind's eye, I can picture Nephi₂ mentioning several prophets in succession, energetically saying, "O repent ye, repent ye!" (Helaman 7:17) and urging the people to avoid the "great destruction" that awaits them (Helaman 9:22).

With one hundred years between them, their approaches to truth and testifying were unique, yet their similarities are inspiring as well. Both men followed God into difficult places. Both relied on previous prophets and scripture to teach. And both testified boldly of Heavenly Father and Jesus Christ. Their distinctive voices remind me that Abinadi and Nephi₂ are real people who did their best to follow God—setting an example for me to follow.

More than two thousand years have passed since their voices were originally heard, and yet they continue to speak, inviting our own voices to join theirs in faith and testimony. We are all in different circumstances. What similarities do we share with Abinadi and Nephi₂? What will we do with the unique voices God has given us?

Chapter 5

The Savior's Voice in the Book of Mormon

If I were to ask, "Who is the main character in the Book of Mormon?" a person might be tempted to say Nephi, Alma, or Mormon. But these answers are clearly wrong. The real main character in the Book of Mormon is Jesus Christ. After all, even when we hear the voice of other narrators, their whole purpose is "to persuade [everyone] to believe in Christ" (2 Nephi 25:23). Within the Book of Mormon, titles and pronouns that refer to Christ occur 7,452 times—an average of more than one reference per verse.[1] Thus, no voice is more vital to study than the voice of Jesus Christ.

At the beginning of his record, Nephi wrote that the "fulness" of his intent was to persuade people to come unto Christ (1 Nephi 6:4). Moroni concluded his words by inviting readers to "come unto Christ, and be perfected in him" (Moroni 10:32). An explicitly stated purpose of the Book of Mormon is to convince all people that "Jesus is the Christ, the Eternal God, manifesting himself unto all nations" (title page).

---

1   Of course, some verses contain multiple references to Christ, while others do not have any. On average, there is one reference to Christ for every 0.88 verses in the Book of Mormon. See John Hilton III and Madison Sinclair, "Jesus Christ in the Book of Mormon" (forthcoming).

Because of the central importance of Jesus Christ, focusing on his voice has been particularly meaningful for me. His words challenge, testify, comfort, and teach truth. In this chapter, I will first briefly contrast the patterns when Jesus Christ is explicitly speaking versus when "the Lord" is cited as the speaker. I will then examine three key words Christ uses in the Book of Mormon and explore what his emphasis on them can mean in our lives. This study has changed the way I think about key gospel principles; I hope it does the same for you.

Jesus Christ and the Lord's Speaking Patterns

As described in chapter 1, when my colleagues and I were parsing the text of the Book of Mormon, one critical issue was how to split apart the different references to the Godhead. We chose to combine all generic references (such as "the Lord God," "God," "the Lord," and so forth) as referring to the voice of "the Lord." When there was an explicit identification or clear textual evidence that we were hearing the words of "the Father," "Jesus Christ," or "the Spirit," we designated those words as belonging to that specific individual. For example, in Mosiah 26:23–24 we read, "It is I that taketh upon me the sins of the world; for it is I that hath created them; and it is I that granteth unto him that believeth unto the end a place at my right hand. For behold, in my name are they called; and if they know me they shall come forth, and shall have a place eternally at my right hand." In this passage, while Jesus Christ is not explicitly named, context makes it clear that he is the speaker.

Dividing the text in this manner assigns 14,161 words to Jesus Christ (5.3 percent of the total text of the Book of Mormon) and 11,971 words to the Lord (4.5 percent of the total text). While to some this might seem like an arbitrary distinction, parsing the text in this way showed several clear differences between the voice of Jesus Christ and the voice of "the Lord."[2] Some of these differences are highlighted in table 5.1.

---

2   Some might wonder why a difference in voice exists in the Book of Mormon between when Jesus Christ specifically is cited as speaking versus the Lord. That a difference exists is statistically certain. But it is not possible to state with certainty why there is a difference. One possibility (and I offer this only as conjecture) is that perhaps when people say, "The Lord said," they might

Table 5.1. Jesus Christ and the Lord's different speaking patterns

Word	Times used by Jesus Christ per 1,000 words spoken	Total times used by Jesus Christ	Times used by the Lord per 1,000 words spoken	Total times used by the Lord	LL value when both use the word[3]
Baptize	2.5	36	0.1	1	24.9
Blessed	3.0	43	1.3	16	9.0
Doctrine	0.7	10	0.2	2	7.1
Father	12.7	180	1.1	13	171.0
Forgive	0.9	13	0	0	N/A
Gentiles	2.7	38	0.8	9	13.9
Gospel	1.2	17	0	0	N/A
Me	12.4	175	5.7	68	32.5
Name	4.5	64	1.3	15	22.0
Thee	1.6	23	7.5	90	54.5
Thy	3.2	46	11.9	143	69.9
You	13.6	192	2.0	24	122.0
Your	5.9	84	2.3	27	21.9
Verily	4.9	71	0	0	N/A

In several instances, Jesus Christ and the Lord have very different patterns in words they use. For example, Jesus heavily uses the words *you* and *your* while the Lord instead employs *thee* and *thy*.

---

not always be speaking the verbatim words of the Lord, but rather putting the general message that the Lord has given them into their own words.

3   As stated previously, an LL score of 6.63 is equivalent to a p value < .01, indicating statistical significance. In other words, in every case in table 5.1 when "the Lord" and "Jesus Christ" use the same word, there is a probability smaller than 1 percent that this happened by chance.

One particularly noteworthy example of the differences in these two voices is the word *verily*, which appears seventy-six times in the Book of Mormon. Of these occurrences, seventy-one are in the voice of Jesus Christ (this word is never said by the Lord).[4] It is striking that this small word is also predominantly used by Jesus Christ in the Bible. For example, the phrase "verily, verily I say unto you" appears twenty-five times in the New Testament, exclusively in the book of John and always in the words of Jesus. This same phrase appears twenty-five times in the Book of Mormon, twenty-four times in the voice of Jesus Christ and once in Mormon's words. The shorter phrase "verily I say" appears fifty-two times in the New Testament (exclusively in Matthew, Mark, and Luke, always in the voice of Jesus). This same phrase appears twenty-three times in the Book of Mormon and is used only by Jesus Christ. To a casual reader of the Book of Mormon, the word *verily* might seem like a "scriptural" word, like *behold* or the phrase "it came to pass," that would be randomly distributed throughout the Book of Mormon. However, this is not the case. The word *verily*, connected with Jesus Christ in the Bible, is also connected with him in the Book of Mormon.

Perhaps more importantly, there are several doctrinally significant words that the Savior uses much more frequently than other speakers. In this chapter I will focus on three of these important words: *baptize*, *name*, and *Father*.

---

4   The word *verily* is used one time each by Alma, Korihor, and Nephi, all of whom use it differently than Jesus Christ does. For example, Nephi says, "He [Isaiah] verily saw my Redeemer" (2 Nephi 11:2). On one occasion Mormon says "Verily, verily" to start a sentence (see Alma 48:17); this is the only time this construction appears in the Book of Mormon outside the words of Jesus Christ.

Baptize[5]

In the Book of Mormon, the word *baptize* first appears in 1 Nephi 10, when Nephi describes a dream Lehi had depicting the work of John the Baptist. The final occurrence of *baptize* is in Moroni 8:10: "Teach parents that they must repent and be baptized, and humble themselves as their little children, and they shall all be saved with their little children." Indeed, from the beginning to the end, Book of Mormon writers consistently emphasize the importance of being baptized.[6] Although the word *baptize* appears throughout the Book of Mormon, it is emphasized to different degrees by individual speakers. Table 5.2 shows how many times major speakers in the Book of Mormon say *baptize*.

Table 5.2. Use of *baptize* by major Book of Mormon speakers

Speaker	Times used per 1,000 words spoken	Times used	Percent of total uses of *baptize* in the Book of Mormon	Percent of total words in the Book of Mormon attributed to speaker
Jesus Christ	2.54	36	30.3%	5.3%
Mormon	0.57	56	47.1%	36.4%
Nephi	0.42	12	10.1%	10.5%
Jacob	0.24	2	1.6%	3.2%

5   This section is adapted from John Hilton III and Jana Johnson, "The Word *Baptize* in the Book of Mormon," *Interpreter: A Journal of Latter-day Saint Faith and Scholarship* 29 (2018): 65–80. Note that in this chapter I'm examining the verb *baptize* as well as its variants *baptized* and *baptizing*. The noun form, *baptism*, was not included in this study. *Baptize* is used much more than *baptism* in the scriptures (257 versus 85 times), particularly in the Book of Mormon (119 versus 26 times).

6   For more insights on baptism in the Book of Mormon, see Noel B. Reynolds, "Understanding Christian Baptism through the Book of Mormon," *BYU Studies Quarterly* 51, no. 2 (2012): 5–37.

Moroni$_2$	0.20	4	3.4%	7.3%
Alma$_2$	0.20	4	3.4%	7.5%
The Lord	0.08	1	0.8%	4.5%

Although Mormon numerically uses *baptize* more than any other speaker, Jesus Christ proportionally uses the word much more than Mormon does.[7] Christ's emphasis on being baptized is not simply a function of his focus on this topic in 3 Nephi 11. In fact, not only does Jesus Christ say *baptize* more per one thousand words than any other speaker, but he also consistently uses the word *baptize* throughout the text.

Table 5.3. Christ's use of *baptize* inside and outside 3 Nephi 11–28

Location	Appearances of *baptize*	Total words spoken	Uses of *baptize* per 1,000 words
Inside 3 Nephi 11–28	25	9,694	2.58
Outside 3 Nephi 11–28	11	4,467	2.46

Table 5.3 illustrates that in addition to regularly saying *baptize* in 3 Nephi 11–28, Jesus Christ also consistently uses the word throughout the entire text of the Book of Mormon. In 3 Nephi 11 he designates the specific manner of baptism; however, apart from that deviation, Christ is fairly consistent in his use of *baptize* throughout the text. He typically focuses on the idea that people should be baptized in his name and receive the Holy Ghost (for example, see 2 Nephi 31:12).

In addition to quantitatively using *baptize* more than other Book of Mormon speakers, Jesus Christ uniquely collocates specific words with *baptize*. For example, Christ is much more likely than any other speaker to associate *name* with *baptize*, as illustrated by table 5.4, which compares the three speakers in the Book of Mormon who use the word *baptize* more than ten times.

---

7   Comparing Jesus's use of *baptize* and *baptized* with all other Book of Mormon speakers provides LL values of 24.3 and 54.7, respectively.

Table 5.4. Appearances of *baptize* and *name* in the same verse

Speaker[8]	Times *baptize* is used per 1,000 words spoken	Number of verses in which *baptize* appears	Number of verses in which *baptize* and *name* appear together	Percent of verses using *baptize* and *name* together
Jesus Christ	2.54	28	17	61%
Mormon	0.57	47	5	11%
Nephi	0.42	7	0	0%

There is a stark difference between these speakers in terms of their propensity to use *baptize* and *name* in the same verse. Christ uses *name* in 61 percent of the verses in which he utilizes *baptize*. Jesus frequently uses phrases like "be *baptized* in my *name*" (3 Nephi 11:38; see also 2 Nephi 31:12; 3 Nephi 11:23, 27, 37; 18:5, 11, 16, 30; 21:6; 27:16, 20; 30:2; Ether 4:18; and Moroni 7:34). In contrast, Mormon employs *name* only 11 percent of the time he speaks of being *baptized*. We never hear Nephi's voice use *baptize* and *name* in the same verse, although Nephi quotes both the Father and Jesus Christ in this way (see 2 Nephi 31:11–12). Importantly, Mormon's use of *name* and *baptize* appears to be related to Christ's.

On several occasions Mormon utilizes the phrase "baptized unto repentance." For example, Mormon writes phrases such as "They did preach the word of God, and they did *baptize unto repentance* all men whosoever would hearken unto their words" (Alma 48:19), and "There were thousands who did join themselves unto the church and were *baptized unto repentance*" (Helaman 3:24). However, a shift takes place after Christ's extensive emphasis on being *baptized* in his *name*. Before 3 Nephi 26, Mormon never speaks of being baptized in the name of Christ. However, *after* Mormon provides an account

---

8   Other speakers who use *baptize* and *name* in the same verse include an angel who speaks in Alma 9:27 (one time) the Father (one time), Jacob (two times), Moroni (one time), and Alma the Elder (one time).

of Christ's ministry to the Lehites,[9] we see several examples where he might previously have employed the phrase "baptized unto repentance" but now substitutes it with a reference to being "baptized in the name of Christ," as illustrated in table 5.5.

Table 5.5. Mormon's descriptions of baptism before and after Christ's ministry to the Lehites

Mormon writing before 3 Nephi 11	Mormon writing after 3 Nephi 25
"Whosoever did not belong to the church who repented of their sins *were baptized unto repentance*, and were *received into the church*" (Alma 6:2).	"And they who *were baptized in the name of Jesus* were *called the church of Christ*" (3 Nephi 26:21).
"*Nephi went forth* among the people, and also many others, *baptizing unto repentance*" (3 Nephi 1:23).	"*The disciples of Jesus were journeying* and were . . . *baptizing in the name of Jesus*" (3 Nephi 27:1).
"There were thousands who did join themselves unto the church and *were baptized unto repentance*" (Helaman 3:24).	"And as many as did come unto them, and did truly repent of their sins, *were baptized in the name of Jesus*" (4 Nephi 1:1).

Why does Mormon employ the phrase "baptized unto repentance" eight times before 3 Nephi 9 and never thereafter? Why does he use the phrase "baptized in the name of Jesus" five times after Christ's visits to the Lehites but never previously? One answer could be that Mormon took his textual cues from the Savior. Perhaps once he understood through his redaction of 3 Nephi the extent to which Christ emphasized being *baptized* in his *name*, he followed suit. If this is the case, it demonstrates an interesting textual way in which Mormon's voice changes to better harmonize with the Savior's voice. Another possibility is that Mormon wanted to stay true to the text of those who went before them. Perhaps those who wrote on the plates

---

9   While people commonly refer to Christ visiting the "Nephites," there were in fact Lamanites among those who heard Christ speak (see 3 Nephi 10:18). Thus, I use the more inclusive term *Lehites* while acknowledging that other groups (e.g., the Mulekites) had also merged with the Lehites.

before Christ's visits spoke of being *baptized unto repentance,* and Mormon simply followed their lead.

Another example of Christ's unique use of *baptize* in the Book of Mormon is in the personal connection he makes between it and himself. Jesus uses phrases like "Whoso believeth in *me* and is *baptized . . .* shall be saved" (3 Nephi 11:33) and "Come unto *me* and be *baptized*" (3 Nephi 21:6). When we look at every possible reference to Christ in the Book of Mormon (such as "come unto *him*" and "be baptized unto the *Lord*"), Jesus Christ is still much more likely to say *baptize* in reference to himself than other speakers are. Christ associates himself with being baptized in twenty-three verses, more than all other speakers combined, making him responsible for 56 percent of the appearances of *baptize* that relate to Christ. This number is disproportionate with the fact that he is responsible for only 30 percent of the appearances of *baptize* in the text.

An additional unique way in which Christ uses the word *baptize* is in his frequent invitations for others to be baptized. Of the 119 instances of *baptize* in the Book of Mormon, 12 are invitations or commands to be baptized.[10] Of those who frequently say *baptize,* only Jesus Christ and Mormon issue invitations to be baptized. Table 5.6 illustrates their relative usage, along with the others who issue invitations to be baptized.

Table 5.6. Invitations to be baptized

Speaker	Times used per 1,000 words spoken	Number of times speaker uses *baptize*	Invitations to be baptized
Jesus Christ	2.54	36	7 (2 Nephi 31:12; 3 Nephi 11:37, 38; 3 Nephi 27:20; 3 Nephi 30:2; Ether 4:18; Moroni 7:34)

---

10   There are also two invitations to be baptized associated with the word *baptism* (out of twenty-six instances of baptism).

The Father	0.70	1	1 (2 Nephi 31:11)
Mormon	0.57	56	1 (Mormon 7:8)
Alma₂	0.20	4	2 (Alma 5:62; 7:14)
The Lord	0.08	1	1 (Mormon 3:2)

From table 5.6, we see that while Christ is responsible for about 30 percent of the instances of *baptize* in the Book of Mormon, he is disproportionately responsible for 58 percent of the invitations to be baptized. Except for 2 Nephi 31:12,[11] all these invitations are associated with the concept of repentance. Clearly Christ places emphasis on the importance of repenting and being baptized.

In addition to Christ's distinctive use of *baptize* within the Book of Mormon, it is interesting to note his unique patterns in using *baptize* in the Book of Mormon as opposed to the New Testament.[12] In contrast to his frequent use of *baptize* in the Book of Mormon, in the four Gospels Christ says *baptize* only 0.25 times per 1,000 words. Put differently, given any 1,000 words, Christ is ten times more likely to use the word *baptize* in the Book of Mormon than in the New Testament. We find one possible explanation for this in 1 Nephi 13:26, 28, when an angel speaking to Nephi says, "For behold, they have taken away from the gospel of the Lamb many parts which are plain and most precious; and also many covenants of the Lord have they taken away. . . . Wherefore, thou seest that . . . there are many plain and precious things taken away from the book, which is the book of the Lamb of God." Perhaps some of the "covenants of the Lord" that were taken away were some of Christ's biblical teachings about baptism. If this were the case, it could account for the drastic differences in Christ's use of *baptize* in the Book of Mormon and the New Testament.[13]

---

11 Note that repentance is addressed in the surrounding verses.

12 *Baptize* appears about as frequently in the Book of Mormon as in the New Testament (0.42 times per 1,000 words in the Book of Mormon and 0.41 times per 1,000 words in the King James Version of the New Testament).

13 Another plausible explanation is that the Nephites were particularly confused about baptism. In 3 Nephi 11:28 Christ suggests that there had been argu-

Christ also uses *baptize* differently in the Book of Mormon and the New Testament. Primarily, in the four Gospels Christ's use of *baptize* centers around the phrase "baptized with the baptism that I am baptized with."[14] However, Christ never uses this phrase in the Book of Mormon. Similarly, most of the phrases Christ uses in the Book of Mormon are not used in the New Testament. For example, although Christ frequently associates baptism with his name in the Book of Mormon, Christ collocates *name* and *baptize* in only one New Testament verse (Matthew 28:19).[15] While Christ frequently extends invitations to be baptized in the Book of Mormon, he never employs *baptize* as part of any invitation to others to be baptized in the New Testament.[16] It is clear that Jesus Christ focuses on the word *baptize* in unique ways in the Book of Mormon, both within the text itself and in comparison with his words in the New Testament.

Name

The word *name* appears 338 times in the Book of Mormon; in 64 of these instances (19 percent of the total), it is used by Jesus Christ. Proportionally speaking, Jesus Christ uses this word more than anybody else in the Book of Mormon; only one speaker even comes

---

ments among the Nephites about baptism: "According as I have commanded you thus shall ye baptize. And there shall be no disputations among you, as there have hitherto been; neither shall there be disputations among you concerning the points of my doctrine, as there have hitherto been." We might also look to the compilers of these records for an explanation of Christ's different uses of *baptize*. With limited space and resources, Mormon had to decide what was most valuable to include in the record. It is possible that Christ spoke very similarly to the Nephites as he did to those in Jerusalem, but Mormon saw baptism as being a particularly important concept and other things as being less so. Similarly, those who recorded Christ's words in the New Testament may have felt it more necessary to focus on certain other points of Christ's doctrine.

14   Matthew 20:22–23; Mark 10:38–39; and Luke 12:50.

15   In the New Testament, *baptize* and *name* appear together in Matthew 28:19; Acts 2:38; 8:12, 16; 10:48; 19:5; 22:16; and 1 Corinthians 1:13, 15.

16   Neither does he extend any such invitations using the word *baptism*.

close to Christ's usage.[17] Table 5.7 shows how many times major speakers in the Book of Mormon say *name*.

Table 5.7. Use of *name* by major Book of Mormon speakers

Speaker	Times used per 1,000 words spoken	Times used	Percent of total uses of *name* in the Book of Mormon	Percent of total words in the Book of Mormon attributed to speaker
Jesus Christ	4.4	63	20.7%	5.3%
King Benjamin	3.8	16	5.3%	1.6%
Jacob	1.6	14	4.6%	3.2%
Moroni$_2$	1.4	27	8.9%	7.3%
Amulek	1.3	4	1.3%	1.2%
Isaiah	1.1	9	3.0%	3.0%
Samuel the Lamanite	1.0	3	1.0%	1.1%
Mormon	0.9	89	29.3%	36.4%
The Lord	0.9	11	3.6%	4.5%
Nephi	0.7	20	6.6%	10.5%
Moroni$_1$	0.7	2	0.7%	1.1%
Alma	0.6	12	3.9%	7.5%
Helaman	0	0	0%	1.9%
Lehi$_1$	0	0	0%	1.7%
Abinadi	0	0	0%	1.0%

17   Comparing Jesus's use of *name* with all other Book of Mormon speakers provides an LL value of 86.6.

There are three principal ways in which Christ refers to his name.[18] Most frequent is how he speaks of being baptized in his name (described in the previous section).

The second most frequent is in his exhortations to ask, pray to, or call on the Father in Christ's *name*. On five occasions Jesus tells his followers to "ask the Father in *my name*";[19] five additional times Christ tells people to "pray unto the Father in *my name*";[20] and five more times he invites people to "call on the Father in *my name*."[21]

Christ's consistent invitations to pray to the Father in his name emphasize the importance of his Father and show the unity that they have (discussed further in the next section). In addition, the command to call on the Father *in Christ's name* reminds us that "there shall be no other name given nor any other way nor means whereby salvation can come unto the children of men, only in and through the name of Christ" (Mosiah 3:17). We pray in *the name of Jesus Christ*, reminding us that it is through the Savior that we converse with, and eventually will be brought back into the presence of, the Father.

The third primary way that Christ uses *name* is to connect it with the name of his Church. Shortly after the Savior's appearance to the Nephites, a group of his disciples was disputing about what the name of the Church should be. During their discussion, Jesus himself appeared to them once again and asked, "How be it my church save it be called in my *name*? For if a church be called in Moses' *name* then it be Moses' church; or if it be called in the *name* of a man then it be the church of a man; but if it be called in my *name* then it is my church, if it so be that they are built upon my gospel. . . . Ye shall call whatsoever things ye do call, in my *name*" (3 Nephi 27:8–9).

In a modern context, the name of his Church continues to matter to Jesus Christ. In the beginning of the Restoration, the name of

---

18 Aside from these more frequently appearing patterns, Jesus uses the word *name* in several different ways. For example, he invites people to believe on his name (e.g., 3 Nephi 9:17), take on his name (e.g., 3 Nephi 27:5), and go forth in his name (e.g., Mosiah 26:20).

19 See 3 Nephi 16:4; 17:3; 18:20; 27:28. Moroni$_2$ is the only other person to use this phraseology (see Mormon 9:21, 27; Moroni 10:4).

20 See 3 Nephi 18:19, 21, 23, 30; 20:31.

21 See 3 Nephi 21:27; 27:7, 9; Ether 4:15; Moroni 2:2.

the Church was "the Church of Christ" (Doctrine and Covenants 20:1), and it was later changed to become "The Church of Jesus Christ of Latter-day Saints" (Doctrine and Covenants 115:4). For many years I thought that all that happened was that Church leaders simply later added the phrase "Latter-day Saints." But in fact, although the restored Church was originally called "The Church of Christ," in 1834 Church leaders voted to change the name to "The Church of the Latter-day Saints."[22]

The name of Jesus was removed.

The title page for the 1835 Doctrine and Covenants reads "The Church of the Latter-day Saints." This same name for the Church also appears on the Kirtland Temple. Thus, when Jesus revealed in 1838 that the Church should be called "The Church of Jesus Christ of Latter-day Saints" (Doctrine and Covenants 115:4), he wasn't adding "Latter-day Saints"; he was restoring *his* name to the name of *his* church.[23]

Christ's proportional use of the word *name* is dramatically higher than that of nearly every other speaker in the Book of Mormon. Jesus Christ focuses on being baptized in his *name*, asking the Father and calling upon him in prayer in Christ's *name*, and calling the Church after his *name*. Collectively, this emphasis on his *name* reminds us that Jesus should be at the center of everything we do.

Father

The word *Father* (with a capital *F*) appears 271 times in the Book of Mormon, and 171 of these occurrences come from the words of Jesus Christ. Although twenty-one other individuals use this word,

---

22 K. Shane Goodwin, "The History of the Name of the Savior's Church: A Collaborative and Revelatory Process," *BYU Studies Quarterly* 58, no. 3 (2019): 16.

23 In the October 2018 general conference, President Russell M. Nelson similarly emphasized employing Christ's name in how we refer to his Church: "The Lord [has] impressed upon my mind the importance of the name He decreed for His Church, even The Church of Jesus Christ of Latter-day Saints. . . . The name of the Church is not negotiable. When the Savior clearly states what the name of His Church should be . . . He is serious." Russell M. Nelson, "The Correct Name of the Church," *Ensign*, November 2018, 87.

no other Book of Mormon speaker comes close to using *Father* as frequently as Jesus Christ does,[24] as illustrated in table 5.8.

Table 5.8. Use of *Father* by major Book of Mormon speakers

Speaker	Times used per 1,000 words spoken	Times used	Percent of total uses of *Father* in the Book of Mormon	Percent of total words in the Book of Mormon attributed to speaker
Jesus Christ	12.1	171	63.1%	5.3%
Abinadi	2.9	8	3.0%	1.0%
Mormon	0.3	29	10.7%	36.4%
Nephi	0.6	16	5.9%	10.5%
Jacob	0.4	3	1.1%	3.2%
Moroni$_2$	0.9	17	6.3%	7.3%
Isaiah	0.1	1	0.4%	3.0%
Alma$_2$	0.1	2	0.7%	7.5%
The Lord	0.2	2	0.7%	4.5%
King Benjamin	0.2	1	0.4%	1.6%
Amulek	0.6	2	0.7%	1.2%
Samuel the Lamanite	0.3	1	0.4%	1.1%

Although he speaks only 5 percent of the Book of Mormon text, Jesus Christ accounts for 63 percent of all uses of *Father*. Five major ways Christ speaks of his Father regard prayer, commandments, quotations from him, his unity with the Father, and covenants. Let's briefly explore each of these themes.

---

24   Comparing Jesus's use of *Father* with all other Book of Mormon speakers provides an astronomical LL value of 660.

The most frequent way that Jesus employs the word *Father* is in conjunction with prayer. As discussed in the previous section, on fifteen occasions Christ speaks of *calling on, praying to,* or *asking the Father* in his *name.* In addition, Christ uses the word *Father* several times in the prayers he offers. Jesus prays to the Father nine times in the Book of Mormon, beginning in 3 Nephi 13, when he provides a model for prayer beginning with "Our *Father* who art in heaven, hallowed be thy name" (3 Nephi 13:9). Each occurrence of Jesus praying in the Book of Mormon includes an address to the Father, highlighting this as an important component of prayer.[25]

Another way that Jesus uses the word *Father* is in talking about his commandments. *Commandments* and *Father* appear together fifteen times in Christ's voice in the Book of Mormon, with the Savior often emphasizing the importance of his Father's commandments. For example, in 3 Nephi 11:32 Jesus says, "I bear record that *the Father commandeth* all men, everywhere, to repent and believe in me." Jesus gives the people the commands of his Father (see 3 Nephi 12:19) and speaks of his efforts to do what his Father has commanded him to do (see 3 Nephi 15:14–16:3). He is also clear that he will fulfill the Father's commandments; in 3 Nephi 18:27 he declares, "I must go unto *my Father* that I may fulfil other *commandments* which he hath given me."

Christ also emphasizes the Father by quoting him; he uses the phrase "saith the *Father*" thirteen times.[26] For example, in 3 Nephi 16:8 Jesus states, "Wo, *saith the Father,* unto the unbelieving of the Gentiles" in the latter days. Two verses later, in describing what will happen if the Gentiles reject the gospel, Jesus says, "Behold, *saith the Father,* I will bring the fulness of my gospel from among them"

---

25 In 3 Nephi 17:15 Christ prays by kneeling on the ground and then directly addressing the Father. In the next chapter, he tells the people that they have all witnessed that he "prayed unto the Father" (3 Nephi 18:24). This pattern continues in 3 Nephi 19, where Christ uses phrases such as "Father, I thank thee" and "Father, I pray thee" (3 Nephi 19:20–21).

26 One of these thirteen is the derivative phrase "Thus said the Father" (3 Nephi 24:1). The only other person in the Book of Mormon to use the phrase "saith the Father" is Nephi (see 2 Nephi 31:20). Nearly all the quotations of the Father in the Book of Mormon come from Jesus Christ.

(3 Nephi 16:10). Christ continues quoting his Father regarding this theme of destruction for the Gentiles if they harden their hearts, continuing with "I will return their iniquities upon their own heads, *saith the Father*" (3 Nephi 20:28). Christ's longest quote from his Father comes in 3 Nephi 24–25, when he specifically attributes the words of Malachi 3–4 to him.

Jesus also uses the word *Father* in the context of describing their unity. Christ speaks of his unity with the Father ten times.[27] He says he was "*with the Father* from the beginning" and teaches, "*I am in the Father,* and the Father in me" (3 Nephi 9:15). Christ also frequently says, "The *Father and I are one*" (3 Nephi 20:35; 28:10; see 11:27) and declares, "*The Father, and I,* and the Holy Ghost *are one*" (3 Nephi 11:36).

A final theme of Jesus using *Father* relates to covenants. *Father* and *covenant* are used together by Jesus Christ nine times in the Book of Mormon. He most commonly uses it to teach how the Father's covenant to his people will be fulfilled. In various ways, Jesus says that he came to fulfill the covenants the Father made with his covenant people. For example, in 3 Nephi 16:5 Jesus declares that he will gather his people together and "*fulfil the covenant which the Father hath made* unto all the people of the house of Israel." Then he connects his audience with the house of Israel, declaring, "*Ye are of the covenant which the Father made* with your fathers" (3 Nephi 20:25). Jesus promises that "this *covenant which the Father hath covenanted* with his people [will] be fulfilled" (3 Nephi 20:46). Jesus points to the fulfilling of covenants in the latter days, stating that when the Book of Mormon comes forth to the descendants of Lehi, they will know that "the work of *the Father hath already commenced unto the fulfilling of the covenant* which he hath made unto the people who are of the house of Israel" (3 Nephi 21:7).

Therefore, What?

Identifying and analyzing words that Christ emphasizes in the Book of Mormon can help us see what is important to him—topics such

---

27 See 3 Nephi 9:15; 11:27, 32, 36; 19:23, 29; 20:35; 28:10; Ether 3:14; 4:12.

as the ordinance of baptism, his name, and the Father.[28] More than any other speaker, Christ personally associates himself with baptism, connecting it with coming to him and his own name. More than any other speaker, he personally invites people to be baptized. Seeing how often he speaks of baptism has deepened my understanding of how important baptism is to the Savior and, therefore, how important it should be to me. Christ's emphasis on this ordinance can motivate us to attach more meaning to it and to be bolder in inviting others to be baptized.

Jesus Christ's *name* is personally important to him. The Savior's consistent teachings in the Book of Mormon regarding his name perhaps stand in contrast to Doctrine and Covenants 107:4, which states that "out of respect or reverence to the name of the Supreme Being, to avoid the too frequent repetition of his name," the term *Melchizedek Priesthood* was used by ancient Church members instead of "the Holy Priesthood, after the Order of the Son of God" (Doctrine and Covenants 107:3). These verses suggest caution in frequent usage of the name of Christ.

However, the Savior himself in the Book of Mormon says, "In *my name* shall [my people] be called" (Mosiah 26:18); "Go forth in *my name*" (Mosiah 26:20); "Believe on *my name*" (3 Nephi 9:17); "In *my name* shall ye baptize" (3 Nephi 11:23); "Call on the Father in *my name*" (3 Nephi 21:27); and "Whatsoever ye shall do, ye shall do it in *my name*" (3 Nephi 27:7). Christ's emphasis on his name suggests a point of balance—yes, we should avoid using his name in a casual way. At the same time, for some the danger might not be using his name too frequently but rather not using his name enough.

A young mother recently shared the following insight with me: "I've used Christ's name more since I've had children. I want the Savior to be very real to them. The first thing a child does when they meet somebody is ask them their name. I want my children to know who Jesus is and know that he is their friend. So we use his name a lot in our house!"

---

28 Other words could be added to this list. For example, Jesus Christ disproportionately speaks of Gentiles. See John Hilton III et al., "Gentiles in the Book of Mormon," *Interpreter: A Journal of Latter-day Saint Faith and Scholarship* 33 (2019): 267–88.

She's exactly right. After all, as Elder Neil L. Andersen stated, "You and I speak of Jesus Christ, but maybe we can do a little better. If the world is going to speak less of Him, who is going to speak more of Him? We are! Along with other devoted Christians!"[29]

In 2019 Elder Ronald A. Rasband gave an address to the seminary and institute leaders of the Church. He spoke about the sobering realities of suicide and said that we must help those in desperate circumstances connect with those who can help them. He encouraged teachers to find new ways to help those who are deeply struggling. He specifically suggested, "Try just saying the name 'Jesus Christ' in a perilous setting with one who has lost hope. Just calling upon Him by name, with reverence, can make a difference in a difficult moment."[30] There is power in the name of Jesus Christ.

Christ's consistent speaking of his *Father* shows us their unity. At times in my life, in response to people who say that Jesus Christ and God the Father are literally the same being, I've focused on their differences. Although they *are* different individuals, it might be helpful for us to focus more on their unity than we sometimes do. As Elder Jeffrey R. Holland taught, "Part of the reason we are so misunderstood by others in the Christian tradition is because in stressing the individual personages of the Godhead, we have not followed that up often enough by both conceding and *insisting* upon Their unity in virtually every other imaginable way. For this we have reaped needless criticism, and we have made our . . . position harder to be understood than it needs to be."[31] Christ's emphasis on linking himself with the Father teaches of the unity that exists between the members of the Godhead and points to a unity we should strive for. Just as Christ is completely one with his Father, so too can we be united to Christ and the Father as we do their work.

The words Jesus Christ chose to use are significant. As we study the Savior's voice, we can better come to know what matters to him

---

29   Neil L. Andersen, "We Talk of Christ," *Ensign*, November 2020, 89.

30   Ronald A. Rasband, "Jesus Christ Is the Answer" (evening with a General Authority, February 8, 2019).

31   Jeffrey R. Holland, "Knowing the Godhead," *Ensign*, January 2016, 37–38.

and make those things more central in our own lives. Focusing more on baptism has changed my experience in sacrament meeting, the temple, and baptismal services. Concentrating more purposefully on Christ's name has changed both what I say at the dinner table and share on social media. Pondering the unity of Christ and his Father increases my desire that the Savior's prayer will be answered: "I pray unto thee for . . . all those who shall believe on [my disciples'] words, that they may believe in me, that I may be in them as thou, Father, art in me, that we may be one" (3 Nephi 19:23; see also 3 Nephi 19:19; John 17:21–22).

Part 2

Voices in Harmony

Chapter 6
Intertextuality in the Book of Mormon

In the previous chapters we have focused on individual voices in the Book of Mormon. But how do these voices intertwine and harmonize with each other? After all, as Ralph Waldo Emerson wrote, "All minds quote. Old and new make the warp and woof of every moment. There is no thread that is not a twist of these two strands. By necessity, by proclivity, and by delight, we all quote."[1]

Emerson here likens quotations to the work of a weaver. Just as a weaver intertwines strands of yarn ("warp and woof") into a beautiful tapestry, authors often construct their work by interlacing concepts and words first uttered by their predecessors. Literary critic Roland Barthes uses the same metaphor as Emerson, writing that text is "entirely woven of quotations, references, echoes: cultural languages . . . , antecedent or contemporary, which traverse it through and through, in a vast stereophony."[2]

---

1   *The Complete Works of Ralph Waldo Emerson*, vol. 8, *Letters and Social Aims* (New York: W. H. Wise, 1920 [1875]), 178, cited in Richard L. Schultz, *The Search for Quotation: Verbal Parallels in the Prophets* (Sheffield, England: Sheffield Academic Press, 1999), 9.

2   Roland Barthes, "From Work to Text," in *The Novel: An Anthropology of Criticism and Theory, 1900–2000*, ed. Dorothy J. Hale (Malden, MA: Blackwell, 2006), 238.

Intertextuality, a word coined by Julia Kristeva,[3] has been defined in different ways by various scholars. In a broad sense it can be seen as the connection between two texts when one text influences another thematically, through specific vocabulary, or through some other relationship. Instances of intertextuality appear throughout literature; Virgil borrowed from Homer, and Dante in turn referred to both.[4] A more recent example of intertextuality in pop culture could be *West Side Story*, which heavily borrows from *Romeo and Juliet*.

In some instances, authors utilize a form of intertextuality by quoting another person (with or without citing a source). For example, in a general conference address, President Dieter F. Uchtdorf said, "Our second key relationship is with our families. Since 'no other success can compensate for failure' here, we must place high priority on our families."[5] This statement provides a readily recognizable example of intertextuality. Although President Uchtdorf did not verbally cite a source here, many Latter-day Saints familiar with President David O. McKay's teachings would have recognized that President Uchtdorf had just woven in a familiar statement with his own. In instances such as this one, authors may specifically create textual connections they want readers to notice. In other instances, an allusion could happen unintentionally when one author subconsciously borrows ideas from another.

Intertextuality can be a valuable approach to studying scripture; indeed, over the past decades many researchers have worked to find intertextual connections between the Old and New Testaments. This has great value, for when we identify Old Testament text in the New

---

3   See Julia Kristeva, *Semeiotike: Recherches pour une sémanalyse* (Paris: Éditions du Seuil, 1969).

4   See Michael Dunne, *Intertextual Encounters in American Fiction, Film, and Popular Culture* (Bowling Green, OH: Bowling Green State University Popular Press, 2001), 19.

5   Dieter F. Uchtdorf, "Of Things that Matter Most," *Ensign*, November 2010, 21. President Uchtdorf was referring to the phrase "No other success can compensate for failure in the home." While this statement has often been attributed to President McKay, he was quoting from another source (more intertextuality!). See J. E. McCulloch, *Home: The Savior of Civilization* (1924), 42; and David O. McKay, in Conference Report, April 1935, 116.

Testament, it not only gives us insight into the message of the New Testament author but also may provide us additional interpretations of the Old Testament passage. In many instances it appears that New Testament authors intentionally use Old Testament texts to bolster their arguments.

For example, Paul writes to the Corinthians seeking financial contributions to assist others in need: "For I mean not that other men be eased, and ye burdened: But by an equality, that now at this time your abundance may be a supply for their want, that their abundance also may be a supply for your want: that there may be equality: **As it is written**, *He that had gathered much had nothing over; and he that had gathered little had no lack*" (2 Corinthians 8: 13–15).

The phrase "as it is written" is a quotation formula signaling to the reader that Paul is utilizing another text. Here Paul references Exodus 16:16–18: "Gather of [the manna] every man according to his eating, an omer for every man. . . . And the children of Israel did so, and gathered, some more, some less. And when they did mete it with an omer, *he that gathered much had nothing over, and he that gathered little had no lack*."

When writing to those who had more than sufficient for their needs, Paul invoked the account of Israelites receiving manna in the wilderness. Paul asserted that God's provision of manna ensured that everyone had enough, regardless of how much he or she had gathered. Commenting on the passage, Peter Balla writes, "[Paul] finds a text in scripture that can strengthen his argument that the Corinthians should support the poor in Jerusalem. In the original setting the phrases 'to abound' and 'to lack' referred to the individuals in Israel: each person had the right amount for himself or herself. . . . Although some people had gathered more than others, they had no surplus because they needed just that much. . . . In the Corinthian context the apostle argues that at a certain time God provides some members of the church with more so that they may help those who have less at that time."[6] When we understand the context of Paul's quotation, his argument becomes much stronger.[7]

This instance of intertextuality is relatively easy to identify, since it begins with a quotation formula. However, many textual connections are not so clearly marked. For example, John 1:1 states, "In the beginning was the Word, and the Word was with God, and the Word was God" (John 1:1). Nothing in the verse signals a textual connection; however, a careful reader may remember the first words of Genesis: "In the beginning God created the heaven and the earth" (Genesis 1:1). By using the phrase "in the beginning," the author of the Gospel of John communicates to readers that Christ's ministry did not begin with his baptism; rather, the Savior has always existed and was instrumental in the creation of all things (see John 1:3).[8]

Similar types of textual connections—including both those with quotation formulas and those with more subtle allusions—appear in the Book of Mormon. This intertextuality provides harmonies among distinctive Book of Mormon voices. As we will see in the following chapters, individuals in the Book of Mormon have unique ways of interweaving their words with others. But to determine whether such textual connections are more likely intentional or coincidental, we must discover and examine shared text among speakers. Indeed, one of the difficulties in uncovering intentional intertextual connections is discerning whether one author was in fact quoting from another or whether the apparent quotation could more feasibly be explained in a different way. In the case of Paul quoting Exodus, the reference to Exodus is relatively recognizable. In other instances, it may not be clear if a later prophet intended to quote a previous

---

6   Peter Balla, "2 Corinthians," in *Commentary on the New Testament Use of the Old Testament*, ed. G. K. Beale and D. A. Carson (Grand Rapids, MI: Baker Academic, 2007), 775.

7   For another biblical example, compare Luke 23:46 with Psalm 31:5. The context of Christ's final words illustrates the redemptive powers of God, powers that Christ was about to make more fully manifest.

8   Andreas J. Köstenberger writes that this textual connection "locates Jesus' existence in eternity past with God and sets the stage for John's lofty Christology." Andreas J. Köstenberger, "John," in Beale and Carson, *Commentary on the New Testament Use of the Old Testament*, 421.

prophet or if the textual connection is simply coincidental. Biblical scholars have debated criteria for validating proposed allusions, a subject to which I now turn.

Criteria for Determining Allusions

Having criteria to determine whether two passages are related to each other is important because "little or no consensus has emerged regarding what distinguishes a quotation from a mere verbal coincidence or vague reminiscence or which criteria are most useful for correctly identifying, explaining the origin of, and assessing the significance of literary borrowing."[9]

It is understandable that scholars disagree about what constitutes allusions. Over a century ago Robert Baker Girdlestone cautioned, "We must be on our guard against mistaking resemblances for references. Some expressions may have been common property to several Hebrew writers; they may have almost become idioms in the language; and we cannot say that the writers borrowed them from one another."[10] For example, in the Book of Mormon the phrase "lifted up in . . . pride" appears seventeen times. While there may be intentional textual connections in the various places where this phrase occurs, it is also possible that was simply a commonly employed phrase.

Lincoln Blumell points out, "With the aid of electronic databases and search engines where a word, root of a word, or even a short phrase, can be readily searched across a huge corpus, if one is willing to look hard enough, they can usually find numerous scriptural echoes and reminiscences. However, the obvious problem with this is that just because one can find a rare word or a distinct [scriptural] phrase . . . , it does not automatically guarantee the author . . . was necessarily echoing or reminiscing that passage."[11] The term

---

9   Schultz, *Search for Quotation*, 18.

10   Robert Baker Girdlestone, *The Foundations of the Bible: Studies in Old Testament Criticism* (London: Eyre and Spottiswoode, 1890), 50, cited in Schultz, *Search for Quotation*, 25.

11   Lincoln H. Blumell, *Lettered Christians: Christians, Letters, and Late Antique Oxyrhynchus* (Leiden: Brill, 2012), 220.

parallelomania[12] has been employed to describe having such a broad standard for parallels that the so-called parallels become meaningless and some textual connections may not be as significant as they initially seem.[13]

Some parallels are simply stronger than others. As biblical scholar Richard B. Hays states, "Quotation, allusion, and echo may be seen as points along a spectrum of intertextual reference, moving from the explicit to the subliminal. As we move farther away from overt citation, the source recedes into the discursive distance, the intertextual relations become less determinate, and the demand placed on the reader's listening power grows greater. As we near the vanishing point of the echo, it inevitably becomes difficult to decide whether we are really hearing an echo at all, or whether we are only conjuring things out of the murmurings of our own imaginations."[14] Thus, it is important to carefully analyze similar phrases to determine the likelihood that an author is deliberately alluding to another text.

To discern whether intentional intertextuality (rather than distant echo) exists in specific passages, some scholars have developed criteria to use. For example, Hays wrote an influential book on intertextuality in the Bible. He proposed using the following seven criteria to distinguish between real and illusory allusions:

1. Availability. Was the proposed source of the echo available to the author and/or original readers?

2. Volume. The volume of an echo is determined primarily by the degree of explicit repetition of words or syntactical patterns, but other factors may also be relevant [such as] how distinctive or prominent is the precursor text within Scripture.

---

12 See Samuel Sandmel, "Parallelomania," *Journal of Biblical Literature* 81, no. 1 (1962): 1–13.

13 See Benjamin L. McGuire, "Finding Parallels: Some Cautions and Criticisms," parts 1 and 2, *Interpreter: A Journal of Latter-day Saint Faith and Scholarship* 5 (2013): 1–104, https://journal.interpreterfoundation.org /finding-parallels-some-cautions-and-criticisms-part-one/, https://journal .interpreterfoundation.org/finding-parallels-some-cautions-and-criticisms -part-two/.

14 Richard B. Hays, *Echoes of Scripture in the Letters of Paul* (New Haven, CT: Yale University Press, 1993), 23.

3. Recurrence. How often does [the author] elsewhere cite or allude to the same scriptural passage?

4. Thematic Coherence. How well does the alleged echo fit into the line of argument that [the author] is developing?

5. Historical Plausibility. Could [the author] have intended the alleged meaning effect?

6. History of Interpretation. Have other readers, both critical and pre-critical, heard the same echoes?

7. Satisfaction. With or without clear confirmation from the other criteria listed here, does the proposed reading make sense?[15]

While some debate continues to exist regarding specific scriptural passages, criteria like those proposed by Hays have helped scholars identify multiple instances of intertextuality between the Old and New Testaments. Speaking specifically of the writings of Paul, Hays states, "The Pauline quotations and allusions have been cataloged, their introductory formulas classified, their relation to various Old Testament text-traditions examined, their exegetical methods compared to the methods of other interpreters within ancient Christianity and Judaism. The achievements of such inquiries are by no means to be disparaged: they have, as it were, unpacked and laid out the pieces of the puzzle."[16]

While this may be true of Pauline allusions and other intertestamental connections, the textual connections between the words of various Book of Mormon speakers remain to be completely investigated in this manner. The Book of Mormon is rich in intertextuality, full of connections to the Bible, and replete with internal references to itself. Although the focus in this and the following chapters is to describe intertextual connections *within* the Book of Mormon (perhaps these could be called *intratextual* connections), let us first

---

15 Hays, *Echoes of Scripture*, 29–31. Shortly before Hays published this book, Noel B. Reynolds set forth similar criteria in "The Brass Plates Version of Genesis," in *By Study and Also by Faith*, ed. John M. Lundquist and Stephen D. Ricks (Salt Lake City: Deseret Book, 1990), 2:138.

16 Hays, *Echoes of Scripture*, 9.

briefly consider intertextual links between the Book of Mormon and the Bible.[17]

Intertextuality between the Book of Mormon and the Bible

The Book of Mormon is textually connected to the Bible. Large sections of Isaiah appear in the Book of Mormon (2 Nephi 12–24; compare Isaiah 2–12), and a version of the Sermon on the Mount is also present (3 Nephi 12–14; compare Matthew 5–7). Several smaller biblical allusions appear throughout the Book of Mormon. Christ utilizes the words of both Micah and Malachi. Nephi, Abinadi, and others refer to the words of Moses. The existence of these connections can at times help us gain more meaning from the text. Although some of these textual connections are easily identifiable, others are much more subtle.

Consider the following example. Textual evidence suggests that Jacob, in constructing his book, utilized Psalm 95. In Jacob 1:7 he records, "Wherefore we labored diligently among our people, that we might persuade them to come unto Christ, and partake of the goodness of God, *that they might enter into his rest*, lest by any means *he should swear in his wrath they should not enter in, as in the provocation in the days of temptation while the children of Israel were in the wilderness*." The italicized portions of this verse bear a clear connection to Psalm 95:8–11, which states, "Harden not your heart, *as in the provocation, and as in the day of temptation in the wilderness. . . . Forty years long was I grieved with this generation . . . unto whom I* *sware in my wrath that they should not enter into my rest*."

This shared text cannot be coincidental. This is doubly the case when we see another allusion to Psalm 95 toward the end of Jacob's record. In Jacob 6:6 he exhorts, "*Yea, today, if ye will hear his voice,*

---

17   The volume *They Shall Grow Together: The Bible in the Book of Mormon*, ed. Charles Swift and Nicholas J. Frederick (Provo, UT: Religious Studies Center, Brigham Young University; Salt Lake City: Deseret Book, 2022), contains several extended examinations of intertextuality between the Bible and the Book of Mormon. See also Nicholas J. Frederick, "The Bible and the Book of Mormon: A Review of Literature," *Journal of Book of Mormon Studies* 28, no. 1 (2019): 205–36.

harden not your hearts; for why will ye die?" These words directly echo Psalm 95:7–8: "*To day if ye will hear his voice, harden not your heart.*"[18] Thus Jacob alludes to Psalm 95 at the beginning of his book (Jacob 1:7) and as he nears the end of it (6:6).[19]

Psalm 95 is an important psalm of worship. It is a hymn of praise connected with the Feast of Tabernacles, one of the three major Mosaic festivals. As such, it certainly could predate the Babylonian exile and have been in common use before Lehi's day.[20] In context, Psalm 95:7–8 refers to an event in which the Israelites, while camped at Meribah, complained against Moses, leading Moses to miraculously provide water from a rock (see Exodus 17:1–7; Numbers 20:1–13). Commenting on the connection between Psalm 95 and Exodus 17, Catherine Thomas writes, "The Provocation refers not only to the specific incident at Meribah but to a persistent behavior of the children of Israel that greatly reduced their spiritual knowledge. . . . After a succession of provocations, the Israelites in time rejected and lost the knowledge of . . . the great plan of grace inherent in the doctrine of the Father and the Son."[21]

By invoking Psalm 95, Jacob could be reminding us of a story of hardened hearts during the Exodus; he invites us to learn from them, harden not our hearts, and come unto Christ. Jacob wants us to choose today which path we will take. It may be that Jacob saw in the people of his day many similarities to the rebellious Israelites

---

18 Hebrews chapters 3 and 4 and Alma 12:35 also contain extensive references to Psalm 95. Although an extended discussion of these texts is beyond the scope of this chapter, Peter E. Enns discusses the relationship between Psalm 95 and Hebrews 3:1–4:13; see Peter E. Enns, "Creation and Re-creation: Psalm 95 and Its Interpretation in Hebrews 3:1–4:13," *Westminster Theological Journal* 55 (1993): 255–80.

19 While Jacob's record extends into chapter 7, chapter 6 clearly represents a conclusion of sorts (see Jacob 6:12–13).

20 For a discussion on the dating of Psalm 95, see Marvin E. Tate, *Psalms 51–100*, Word Biblical Commentary 20 (Dallas: Word Books, 1990).

21 M. Catherine Thomas, "The Provocation in the Wilderness and the Rejection of Grace," in *Sperry Symposium Classics: The Old Testament*, ed. Paul Y. Hoskisson (Provo, UT: Religious Studies Center, Brigham Young University; Salt Lake City: Deseret Book, 2005), 164–76.

in the wilderness. By echoing Psalm 95, Jacob ultimately encourages them (and us) to "enter into [God's] rest" and "obtain eternal life" (Jacob 1:7; 6:11). Seeing the connections between Jacob's writing and Psalm 95 can help us better understand Jacob's words and message.[22] Many other instances of intertextuality exist between the Bible and the Book of Mormon. For example, Grant Hardy notes several textual connections between Abinadi and Moses, such as the fact that both read the Ten Commandments, both shine brightly, and both speak to blasphemous rulers who say, "Who is the Lord?" (Exodus 5:2; Mosiah 11:27).[23]

Examples of Textual Connections within the Book of Mormon

But what of intertextuality *within* the Book of Mormon? The possibility that Book of Mormon prophets quote each other should not be surprising. In essence, the only requirement for one person to be able to quote from another is access to the other person's words. The text of the Book of Mormon makes it clear that speakers who lived in later time periods had access to the teachings of earlier prophets. Nephi explicitly intended for his words to go forth among his people, stating that the small plates "should be kept for the instruction *of my people*, who should possess the land" (1 Nephi 19:3). Nephi clearly wanted the small plates to remain in circulation. Amaleki expressed his plan to accomplish that purpose by giving the small plates to King Benjamin (see Omni 1:25). Benjamin passed on the records

---

22 For more insight on this passage, see John Hilton III, "Old Testament Psalms in the Book of Mormon," in *Ascending the Mountain of the Lord: Temple, Praise, and Worship in the Old Testament*, ed. David R. Seely, Jeffrey R. Chadwick, and Matthew J. Grey (Provo, UT: Religious Studies Center, Brigham Young University, 2013), 291–311.

23 See Grant Hardy, *Understanding the Book of Mormon: A Reader's Guide* (New York: Oxford University Press, 2010), 157–60. As another proposed example of intertexuality between the Book of Mormon and the Old Testament, Ben McGuire suggests textual connections between Nephi slaying Laban and David killing Goliath. See Ben McGuire, "Nephi and Goliath: A Case Study of Literary Allusion in the Book of Mormon," *Journal of Book of Mormon Studies* 18, no. 1 (2009): 16–31.

to Mosiah₂ (see Mosiah 1:16), who in turn gave "all the records" in his possession to Alma (Mosiah 28:20). Although Mormon was apparently not aware of the small plates when he began his record (see Words of Mormon 1:3), it is not clear at what point this record might have disappeared from the view of recordkeepers.

King Benjamin also wanted his words to be known; he "caused that the words which he spake should be written and sent forth among those that were not under the sound of his voice, that they might also receive his words" (Mosiah 2:8). This was not the only sending forth of the written prophetic word. In Alma 63:12 Mormon tells us, "All those engravings which were in the possession of Helaman [these likely included the small plates, as well as the words of Alma, Amulek, Abinadi, King Benjamin, and others] were written and sent forth among the children of men throughout all the land."

When preaching to the people of Ammonihah, Alma alluded to King Benjamin's words, suggesting that the people of Ammonihah may have had access to the prophetic word of a previous generation.[24] In his address to the financially poor Zoramites, Alma clearly referred to Zenos, Zenock, and Moses, leading one to believe that even these individuals with lower socioeconomic status were familiar with teachings from the brass plates.[25] Helaman₂'s counsel to his sons Nephi and Lehi makes it plain that they had access to the works of previous prophets.[26] He says, "O remember, remember, my sons, the words which king Benjamin spake unto his people. . . . And remember also the words which Amulek spake unto Zeezrom, in the city of Ammonihah" (Helaman 5:9–10). It is noteworthy that

---

24   For example, see Alma 13:28; compare Mosiah 3:19.

25   See Alma 33:3–20. The brass plates were original records that Lehi's family took with them on their journey to the promised land.

26   John W. Welch writes, "Nephi and Lehi likely used the precise words of King Benjamin in their preaching, just as their father had quoted to them some of the words of King Benjamin: 'Remember that there is no other way nor means whereby man be saved, only through the atoning blood of Jesus Christ' (Helaman 5:9; compare Mosiah 3:18; 4:8)." John W. Welch, "Textual Consistency," in *Reexploring the Book of Mormon*, ed. John W. Welch (Salt Lake City: Deseret Book; Provo, UT: FARMS, 1992), 22–23. See also the relationship between Alma 36:22 and 1 Nephi 1:8, discussed in that same chapter.

Helaman expressly refers to Amulek, indicating that whatever records Helaman had obtained specifically attributed the same words to Amulek that we now also have Amulek recorded as speaking (see Helaman 5:10; compare Alma 11:34, 37). Later textual evidence suggests that words from Alma, Amulek, and Zeezrom were circulated among the people generally. When speaking to a group of Lamanites and apostate Nephites, Aminadab said, "You must repent, and cry unto the voice, even until ye shall have faith in Christ, who was taught unto you by Alma, and Amulek, and Zeezrom [words which had been given some forty-five years previously]" (Helaman 5:41).[27]

Exploring intertwining voices within the Book of Mormon is a fruitful area of study. The fact that later Nephite prophets had access to the voices of earlier ones opens the possibility for intentional intertextual quotations and allusions within the Book of Mormon. While much work remains, researchers have already found several instances of intertextual allusions in the Book of Mormon. For example, John Welch points to close parallels between King Benjamin's speech and many of Alma's words:

> In establishing the church of God in the first years of the reign of judges, Alma implemented many of the religious and social policies articulated by Benjamin. Alma required that all those who "had taken upon them the name of Christ" (Alma 1:19; compare Mosiah 5:9) should "impart of their substance" to the poor and the needy, "every man according to that which he had" (Alma 1:27; compare Mosiah 4:26); that no church leader should "[esteem] himself above his hearers" (Alma 1:26; compare Mosiah 2:26); that the names of all hardened transgressors "were blotted out" (Alma 1:24; compare Mosiah 5:11); that "every man receiveth

---

27   The fact that these words had been spoken several decades previously indicates a reliance on oral or written traditions as opposed to people having heard the words firsthand, as in Helaman 5. It is also clear that a wide variety of people had access to the words on the brass plates, including both the wealthy priests of King Noah and the poor Zoramites (see Mosiah 12:20–21 and Alma 33:15). However, the fact that these words were circulated does not necessarily indicate widespread literacy among the Nephites. It is possible that the words were given to literate people in the community who then read them to others. Either way, it suggests many people in the Book of Mormon were familiar with the teachings of earlier Nephite prophets.

wages of him whom he listeth to obey" (Alma 3:27; compare Mosiah 2:32); [and] that all should strive to retain "a remission of their sins" (Alma 4:14; compare Mosiah 4:12).[28]

These extensive connections between King Benjamin and Alma suggest the ongoing importance of King Benjamin's final discourse. Another scholar who has uncovered multiple instances of intertextuality is Grant Hardy. For example, he identifies eight connections between Abinadi's ministry and Alma and Amulek's in Ammonihah. He also shows how Moroni extensively quotes from previous Book of Mormon authors in each of his farewells (Mormon 9, Ether 12, and Moroni 10). My favorite of Hardy's intertexuality discoveries is what he terms "a verbal curtain call."[29] Hardy shows that in Moroni's final words Moroni alludes to the last words of Nephi, Mormon, Amaleki (the final author of the small plates), Lehi, Enos, and Jacob.

For example, in Moroni's final farewell, he alludes to Nephi's references to seeing readers at the bar of God (Moroni 10:27; compare 2 Nephi 33:11) and states that God will show modern readers that Moroni's words are true (Moroni 10:28–29; compare 2 Nephi 33:11, 14). Additionally, he alludes to Amaleki and Mormon when he gives the exhortation to "come unto Christ, and lay hold upon every good gift" (Moroni 10:30; compare Omni 1:26; Moroni 7:19, 20, 25). Moroni alludes to some of Lehi's final words when he says, "Awake, and arise from the dust" (Moroni 10:31; compare 2 Nephi 1:14, 23; see also Isaiah 52:1–2). In addition, in the last verse in the Book of Mormon, Moroni uses phrases such as "Now I bid unto all, farewell. I soon go to rest" and "before the pleasing bar of the great Jehovah"—echoing some of the final words written by Enos and Jacob (Moroni 10:34; compare Enos 1:27; Jacob 6:13).[30]

Hardy notes, "Moroni puts on a striking display of allusive virtuosity as he borrows from the farewell speeches of his predeces-

---

28   John W. Welch, "Benjamin, the Man: His Place in Nephite History," in *King Benjamin's Speech: "That Ye May Learn Wisdom,"* ed. John W. Welch and Stephen D. Ricks (Provo, UT: FARMS, 1998), 44.

29   Hardy, *Understanding the Book of Mormon*, 262.

30   These allusions are explained in greater depth in Hardy, *Understanding the Book of Mormon*, 262–63.

sors."[31] Seeing this pattern of quotations—Moroni crafting his last words from quotations of the last words of earlier prophets—helps us see Moroni as a careful writer, an author who thought carefully about his last words and how he could maximize their impact. It also demonstrates a literary beauty that we might miss if we were not attuned to how Moroni is using different individual voices that appear in the Book of Mormon.

Notwithstanding the many examples of intertextuality that have been discovered and explained by scholars to date, much more remains to be uncovered. In contrast to the many books exclusively devoted to textual allusions between the Old and New Testaments, researchers have written relatively little regarding textual relationships within the Book of Mormon. Perhaps one reason this is the case is that the Book of Mormon presents some unique challenges in terms of uncovering textual allusions.

Unique Considerations of Intertextuality in the Book of Mormon

In addition to the general question of what constitutes a true allusion (discussed above), there are at least three specific issues that we must address when seeking to identify textual allusions within the Book of Mormon. These issues are as follows: (1) the potential for the brass plates as the original source for apparently intra–Book of Mormon citations, (2) parallels between Book of Mormon phrases and those appearing in the New Testament, and (3) allusions that may be exaggerated or obscured through the process of translation. Let us examine each of these issues in turn.

Do allusions come from the brass plates?

The brass plates were records that the early Book of Mormon peoples brought with them to the Americas from Jerusalem. From the context of the Book of Mormon, it appears that these brass plates were similar in some respects to the Old Testament (see 1 Nephi 13:23). In addition, the brass plates contained writings from prophets not mentioned in the Old Testament. The presence of an additional

---

31 Hardy, *Understanding the Book of Mormon*, 263.

record such as the brass plates presents a problem when looking for textual connections within the Book of Mormon because we cannot be certain whether a proposed allusion from a later Book of Mormon prophet to an earlier one demonstrates a textual connection between the two speakers or whether both were referring to the brass plates.

Some quotations in the Book of Mormon clearly appear to be related to the brass plates, such as references to Isaiah. But it is not always clear if a quotation in the Book of Mormon comes from an earlier Book of Mormon prophet or another source. For example, Alma's phrase "They had become carnal, sensual, and devilish" (Alma 42:10) seems to be an allusion to Abinadi's statement regarding "all mankind becoming carnal, sensual, devilish" (Mosiah 16:3). The words *carnal*, *sensual*, and *devilish* do not appear in the Bible, and they appear in the Book of Mormon only in these two verses. However, it is possible that they occurred in the brass plates. Thus, while we can assert a textual connection between Abinadi and Alma, it's technically possible that both are referring to Zenos or another author on the brass plates.[32]

The brass plates were passed from one prophet to another and could be the source of many textual connections in the Book of Mormon.[33] Because we do not have access to the brass plates, it is ultimately impossible to tell whether a quote originates with a Book of Mormon speaker or the brass plates. Nevertheless, if two speakers in the Book of Mormon use similar phrases and these phrases do not appear in the Old Testament, the probability increases that one Book of Mormon prophet is referring to another, particularly when there are multiple textual allusions in quick succession.

---

32 The words *carnal*, *sensual*, and *devilish* do collocate in the Book of Moses. Reynolds argues that their appearance in the Book of Mormon "demands a source in a prominent text or ritual. The book of Moses provides both." Reynolds, "Brass Plates Version of Genesis."

33 The brass plates are explicitly mentioned as being passed from King Benjamin to Mosiah$_2$ (Mosiah 1:16), from Mosiah$_2$ to Alma (Mosiah 28:20), from Alma to Helaman$_2$ (Alma 37:3), and from Nephi$_2$ to Nephi$_3$ (3 Nephi 1:2). Mormon also demonstrates an awareness of what was written on the brass plates (3 Nephi 10:17).

Parallels with the New Testament

A second issue that must be addressed is what to do when Book of Mormon intertextuality takes place with phrases from the New Testament. Consider the following example: Abinadi states, "Even *this mortal shall put on immortality, and this corruption shall put on incorruption*, and shall be brought *to stand before the bar of God, to be judged of him according to* their works" (Mosiah 16:10). This phrase is nearly identical to one Alma says while teaching the people of Zarahemla: "Do you . . . view *this mortal body raised in immortality, and this corruption raised in incorruption, to stand before God to be judged according to* the deeds which have been done in the mortal body?" (Alma 5:15).

There is an unmistakable connection between these verses. However, they are both similar to 1 Corinthians 15:53–54: "For this corruptible must *put on incorruption*, and *this mortal must put on immortality*. So when this *corruptible shall have put on incorruption*, and *this mortal shall have put on immortality*, then shall be brought to pass the saying that is written, Death is swallowed up in victory." The question then arises: Are the connections in Alma 5:15 and Mosiah 16:10 between each other or the New Testament?

The presence of the New Testament in the Book of Mormon can be a stumbling block; some people have suggested that the Book of Mormon cannot be an ancient work because of its textual connections to the New Testament. Brigham Young University religion professors Nicholas J. Frederick and Joseph M. Spencer summarized responses to this criticism as follows:

> The most traditional approach has been to argue (or at least to assume) that New Testament language appears in the Book of Mormon because that's what was inscribed on the gold plates by its ancient authors. On this view, there's no direct dependence of the Book of Mormon on the New Testament. The two have similar language because God reveals the same things from one generation to another. A slight variation on this view might be the idea that the ancient authors of the Book of Mormon were given, through divine experiences, to know the language of the New Testament and to use it in their writings. . . .

Another set of approaches . . . allow for a looser notion of translation, suggesting that the English text might take certain liberties with the underlying gold-plates text. That is, these approaches take the Book of Mormon's English text as introducing New Testament language into a text that wasn't originally worded that way. . . . To translate needn't be to produce a slavish reproduction of content in one language into another; it can also be to couch the content of the original in language and imagery more familiar to the target audience. . . . Those who embrace this looser notion of translation tend to see a variety of reasons for a less literal translation. New Testament language makes the Book of Mormon more intelligible to a latter-day (and largely Christian) audience. It also lends rhetorical authority to the Book of Mormon, allowing it to speak in the voice of authoritative scripture.[34]

Frederick and Spencer effectively argue that there are a variety of possible explanations for the presence of the New Testament text in the Book of Mormon. Several resources are available for those interested in further studies on this topic.[35] In this book, while I identify the connections to the New Testament when they appear, my focus is on the connections *within* the Book of Mormon.

In this case, in the Book of Mormon the words *mortal, immortality, corruption,* and *incorruption* appear together only in the words

---

34 Nicholas J. Frederick and Joseph M. Spencer, "The Book of Mormon and the Academy," *Religious Educator* 21, no. 2 (2020): 183–84. When commenting on the similarities in language between Moroni 7:45 and 1 Corinthians 13:4–7, Elder Jeffrey R. Holland wrote, "The fact that Paul uses comparable language without having the benefit of Mormon and Moroni's text suggests the possibility of an ancient source available to both Book of Mormon and New Testament writers. It may also simply be another evidence that the Holy Ghost can reveal a truth in essentially the same words to more than one person." Jeffrey R. Holland, *Christ and the New Covenant: The Messianic Message of the Book of Mormon* (Salt Lake City: Deseret Book, 1997), 413.

35 Nicholas J. Frederick has a large body of work examining the relationship between the New Testament and the Book of Mormon. For example, see his articles "The Book of Mormon and Its Redaction of the King James New Testament: A Further Evaluation of the Interaction between the New Testament and the Book of Mormon," *Journal of Book of Mormon Studies* 27 (2018): 44–87; and "Finding Meaning(s) in How the Book of Mormon Uses the New Testament," *Journal of Book of Mormon Studies* 30 (2021): 1–35.

of Alma and Abinadi. Thus, even if New Testament language influenced the translation of the Book of Mormon, it did so very unevenly. Moreover, both Alma and Abinadi include the shared phraseology "stand before God to be judged," which isn't found in 1 Corinthians. In other words, the presence of New Testament phraseology does not explain why such phrases occurred only in those two instances in the Book of Mormon—clearly there is some relationship between the words of Alma and Abinadi.[36] In the following chapters, I focus on what we can learn from instances of shared text within the Book of Mormon, regardless of their potential connection with the New Testament.

The translation process

The Book of Mormon is unique in that it is both an abridged and a translated work. Thus it can be difficult to determine if minor textual similarities (or differences) are a result of Mormon's abridgment or Joseph Smith's translation or are part of the text from an original writer. For example, are the textual connections between Samuel the Lamanite and Alma the result of Samuel's study of Alma's words, the two both receiving similar inspiration, Mormon's careful editing, or some other source? While such questions cannot be fully answered, this should not diminish the importance of those textual connections and discourage efforts to explore how they might be related.

Perhaps the more important issue is determining whether phrases are sufficiently similar to suggest a clear connection. For example, Mosiah 4:6 and Mosiah 10:19 both speak of a person or people "put[ting] . . . trust in the Lord." These are the only instances in the Book of Mormon in which these specific phrases (including their variants) appear in the same verse. However, similar phrases speaking of "putting [your] trust in God" appear four times in the Book of Mormon (Mosiah 7:19; Alma 36:3; 38:5; 57:27). More instances occur of "putting [your] trust in him" (Mosiah 7:33; 23:22; 29:20; Alma 36:27; 61:13; Helaman 12:1). Are these different passages related to one another, or are they simply common ways of expressing

---

36   See Hardy, *Understanding the Book of Mormon*, 302.

an important way of living? To answer questions such as this one, let us return to the subject of identifying allusions.

Guiding Principles for Finding Allusions in the Book of Mormon

As described previously, Hays and others have set forth criteria for finding allusions within specific contexts of intertextuality. Given the unique considerations of intertextuality in the Book of Mormon described previously, I believe that a similar set of guidelines can be employed for determining the likelihood that one Book of Mormon passage is related to another.[37] Throughout the rest of the chapters in this book, I will implicitly draw on the following four criteria in determining whether intertextual allusions within the Book of Mormon are in fact intentional:

1. *Source.* The following questions should be satisfactorily answered to determine if one prophet's words could be legitimately construed as using another source: Does it seem plausible that a later author could have had access to the purported source? Is there another source that may be a more likely candidate for the allusion (either from the brass plates or a different Book of Mormon prophet)?

2. *Uniqueness.* This criterion addresses the extent to which phrases are unique. The more frequently phrases appear (both within the Book of Mormon and in scripture generally), the more difficult it is to establish that any two of those phrases are uniquely connected. Even if a phrase were to appear frequently in the Doctrine and Covenants (obviously not a source text for the Book of Mormon), this frequent appearance might indicate that the phrase was simply a part of Joseph Smith's vocabulary. In the following chapters, tables will illustrate how frequently a phrase appears in scripture. The purpose of these tables is to show

---

37 These criteria are based on the studies by Hays and Reynolds mentioned previously. In addition, Nicholas J. Frederick proposes similar criteria in his article "Evaluating the Interaction between the New Testament and the Book of Mormon: A Proposed Methodology," *Journal of Book of Mormon Studies* 24 (2015): 1–30.

the extent to which a phrase appears to be unique to any two passages or speakers.[38]

3. *Length.* Length answers the question "How long is the proposed echo?" Longer identical phrases argue for stronger connections than shorter ones.

4. *Context.* This criterion addresses issues such as the following: Are the contexts in which the phrases are used similar? Are there words surrounding the phrases that indicate a connection? Is there a series of allusions in proximity? Affirmative answers to the foregoing questions would indicate an increased likelihood of intentional allusion.

Evaluating Proposed Connections Considering These Criteria

To see more detailed examples of how these criteria might be specifically applied, I next provide a series of proposed allusions and examine them based on the guidelines just presented. Dozens of examples could be provided; in the interest of brevity, I share only three.[39]

Darkest abyss and marvelous light of God

After an angel commands Alma and the sons of Mosiah to repent in Mosiah 27, Alma declares, "My soul hath been redeemed from the gall of bitterness and bonds of iniquity. I was *in the darkest abyss*; but now I *behold the marvelous light of God*" (Mosiah 27:29). Later, when Ammon (one of the sons of Mosiah) rejoices in the repentance of the Lamanites, he states, "Our brethren, the Lamanites, were in darkness, yea, even *in the darkest abyss*, but behold, how many of them are brought to *behold the marvelous light of God*!" (Alma 26:3).

---

38 In speaking of this concept, Hardy writes, "The possibility of intentionality increases when [connecting phrases occur only in two specific passages]." Hardy, *Understanding the Book of Mormon*, 251.

39 Specific examples of parallel phrases are found throughout the remainder of this book. I will not typically include a written explanation of how these matching phrases meet the criteria explained in this section, for as Richard Hays wrote, "To run explicitly through this series of criteria for each of the texts that I treat would be wearisome." Hays, *Echoes of Scripture*, 32. Nevertheless, I used these criteria in determining whether the intertextual connections I present appear to be significant.

Ammon later mentions that he and his brethren had gone "forth in wrath, with mighty threatening to destroy [God's] church" (Alma 26:18), which is a clear reference to the events of Mosiah 27.

Regarding source criteria, Alma and Ammon were contemporaries and could have been familiar with the other's phraseology. An additional possibility is that Mormon, as the narrator telling both stories, could have put these words into the mouths of both Alma and Ammon to help readers draw comparisons between the two accounts. The phrases "darkest abyss and marvelous light of God" appear only in these two pericopes, arguing for their uniqueness.[40] At ten words, the phrase "in the darkest abyss . . . behold the marvelous light of God" indicates the possibility of a relationship. Regarding context, both Alma and Ammon are speaking of the change that comes from conversion, providing plausibility that this is a genuine connection that deserves to be explored. Perhaps this connection is an intentional rhetorical device meant to help readers see that people who were once in the "darkest abyss" can change their lives and help others "behold the marvelous light of God." Whether it is an individual who has willfully rebelled or an entire people who have made wrong decisions based on the traditions they were taught, all can enter God's marvelous light.

The blood of the saints

In 2 Nephi 26:3 Nephi prophesied that the day of Christ's death will be "great and terrible . . . unto the wicked, for they shall perish . . . because they cast out *the prophets, and the saints* . . . ; wherefore the cry of *the blood of the saints* shall ascend up to God *from the ground against them.*" Nephi also wrote that "they that kill *the prophets, and the saints, the depths of the earth* shall swallow them up" (2 Nephi 26:5).

After Christ's death, great destruction took place in the Americas, and the survivors heard Christ's voice. Christ said, "The great city Moronihah have I covered with earth . . . to hide their iniquities . . . , that *the blood of the prophets and the saints* shall not come any

---

40   In fact, the words *abyss* and *light* appear together only in these two verses.

more unto me against them" (3 Nephi 9:5).[41] In 3 Nephi 9:8 the Savior, speaking of several cities, stated, "All these have I caused to be sunk, and made hills and valleys in the places thereof; and the inhabitants thereof have I buried up in *the depths of the earth*." Christ also explained that he destroyed people so "that *the blood of the prophets and the saints . . .* might not cry unto me *from the ground against them*" (3 Nephi 9:11).

Could the surviving Lehites have been familiar with Nephi's words and thus recognized in Christ's statement their fulfillment? This is one possibility and allows for the potential allusions to pass the source criterion. Perhaps by using Nephi's words, Christ reminded the Nephites, as well as modern readers, that this destruction was a fulfillment of prophecy. He also may have been offering hope to the survivors that salvation through Christ, of which Nephi had prophesied, would also be extended.

At the same time, it is difficult to measure the extent to which the Lehites may have heard Christ's words as echoes of Nephi's writings. It is also possible that Mormon, having recently discovered or read Nephi's record, adjusted the words of the Lord, however slightly, to create allusions for modern audiences—clearly showing that prophetic words are fulfilled.

Whether the allusions to Nephi come directly from Jesus Christ or are mediated through Mormon's abridgment, this tight clustering of relatively lengthy phrases, combined with their rare use in scripture, provides satisfaction that the uniqueness and length criteria are met. These connections, along with others between Jesus Christ and Nephi, will be further explored in chapter 12.

That I might rid my garments

In prefacing his discourse on pride and chastity, Jacob says, "I, Jacob, according to the responsibility which I am under to God, to magnify mine office with soberness, and *that I might rid my garments of your sins*, I come up into the temple this day that I might declare unto

---

41   Royal Skousen's *The Book of Mormon: The Earliest Text* (New Haven, CT: Yale University Press, 2009) reads "the blood of the prophets and of the saints."

you the word of God" (Jacob 2:2). King Benjamin similarly says, "I say unto you that I have caused that ye should assemble yourselves together *that I might rid my garments of your* blood, at this period of time when I am about to go down to my grave" (Mosiah 2:28).

In terms of the source criterion, it seems logical that King Benjamin, who had been given the small plates, would be familiar with and able to quote Jacob's words. The specific phrase "that I might rid my garments" of your never appears elsewhere in scripture, and the shorter "rid my/our/their garments" appears four times in scriptures (Jacob 2:2; Mosiah 2:28; Mormon 9:35; and Doctrine and Covenants 61:34). While this suggests uniqueness and makes Jacob the earliest source, similar phrases exist elsewhere. For example, Jacob also speaks of taking off his garments and becoming rid of the blood of the people (see 2 Nephi 9:44), and in Acts 18:6 Paul "shook his raiment, and said unto them, Your blood be upon your own heads; I am clean: from henceforth I will go unto the Gentiles." Thus, while the words *rid* and *garment* appear together in only five verses,[42] this repeated usage possibly represents a traditional idea rather than deliberate borrowing.

As an eight-word phrase, "that I might rid my garments of your" is likely long enough to satisfy the length criterion, although several of the words are not significant. In terms of context, both Jacob and King Benjamin use the phrase in stating one of their purposes of their addresses. In addition, King Benjamin uses several other phrases from Jacob, further increasing the possibility that King Benjamin is deliberately drawing on Jacob. Nevertheless, this is a weaker allusion, and although the phrase "that I might rid my garments of your" could potentially pass all four of these criteria, it is by no means certain that King Benjamin is intentionally alluding to Jacob's words (for more details on this phrase and other connections between Jacob and King Benjamin, see chapter 7).

Therefore, What?

In this chapter we've explored several issues relating to intertextuality in the Book of Mormon. Developing a comprehensive list of Book

---

42 See 2 Nephi 9:44; Jacob 2:2; Mosiah 2:28; Mormon 9:35; and Doctrine and Covenants 61:34.

of Mormon intertextuality is challenging because, as Hays states, "sometimes the echo will be so loud that only the dullest or most ignorant reader could miss it; other times there will be room for serious differences of opinion about whether a particular phrase should be heard as an echo of a prior text."[43] Nevertheless, the difficulty of the task should not dissuade us from pressing forward with the work of identifying and analyzing Book of Mormon intertextuality.

To that end, I have proposed criteria that could be used to evaluate the extent to which proposed textual connections could be intentional and have given examples of how these criteria could be utilized. In the following chapters I will give specific, extended examples of how the different speakers in the Book of Mormon use the distinctive voices of their prophetic predecessors.

When we read the Book of Mormon, we can use a variety of lenses. For example, President Russell M. Nelson invited Church members to read the Book of Mormon and identify references to Jesus Christ.[44] President Ezra Taft Benson spoke of how the Book of Mormon exposes the enemies of Christ.[45] If we read the Book of Mormon specifically with the lens of identifying references to Jesus Christ, we will find different things than if we study its pages looking for the tactics of those who oppose Christ. Using a different lens in our study can help us find additional insights.

For me, identifying intertextuality has been a helpful lens in increasing my understanding and testimony of the Book of Mormon. As I will describe in the following chapters, seeing how Alma used the words of Lehi and Abinadi or learning more about how Jacob's words were employed by later prophets has not only been intellectually stimulating but has also illuminated spiritual lessons I would have otherwise missed. Identifying and examining intertextuality can show us how prophets carefully studied the words of their predecessors, which can motivate us to deepen our own studies. As

---

43 Hays, *Echoes of Scripture*, 29.

44 See Russell M. Nelson, "Sisters' Participation in the Gathering of Israel," *Ensign*, November 2018, 69–70.

45 See Ezra Taft Benson, "The Book of Mormon Is the Word of God," *Ensign*, January 1988, 3.

we now turn to closely examining how Book of Mormon prophets utilize the words of their predecessors in their teaching, we can learn much about how we use scripture as we teach others.

Chapter 7
Jacob's Textual Legacy

As described in chapter 2, Jacob has a unique voice within the Book of Mormon.[1] By studying and comparing his distinct patterns, words, and phrases, we saw that Jacob was a powerful speaker with a testimony to match. In this chapter, we will explore the reach of his voice by identifying how some later Book of Mormon prophets used his words.[2] We will examine three cases in which Jacob's words were cited by later prophets (each case containing several allusions), thus providing a literary legacy of Jacob's testimony and words.

---

1   This chapter is adapted from John Hilton III, "Jacob's Textual Legacy," *Journal of the Book of Mormon and Other Restoration Scripture* 22, no. 2 (2013): 52–65. Used with permission.

2   The present chapter deals with allusions made by Nephi, King Benjamin, and Moroni. These are not the only prophets that share a connection with Jacob. For example, Joseph M. Spencer points out connections between Jacob and Abinadi, stating, "Abinadi is Jacob's unquestionable doctrinal heir" (*An Other Testament: On Typology* [Salem, OR: Salt Press, 2012], 134). Samuel the Lamanite also draws on Jacob (and others), as discussed in chapter 11.

Three Cases of Textual Echoes from Jacob

Case 1: 2 Nephi 9 and 2 Nephi 28

The first prophet who echoed the words of Jacob was not only a prophet, he was Jacob's brother. Though it may seem strange to think of Nephi as being influenced by his younger brother Jacob, the tight connections between 2 Nephi 9 (Jacob's sermon)[3] and 2 Nephi 28 (part of a later sermon given by Nephi) lead one to believe that this is in fact the case. Nephi's allusions in 2 Nephi 28 to Jacob's earlier words in 2 Nephi 9 are summarized in table 7.1.

Table 7.1. Nephi's allusions in 2 Nephi 28 to Jacob's words in 2 Nephi 9

Case #	Nephi's words	Jacob's words	Allusion	Times exact phrase is used elsewhere in scripture
1	2 Nephi 28:13	2 Nephi 9:30	They persecute the meek	0
2	2 Nephi 28:15	2 Nephi 9:42	The wise, and the learned, and the rich, that are puffed up	0
3	2 Nephi 28:15	2 Nephi 9:36	Who commit whoredoms	0 (but the phrase "commit whoredoms" frequently appears)

---

3 Nephi explicitly tells us that he is quoting from Jacob in 2 Nephi 6–10 (see 2 Nephi 6:1).

4	2 Nephi 28:15	2 Nephi 9:36	They shall be thrust down to hell	0 (the phrase "thrust down to hell" appears in Luke 10:15 and Doctrine and Covenants 76:84)
5	2 Nephi 28:23	2 Nephi 9:19, 26	Death, and hell, and the devil	0
6	2 Nephi 28:23	2 Nephi 9:19, 26	Lake of fire and brimstone, which is endless torment	0
7	2 Nephi 28:28	2 Nephi 9:38	And in fine, wo unto all those who	0

In 2 Nephi 28:13 Nephi states that the proud "rob the poor" because of their "fine sanctuaries" and "fine clothing" and that "they persecute the meek" because of their pride. In this instance, we find both conceptual and textual echoes from Jacob's earlier words. Jacob had said, "Because they are rich they despise the poor, and *they persecute the meek*, and their hearts are upon their treasures" (2 Nephi 9:30). In both instances, the proud (wealthy) rob (or despise) the poor and persecute the meek because of their pride (wealth). Pride and riches thus are pinpointed as the cause violating the second great commandment—to love one's neighbor as oneself.[4]

---

4 An interesting difference between the two statements is Jacob's focus on wealth, versus Nephi's focus on pride. Jacob states, "Wo unto the rich who are rich as to the things of the world" (2 Nephi 9:30), not explicitly drawing any distinction between the wealthy who are caught up in pride and the wealthy who use their means to bless humanity. Later, however, Jacob will warn "they that are rich, who are puffed up . . . because of their riches" (2 Nephi 9:42).

Jacob warned, "*Wo* unto *them who commit whoredoms, for they shall be thrust down to hell*" (2 Nephi 9:36). He also taught that happiness would not come to "*the wise, and the learned, and they that are rich, who are puffed up* because of their learning, and their wisdom, and their riches" (2 Nephi 9:42).

Nephi alludes to both these ideas as he declares that "*the wise, and the learned, and the rich, that are puffed up* in the pride of their hearts, . . . and *all those who commit whoredoms*, and pervert the right way of the Lord, *wo*, wo, wo be unto them, saith the Lord God Almighty, *for they shall be thrust down to hell*" (2 Nephi 28:15).

In 2 Nephi 28:23,[5] Nephi warns both those who are pacified by the devil and those who are angry with the truth that "they are grasped with . . . *death, and hell, and the devil*, and all that have been seized therewith must stand before the throne of God, and be judged according to their works, from whence they must go into . . . a *lake of fire and brimstone, which is endless torment*." In making this statement, Nephi alludes to Jacob's teaching that "the atonement satisfieth the demands of his justice upon all those who have not the law given to them, that they are delivered from that awful monster, *death and hell, and the devil, and the lake of fire and brimstone, which is endless torment*" (2 Nephi 9:26; see verse 19). These phrases are unique in scripture, and the words *lake*, *fire*, and *endless* appear together only in these passages and in Jacob 6:10. While Jacob employs these phrases to illustrate the majesty of the Savior's Atonement, Nephi uses them to warn those who are "at ease in Zion . . . and are angry because of the truth of God" (2 Nephi 28:24, 28).

---

5   The 2013 text of 2 Nephi 28:23 states, "They are grasped with death, and hell; and death, and hell, and the devil." Royal Skousen notes that "the current text here in 2 Nephi 28:23 seems to involve a textual dittography. The original manuscript is not extant here, but it appears that Oliver Cowdery repeated the words "death and hell and" as he copied from the original manuscript into the printer's manuscript." Royal Skousen, *Analysis of Textual Variants of the Book of Mormon, Part Two: 2 Nephi 11–Mosiah 16* (Provo, UT: FARMS, 2005), 873. Basing his analysis in part on 2 Nephi 9:19, 26, Skousen recommends removing the first "death and hell and" in this sentence. This emendation only strengthens the textual connection between Jacob's and Nephi's words.

Nephi's final allusion to Jacob in 2 Nephi 28 comes as he states, "*And in fine, wo unto all those* who tremble, and are angry with the truth of God!" (2 Nephi 28:28). Jacob had used a similar phrase as he capped a list of woes by teaching, "*And, in fine, wo unto all those* who die in their sins; for they shall return to God, and behold his face, and remain in their sins" (2 Nephi 9:38). The words *in fine* and *wo* collocate only in these two verses.

In 2 Nephi 28:15–32, Nephi offers eleven instances of *wo*. In 2 Nephi 9:27–38, Jacob provides ten. There are several similarities between these, including specific statements regarding "the rich" and those who commit "whoredoms" (compare 2 Nephi 28:15 with 2 Nephi 9:30, 36). Given the textual and conceptual similarities between Nephi's and Jacob's woes, it is possible that Nephi used the phrase "and in fine, wo unto all those" as a merism to more comprehensively refer back to the woes stated previously by Jacob. (A merism is a statement in which one key phrase can be employed to represent a longer statement.) If this is the case, Nephi employs the unique phrase "and in fine, wo unto all those" as a rhetorical device to link his woes with Jacob's and reemphasize Jacob's warnings.

Why would Nephi quote from Jacob? It would seem like the younger brother would quote the older one, and not the other way around. Perhaps Nephi, the senior leader of the Nephites, wanted to quote his younger brother to prepare the people for the eventual transfer of ecclesiastical authority to Jacob. Perhaps by alluding to Jacob he added additional prophetic credibility to Jacob's words. Or it may simply be that Jacob's sermon in 2 Nephi 9, with more references to "hell" than any other chapter in all of scripture,[6] was a natural text to turn to when Nephi needed to rebuke prideful people.

---

6 *Hell* appears eight times in 2 Nephi 9, followed by five times in 2 Nephi 28, indicating another connection between the chapters. In addition, only one chapter in all scripture (Alma 12) has as many references to "death." Of course, these chapter breaks were not part of the original text, and some chapters are longer than others; thus this is meant to be an approximate comparison, not a precise one.

In addition, Nephi shows a propensity to adhere to the law of witnesses. He specifically states that three witnesses are necessary and writes that he, Jacob, and Isaiah qualify as these three witnesses (see 2 Nephi 11:3). Just as Nephi turns to Jacob's words to testify of Christ, it may also be that Jacob's writings provide an additional witness to Nephi's teachings regarding pride and sin.

Case 2: 2 Nephi 9 and King Benjamin's address[7]

The concept that King Benjamin could have been interested in Jacob's words is easy to establish. Amaleki, the last writer on the small plates (which contained Jacob's words), delivered them to King Benjamin (see Omni 1:25). To receive new prophetic records is not a regular occurrence; thus it seems likely that Benjamin would have carefully studied them.

Textual evidence also suggests that Benjamin's people could have been familiar with Jacob's words. King Benjamin tells his people, "Ye . . . have been taught concerning the records which contain the prophecies which have been spoken by the holy prophets, even down to the time our father, Lehi, left Jerusalem; and also, *all that has been spoken by our fathers until now*" (Mosiah 2:34–35). At least thirteen connections exist between Jacob's words in 2 Nephi 9 and King Benjamin's words. These allusions are outlined in table 7.2.

---

7   The textual connections between King Benjamin and Jacob are particularly interesting when considering the order of translation. It appears that Joseph Smith and Oliver Cowdery began their translation efforts with the early chapters of Mosiah in April of 1829. They then translated 2 Nephi after they arrived in Fayette, New York, in June of 1829. Given that translation witnesses said Joseph never referred to notes, other texts, or previous translations, it is inconceivable that Joseph, if he were the author of the Book of Mormon, could create such similarities between these two sermons when they were about as far removed in translation time as they could be. See John W. Welch, "Timing the Translation of the Book of Mormon: 'Days [and Hours] Never to Be Forgotten,'" *BYU Studies Quarterly* 57, no. 4 (2018): 10–50.

Table 7.2. King Benjamin's allusions to Jacob's words in 2 Nephi 9

Case #	King Benjamin's words	Jacob's words	Allusion	Times exact phrase is used elsewhere in scripture[8]
1	Mosiah 2:15, 17	2 Nephi 9:1, 3	These things that ye	1 (Helaman 5:8)
2	Mosiah 2:26	2 Nephi 9:7	Its mother earth	0 (but Mormon 6:15 is very close)
3	Mosiah 2:28	2 Nephi 9:44	Rid . . . garments	3 (Jacob 2:2; Mormon 9:35; Doctrine and Covenants 61:34)
4	Mosiah 2:33	2 Nephi 9:38	Wo . . . remaineth and dieth in . . . sins	0
5	Mosiah 2:38	2 Nephi 9:16	Whose flame ascendeth up forever and ever	1 (Alma 12:17)
6	Mosiah 2:41	2 Nephi 9:24	To the end . . . the Lord God . . . hath spoken it	0
7	Mosiah 3:19	2 Nephi 9:39	Yields . . . enticings	0

---

8   Later references to the phrase in the Book of Mormon may be allusions to Jacob or Benjamin (or both).

8	Mosiah 3:23	2 Nephi 9:40	I have spoken the words	0 (but Mosiah 5:6 and Mosiah 13:4 are nearly identical, and "spoken the words" occurs 20 times in scripture)
9	Mosiah 3:27	2 Nephi 9:16	And their torment is as a lake of fire and brimstone	0 (but Alma 12:17 is very similar)
10	Mosiah 4:4	2 Nephi 9:54	The remainder of my words	0
11	Mosiah 4:11	2 Nephi 9:40	Remember . . . the greatness of [the Lord]	0
12	Mosiah 4:11	2 Nephi 9:42	In the depths of humility	2 (Mosiah 21:14; Alma 62:41)
13	Mosiah 4:23	2 Nephi 9:30	Who are rich as . . . to the things of this world	0

These allusions can be divided into two sections—structural and doctrinal allusions. Five of Benjamin's allusions to Jacob follow the structural outline with which Jacob taught. After Jacob quotes Isaiah 50–51, he begins the main body of his address by explaining why he read the words of Isaiah. He says, "*I have read these things that ye might know . . . I speak unto you these things that ye may rejoice*" (2 Nephi 9:1, 3). Similarly, after explaining how he has labored as their king, Benjamin says, "*I tell you these things that ye may know. . . .*

I tell you these things that ye may learn wisdom" (Mosiah 2:15, 17).⁹
While perhaps this is simply a common rhetorical method of introducing a topic, the length and similarity of the two phrases suggest at
least the possibility that King Benjamin is employing Jacob's words
or structure. Later King Benjamin explains that he is not responsible for the sins of the people, saying, "I have caused that ye should
assemble yourselves together that I might *rid my garments of your
blood*" (Mosiah 2:28). This echoes Jacob's sentiment in 2 Nephi 9:44
when he shakes his "*garments*" before the people, saying, "I shook
your iniquities from my soul . . . and am *rid of your blood*" (2 Nephi
9:44).¹⁰

Both Jacob and King Benjamin say they have *spoken the words*
that God had commanded them to say (see 2 Nephi 9:40; Mosiah
3:23).¹¹ Finally, both have breaks in their discourses (Jacob's at the
end of 2 Nephi 9, King Benjamin's at the end of Mosiah 3). Before
ending the first part of his discourse, Jacob says, "On the morrow
I will declare unto you *the remainder of my words*" (2 Nephi 9:54).
Similarly, after hearing a response from his listeners, King Benjamin
resumes his address, saying, "I would again call your attention, that
ye may hear and understand *the remainder of my words*" (Mosiah 4:4).

The second set of allusions are more doctrinal in nature. King
Benjamin uses language similar to Jacob to describe his impending
death. He states, "I am also of the dust. And ye behold that I am
old, and am about to yield up this mortal frame to *its mother earth*"
(Mosiah 2:26). Jacob too had described a time when "this flesh must
have laid down to rot and to crumble to *its mother earth*" (2 Nephi
9:7). Perhaps Benjamin employs Jacob's phrase to emphasize that he,
although a king, faces the same issues of mortality as everyone else.

Next, King Benjamin plainly outlines the consequences of not
repenting, stating, "For behold, there is a wo pronounced upon him

---

9   Note that the phrase is used twice in quick succession by both Jacob and
    Benjamin.

10 Another connection with Jacob's words comes from Jacob 2:2, in which
    Jacob says that he is speaking to the people so that "I might rid my garments
    of your sins."

11 Note that in Mosiah 3:23 it may be the angel speaking as opposed to King
    Benjamin.

who listeth to obey that spirit; for if he listeth to obey him, and *remaineth and dieth in his sins . . .*" (Mosiah 2:33). Note that King Benjamin refers to a "wo" that had been previously issued. This statement may allude to Jacob's tenth wo, in which Jacob states, "And, in fine, wo unto all those who *die in their sins*; for they shall return to God, and behold his face, and *remain in their sins*" (2 Nephi 9:38). The words *remain, die,* and *sin* appear together only in these two verses. Benjamin later alludes to another one of Jacob's woes, teaching, "*Wo be unto that man*, for his substance shall perish with him; and now, I say these things *unto those who are rich as pertaining to the things of this world*" (Mosiah 4:23). This clearly echoes Jacob's statement "*Wo unto the rich, who are rich as to the things of the world*" (2 Nephi 9:30).

King Benjamin speaks of specific consequences for the unrepentant sinner. He states that those who die as enemies to God will receive pain "like an unquenchable *fire, whose flame ascendeth up forever and ever*" (Mosiah 2:38). Benjamin also says[12] (speaking of the wicked), "*Their torment is as a lake of fire and brimstone, whose flames* are unquenchable, and whose smoke *ascendeth up forever and ever*" (Mosiah 3:27). These phrases directly echo Jacob's teaching that, speaking of the filthy, "*their torment is as a lake of fire and brimstone, whose flame ascendeth up forever and ever* and has no end" (2 Nephi 9:16).[13]

As King Benjamin explains to his people how they can avoid this fate and retain a remission of their sins, he exhorts them to "*remember*, and always retain in remembrance, the *greatness of God*, and . . . humble yourselves even *in the depths of humility*, calling on the name of the Lord daily" (Mosiah 4:11).[14] Similarly, Jacob tells his people to "*remember the greatness of the Holy One of Israel*" and states that those who "come down *in the depths of humility*" will receive answers to their prayers (2 Nephi 9:40, 42).

In two instances Benjamin utilizes Jacob's words to contrast points Jacob had made. Benjamin says, "Consider on the blessed and happy state of those that keep the commandments of God. *If they*

---

12 King Benjamin is quoting the Lord in this passage.

13 An even stronger connection with these verses may be in Jacob 6:10.

14 The phrase "retain in remembrance" in this verse may be an allusion to Jacob 1:11.

hold out faithful to the end they are received into heaven, that thereby they may dwell with God in a state of never-ending happiness. O remember, remember that these things are true; *for the Lord God hath spoken it*" (Mosiah 2:41). This text is similar to Jacob's, although Jacob's words represent the opposite end of the spectrum: "*If they will not repent and . . . endure to the end, they must be* damned; *for the Lord God*, the Holy One of Israel, *has spoken it*" (2 Nephi 9:24). Where Benjamin speaks of "the righteous," Jacob tells of those who will "not repent." Benjamin refers to those who "hold out faithful to the end," while Jacob talks about those who will "not . . . endure to the end." Benjamin speaks of "a state of never ending happiness" in contrast to Jacob's reference to the "damned." By using antonyms, Benjamin may have been juxtaposing the happiness that awaits the righteous with the damnation Jacob spoke of that awaits those who do not repent.

A second example of what appears to be textual contrasting occurs between Mosiah 3:19 and 2 Nephi 9:39. Benjamin[15] teaches, "For the natural man is an enemy to God, and has been from the fall of Adam, and will be, forever and ever, unless he *yields to the enticings of the Holy Spirit*, and putteth off the natural man and becometh a saint through the atonement of Christ the Lord" (Mosiah 3:19). By *yielding to the enticings of the Holy Spirit*, one can overcome the natural man. In contrast, Jacob explains, "Remember . . . the awfulness of *yielding to the enticings of that cunning one*. Remember, to be carnally-minded is death" (2 Nephi 9:39).

It seems that this word choice must have been intentional (all variants of the words *yield* and *entice* appear together only in these two verses). Yielding to the enticings of the Spirit leads to becoming a saint. Yielding to the enticings of Satan leads to death. Jacob refers to the "awfulness" of yielding to the devil, while Benjamin associates words such as "patient" and "full of love" with yielding to the Spirit. Thus Benjamin turns Jacob's statement about the awful consequences of *yielding to the enticings* of the devil into a positive statement about *yielding to the enticings* of the Spirit.

In addition to the textual allusions noted above, there are additional echoes that, while lacking specific textual similarities,

---

15   At this point in the text, Benjamin appears to be quoting the angel who spoke to him.

demonstrate important doctrinal connections between 2 Nephi 9 and Mosiah 2–5. Jacob was the first to explain that "the atonement satisfieth the demands of his justice upon all those who have not the law given to them" (2 Nephi 9:26). This doctrine is not stated before or after in the Book of Mormon until King Benjamin states that Christ's "blood atoneth for the sins of those . . . who have died not knowing the will of God concerning them" (Mosiah 3:11).[16] Thus Benjamin echoes not only the sterner portions of Jacob's message but also those pertaining to the Savior's Atonement.

The connection on the important point of redemption for those without law is strengthened when we see that after teaching this principle, both Jacob and Benjamin provide a warning for those who know better. Jacob states, "Wo unto him that has the law given, yea, that has all the commandments of God, like unto us, and that transgresseth them, and that wasteth the days of his probation, for awful is his state!" (2 Nephi 9:27). Similarly, King Benjamin says, "But wo, wo unto him who knoweth that he rebelleth against God! For salvation cometh to none such except it be through repentance and faith on the Lord Jesus Christ" (Mosiah 3:12).

Another doctrinal connection between the two sermons concerns the name of the Messiah. Jacob was the first recorded person in the Book of Mormon to reveal that the name of the Redeemer would be "Christ" (2 Nephi 10:3). Jacob recounts that his information came from an angel. Nephi later expands on this, stating that the prophetic word, as well as the word of an angel, had revealed that the Savior's name would be "Jesus Christ, the Son of God" (2 Nephi 25:19). Based on the word of an angel, Benjamin further develops this revelation, stating that the Lord will be called "Jesus Christ, the Son of God, the Father of heaven and earth, the Creator of all things from the beginning" (Mosiah 3:8).

From the foregoing, it appears Benjamin utilized Jacob's words in 2 Nephi 9 in the creation of his final address to his people. It's possible that Benjamin was simply influenced by Jacob's language as he studied Jacob's words in preparation for his own discourse. But could

---

16   Abinadi (who likely spoke before King Benjamin chronologically) also alludes to this principle in Mosiah 15:24–25.

there be another reason that this speech might have particularly interested Benjamin?

John W. Welch has pointed out that Benjamin faced the difficult task of unifying two groups of people—the Nephites and Mulekites. These two distinctive groups had different ancestry, language, and customs and had only recently united (see Omni 1:17–19). Welch writes, "The key function achieved by Benjamin's speech was to bring the entire population—both Nephites and Mulekites—under a single covenant of loyalty to God and to Mosiah, the new king."[17]

While the exact circumstances of Jacob's address in 2 Nephi 6–10 are unknown, Brant Gardner speculates that Jacob was teaching a combined group of people, some of whom were Nephites and others who were indigenous people with whom the Nephites had come in contact.[18] Gardner believes that the way Jacob structured his speech can be seen as a way of including indigenous peoples as part of the Nephite covenant people. If this were the case, it would add relevance as to why King Benjamin would find meaning in Jacob's words. Perhaps Benjamin saw himself faced with the task of devising a speech intended to unify two distinct groups, and so he turned to Jacob, who had earlier done something similar.

Case 3: Jacob and Moroni

Moroni, the final author of the Book of Mormon, has been noted as one who is fond of alluding to previous Book of Mormon writers.[19] Moroni frequently employs phrases like ones stated by Jacob, and there are at least nine phrases that are exclusively used (or nearly so) by Jacob and Moroni. These allusions may be the most important ones in this chapter because the only people for which Moroni could have been making them is his latter-day audience—us. These connections are summarized in table 7.3.

---

17 John W. Welch, "Benjamin, the Man: His Place in Nephite History," in *King Benjamin's Speech: "That Ye May Learn Wisdom,"* ed. Stephen D. Ricks and John W. Welch, 48–49.

18 See Brant Gardner, *Second Witness: Analytical and Contextual Commentary on the Book of Mormon* (Salt Lake City: Greg Kofford Books, 2007), vol. 2.

19 See Grant Hardy, *Understanding the Book of Mormon* (New York: Oxford University Press, 2010), 250–63.

Table 7.3. Moroni's allusions to Jacob

Case #	Moroni's words	Jacob's words	Allusion	Times exact phrase is used elsewhere in scripture
1	Mormon 8:37, 39	Jacob 2:19	The naked and . . . the sick and the afflicted	0 (*naked, sick,* and *afflicted* also appear together in Alma 4:12; 34:28)
2	Mormon 9:2, 5	Jacob 3:8	When ye shall be brought . . . before . . . God	0
3	Mormon 9:14	2 Nephi 9:15	Then cometh the judgment	0
4	Mormon 9:14	2 Nephi 9:16	Filthy shall be filthy still . . . righteous shall be righteous still	0 (but Revelation 22:11 is very similar)
5	Mormon 9:17	Jacob 4:9	Created . . . power of his word	2 (Doctrine and Covenants 29:30; Moses 1:32)
6	Ether 8:25	2 Nephi 9:9	Who beguiled our first parents	0
7	Moroni 10:26	2 Nephi 9:38	Wo . . . die in their sins	1 (Mosiah 2:33)
8	Moroni 10:34	2 Nephi 9:13	The paradise of God . . . spirit . . . body	0
9	Moroni 10:34	Jacob 6:13	Meet you before the pleasing bar	0

Five of these allusions come from Moroni's first farewell message that appears in Mormon 8–9. Moroni chastises future readers, asking, "Why do ye adorn yourselves with that which hath no life, and yet suffer *the hungry*, and the needy, and *the naked, and the sick and the afflicted* to pass by you, and notice them not?" (Mormon 8:39). Perhaps Moroni intentionally alludes to Jacob's words to illustrate to latter-day readers that they are like former-day materialistic Nephites. It may be that Moroni wanted us to see that Jacob's counsel regarding riches still applies: "Ye will seek [riches] for the intent to do good—to clothe *the naked*, and to feed *the hungry*, and to liberate the captive, and administer relief to *the sick and the afflicted*" (Jacob 2:19).

Moroni continues his rebuke to modern readers, stating, "*When ye shall be brought* to see your nakedness *before God*, . . . it will kindle a flame of unquenchable fire upon you. O then . . . cry mightily unto the Father . . . that perhaps ye may be found spotless, pure, fair, and *white*" (Mormon 9:5–6). Jacob also discussed the dread that would come to those who had to stand before God in their sins. He said, "I fear that unless ye shall repent of your sins that their skins will be *whiter* than yours, *when ye shall be brought* with them *before* the throne of *God*" (Jacob 3:8).

Moroni may echo Jacob in these passages because he wants modern readers to prepare for the Judgment. He later follows Jacob in outlining a series of events—death, resurrection, and final judgment. Table 7.4 demonstrates how within two verses there are multiple relationships (both conceptual and textual) between Moroni's and Jacob's words.

Table 7.4. Relationships between Mormon 9:13–14 and 2 Nephi 9:15–16

Mormon 9:13–14	2 Nephi 9:15–16
The death of Christ bringeth to pass the resurrection, which bringeth to pass a redemption from an endless sleep, *from which sleep all men shall be awakened by the power of God* when the trump shall sound; and they shall come forth, both small and great, and *all shall stand before his bar.* . . .	And it shall come to pass that *when all men shall have passed from this first death unto life*, insomuch as they have become immortal, *they must appear before the judgment-seat of the Holy One* of Israel; and *then cometh the judgment, and then must they be judged according to the holy judgment of God.*
And *then cometh the judgment of the Holy One upon them*; and then cometh the time that *he that is filthy shall be filthy still; and he that is righteous shall be righteous still*; he that is happy shall be happy still; and he that is unhappy shall be unhappy still.	And assuredly, as the Lord liveth, for the Lord God hath spoken it, and it is his eternal word, which cannot pass away, that *they who are righteous shall be righteous still, and they who are filthy shall be filthy still.*

Both prophets state that because of Christ all men will be resurrected and be judged of God. Both teach that the Judgment will be a restoration of what we already are. Moroni's use of Jacob's words adds a second witness to his own and shifts Jacob's testimony forward in time, reiterating its relevance to modern readers—after all, Jacob's words were primarily directed at people of his own day, whereas Moroni is clearly speaking to a modern audience. Perhaps Moroni was merely influenced by Jacob's words; however, it is also possible that these consistent allusions to Jacob are Moroni's way of urging his readers to go back to the beginning and read Jacob's words more carefully, with a renewed understanding that they are intended for latter-day readers.

As Moroni turns his attention toward the miraculous power of God, he again alludes to Jacob. Moroni uses Jacob's teachings about the power of God to illustrate that miracles can continue in the present time. Table 7.5 illustrates several connections between Moroni's and Jacob's words.

Table 7.5. Relationships between Mormon 9:16–17 and Jacob 4:8–9

Mormon 9:16–17	Jacob 4:8–9
Behold, *are not the things that God hath wrought marvelous in our eyes?* Yea, and *who can comprehend the marvelous works of God?* Who shall say that it was not a miracle that *by his word* the heaven and the earth should be; and by the power of his word man was created of the dust of the earth; and by the power of his word have miracles been wrought?	Behold, *great and marvelous are the works of the Lord.* How unsearchable are the depths of the mysteries of him; and *it is impossible that man should find out all his ways.* For behold, *by* the power of *his word man came upon the face of the earth, which earth was created by the power of his word. Wherefore, if God being able to speak and the world was, and to speak and man was created,* O then, why not able to command the earth, or the workmanship of his hands upon the face of it, according to his will and pleasure?

Another of Moroni's allusions to Jacob comes in Ether 8 as Moroni discusses the evils of secret combinations. He states that "[*secret combinations* are] built up by the *devil,* who is *the father of all lies*;[20] even that same liar *who beguiled our first parents,* yea, even that same liar who hath caused man to commit *murder* from the beginning" (Ether 8:25). Similarly, Jacob speaks of secret combinations,[21] stating that the wicked "become devils, angels to a *devil,* to be shut out from the presence of our God, and to remain with *the father of lies,* in misery, like unto himself; yea, to that being *who beguiled our first parents* . . . and stirreth up the children of men unto *secret combinations* of *murder*" (2 Nephi 9:9). Perhaps by alluding to Jacob's stern words (which include the context of dwelling eternally with Satan), Moroni hoped to underscore the serious dangers of secret combinations to modern readers.

---

20 The phrase "father of all lies" also appears in 2 Nephi 2:18 and Moses 4:4. The words "father of lies" is used only by Jacob, in 2 Nephi 9:9.

21 Jacob is the first person in the Book of Mormon to use the phrase "secret combinations."

Three final allusions to Jacob appear in Moroni's last words. Moroni writes, "*Wo unto* them *who . . . die in their sins*, and they cannot be saved" (Moroni 10:26). As with Nephi and King Benjamin, Moroni alludes to the tenth of Jacob's ten woes: "*Wo unto* all those *who die in their sins*" (2 Nephi 9:38).

In his final verse, Moroni says, "And now I bid unto all, farewell. I soon go to rest in *the paradise of God*, until my *spirit and body shall again reunite*" (Moroni 10:34). Moroni's imminent death must have made these words from Jacob increasingly relevant: "O how great the plan of our God! For on the other hand, *the paradise of God* must deliver up the spirits of the righteous, and the grave deliver up the body of the righteous; and the *spirit and the body is restored to itself again*" (2 Nephi 9:13). It may be that Moroni found comfort in a phrase Jacob had uttered nearly one thousand years earlier.

One last allusion to Jacob's words is found in Moroni's final phrase. Moroni says, "[I will] *meet you before the pleasing bar of the great Jehovah. . . . Amen*" (Moroni 10:34), echoing an earlier farewell from Jacob: "I shall *meet you before the pleasing bar of God. . . . Amen*" (Jacob 6:13). I wonder if Moroni felt a special kinship with Jacob. Just as Jacob stood in the giant shadow of his mighty older brother Nephi, perhaps Moroni felt small compared to Mormon and looked to Jacob for guidance on how to play the role of the junior author. Moreover, Moroni likely identified with Jacob's words in Jacob 7:26 ("We being a lonesome and a solemn people, wanderers, cast out from Jerusalem, born in tribulation, in a wilderness, and hated of our brethren . . .") in ways that Jacob may not have fully foreseen.

By frequently quoting from Jacob, Moroni applies Jacob's words to modern readers. Jacob originally spoke to Nephites, and it isn't clear that his words were specifically intended for the present day. But by using phrases such as "the naked and . . . the sick and the afflicted" and "the righteous shall be righteous still . . . [and the] filthy shall be filthy still," Moroni brings images from the sermons from Jacob 2 and 2 Nephi 9 directly to the latter-day readers. His frequent allusions reinforce the importance of Jacob's words for readers in the latter days.

Therefore, What?

Jacob is a key figure in the Book of Mormon, and his words had a lasting impact. As discussed in chapter 2, Jacob appears to have a distinctive voice in the Book of Mormon, increasing the probability that later prophets were referring to his actual words. Nephi used Jacob's teachings to underscore the serious consequences of sin. He also may have emphasized Jacob's words to pave the way for Jacob's succession as the spiritual leader of his people and provide a second witness for his teachings. King Benjamin may have employed Jacob's words to provide both doctrinal and structural underpinnings for his address. In addition, he might have seen similarities between the needs of his audience and those originally addressed by Jacob. Moroni frequently quotes from Jacob, perhaps out of general familiarity with his words, feelings of kinship, or a desire to shift Jacob's words forward in time, urging us to carefully return to them.

In this chapter I have focused on Jacob's textual legacy in terms of how it was utilized by Nephi, King Benjamin, and Moroni, and they are not the only ones who employ Jacob's phrases.[22] Taken together, these multiple allusions to Jacob suggest that his words were well known and employed among the Nephites centuries after his death. Although more work remains to explore how doctrines, concepts, and phrases first employed by Jacob are alluded to by later Book of Mormon prophets, this chapter underscores the fact that, while we may have seen him as standing in Nephi's shadow, Jacob was a powerful literary figure in the Book of Mormon. His words influenced not only future generations of modern readers but also later prophets and people in his own dispensation.

Writing about Jacob, John S. Tanner wrote, "No other Book of Mormon author uses the term *dread*. No one else uses *lonesome*, nor can I imagine any other Book of Mormon author writing 'our lives passed away like as it were unto us a dream,' or 'we did mourn out our days.' None is so open about anxiety, none so poetic."[23] If we

---

22 For example, Samuel the Lamanite also draws on Jacob (and others) in his speech (see chapter 11 herein).

23 John S. Tanner, "Jacob and His Descendants as Authors," in *Rediscovering the Book of Mormon*, ed. John L. Sorenson and Melvin J. Thorne (Salt Lake

take Tanner's picture of Jacob, we see a lonely man, perhaps struggling with depression. How would Jacob have felt toward the end of his life if he had known of the textual influence he would have? Perhaps one lesson from Jacob is that even when we feel to "mourn out our days" (Jacob 7:26), our efforts are not in vain.

For an example of what this might look like in the modern day, imagine an early-morning seminary teacher struggling to reach those she makes diligent efforts to teach. She starts to wonder if her sacrifices are worth it. To such a teacher, President Henry B. Eyring said, "I can promise you this: more than one of [your students] will in that future day love whatever you love and be loyal to what you are loyal. And that could come from just one class on one day, even a day in February. You are doing more good than you know."[24] Surely the statement "You are doing more good than you know" applied to Jacob in his labors and can similarly apply in ours.

The same can be said to parents striving to teach their children only to have them step off the path for a time, or to a ministering brother or sister who reaches out to help another only to get rejected. Jacob teaches us that the impact we make is often not seen in the moment, but rather heard and felt in time. As we faithfully serve the Lord, our efforts will be echoed in the hearts of those we love in *his* time and in *his* way. Whether that is sooner or later, we are doing more good than we know.

City: Deseret Book; Provo, UT: FARMS, 1991), 66; emphasis in original.

24 Henry B. Eyring, "Love and Loyalty," introduction to Jeffrey R. Holland, "Our Consuming Mission" (address to Church Educational System religious educators, February 5, 1999).

Chapter 8

There Was More Than One: Abinadi's Influence on the Book of Mormon

As we discovered in chapter 4, Abinadi is a somewhat mysterious figure in the Book of Mormon.[1] He lived in a time when the Nephites were divided into two groups; some lived in the land of Zarahemla (led by King Mosiah), and others were in the land of Nephi (led by King Noah). We know nothing of Abinadi's background; all Mormon tells us is that during a time of great wickedness Abinadi "began to prophesy" (Mosiah 11:20). Abinadi's warnings of affliction and bondage if the people did not repent were not well received. Mormon records that the people "hardened their hearts against the words of Abinadi, and they sought from that time forward to take him. And king Noah hardened his heart against the word of the Lord, and he did not repent of his evil doings" (Mosiah 11:29).

After two years, Abinadi came among the people in disguise and again warned them of God's coming judgments. This time he was captured and brought before King Noah and his priests. After Abinadi preached a powerful discourse on the coming of Christ, King Noah commanded that Abinadi be put to death. "But there

---

1   This chapter is adapted from John Hilton III, "Abinadi's Legacy: Tracing His Influence through the Book of Mormon," in *Abinadi: He Came among Them in Disguise*, ed. Shon D. Hopkin (Provo, UT: Religious Studies Center, Brigham Young University, 2018), 93–116. Used with permission.

was one among them whose name was Alma. . . . He was a young man, and he believed the words which Abinadi had spoken" (Mosiah 17:2). King Noah was angry with Alma the Elder for his objections, cast him out, and sent guards to slay him. I wonder what Abinadi thought at that moment. Had he developed a relationship with Alma the Elder? Did Abinadi see Alma come to his defense? Did he know that after Alma escaped, he carefully recorded Abinadi's words? We simply don't know.

What we do know is that ultimately Abinadi did not escape as Alma did but was "bound . . . and scourged . . . with faggots, yea, even unto death" (Mosiah 17:13). This, however, did not bring an end to the influence Abinadi would have on Alma and later Book of Mormon authors. His words formed a key part of Alma the Elder's teachings (see Mosiah 18:1) and, as we will see, influenced many others.

Grant Hardy has suggested that it would be fruitful for our understanding of the Book of Mormon "to track various phrases throughout the Book of Mormon to determine which Nephite prophets were particularly influenced by their predecessors."[2] Abinadi is one of the first prophets quoted in the extant abridgment of the large plates and as such has potential to be an influential predecessor. Moreover, Abinadi was directly connected with Alma the Elder's conversion, which created a subsequent lineage of recordkeepers, all of whom likely had intense interest in the words of the person who helped convert their ancestor and shaped the doctrinal understanding of the Nephite church.

The purpose of this chapter is to explore how Abinadi's words[3] reverberate through later generations of Book of Mormon prophets. I first focus on Amulek and Alma's use of Abinadi's words while preaching in Ammonihah. I next briefly mention Abinadi's influence

---

2   Grant Hardy, *Understanding the Book of Mormon* (New York: Oxford University Press, 2010), 134.

3   For an extended discussion on the authorship of Mosiah, and the Abinadi pericope specifically, see John W. Welch, *The Legal Cases in the Book of Mormon* (Provo, UT: BYU Press; Neal A. Maxwell Institute for Religious Scholarship, Brigham Young University, 2008), 140–45.

on Alma's words to Corianton (discussed in depth in the following chapter) and then Mormon's use of Abinadi's phraseology. In the final section of this chapter, I provide an extended discussion of the relationship between the words of Abinadi and King Benjamin. Although Amulek, Alma, and Mormon all clearly had access to Abinadi's words, it is not immediately apparent if or how King Benjamin could have accessed Abinadi's words, a subject we will discuss toward the conclusion of this chapter.

Amulek and Alma Preaching in Ammonihah

While on trial in King Noah's court, Abinadi testified that the Father and the Son "are one God, yea, the very Eternal Father of heaven and of earth" (Mosiah 15:1–4).[4] A few verses later Abinadi concludes his message, saying that "redemption cometh through Christ the Lord, who is the very Eternal Father" (Mosiah 16:15). It is difficult to determine exactly what Abinadi meant with these words, but it seems clear that what he was teaching was unorthodox. In fact, it formed the basis of his death sentence (see Mosiah 17:7–8).[5]

Whatever controversy was embedded in this statement, it appears to have been repeated when, while preaching in the land of Ammonihah, Amulek was confronted by Zeezrom, who asked, "Is the Son of God *the very Eternal Father*? And Amulek said unto him: Yea, *he is the very Eternal Father of heaven and of earth*, and all things which in them are" (Alma 11:38–39). The phrase "very Eternal Father" is utilized only in these two pericopes; thus it may be that Amulek appeals to Abinadi's authority as he responds to Zeezrom.[6] Following this allusion to Abinadi's words, Amulek uses a structure similar to Abinadi's by focusing on Christ's Atonement (Mosiah 15:5–6; Alma 11:40), death (Mosiah 15:7; Alma 11:42), and Resurrection (Mosiah 15:8–9; Alma 11:42–44). In addition to teaching with thematic coherence,

---

4   I acknowledge the work of Jaron Hansen and Taze Miller, who helped identify many of the phrases discussed in this section.

5   For additional discussion on this point, see Welch, *Legal Cases in the Book of Mormon*, 193–95.

6   It also seems likely that Zeezrom's question indicates that Zeezrom is familiar with the words of Abinadi.

Amulek also uses phrases that originated with Abinadi, as illustrated in table 8.1.

Table 8.1. Parallel phrases between Abinadi and Amulek

Abinadi	Amulek
But remember that he that persists in his own carnal nature . . . *is as though there was no redemption made.* If Christ had not *come into the world*, speaking of things to come as though they had already come, there could have been no *redemption*. And if Christ had not risen from the dead, or have *broken the bands of death* that the grave should have no victory . . . (Mosiah 16:5–7)	And he shall *come into the world* to *redeem* his people; and he shall take upon him the transgressions of those who believe on his name . . . , and salvation cometh to none else. Therefore the wicked remain *as though there had been no redemption made*, except it be the *loosing of the bands of death*; for behold, the day cometh that all shall rise from the dead and stand before God. (Alma 11:40–41)

Some of these phrases are unique and suggest intentional borrowing. For example, the words *as though* and *redemption* appear together in only five verses of scripture, and Abinadi is the first to use these words together in the Book of Mormon.[7] Moreover, the phrase "bands of death" originates with Abinadi.[8] Amulek may be attempting to bolster his own authority by using Abinadi's words, or perhaps he's manifesting his acceptance and belief of Abinadi's words.[9]

---

7   See Mosiah 16:5–6; Alma 11:41; 12:18; Moroni 7:38.

8   The phrase "bands of death" first appears in Mosiah 15:8 and is used thirteen times in the Book of Mormon and once in the Doctrine and Covenants. In addition, the words *band* and *death* appear together in Psalms 73:4; 107:14; and Ecclesiastes 7:26. See also Scripture Central, "Why Does Abinadi Use the Phrase 'the Bands of Death'?," KnoWhy #93, Book of Mormon Central, May 5, 2016, https://knowhy.bookofmormoncentral.org/knowhy/why-does -abinadi-use-the-phrase-the-bands-of-death.

9   Amulek revisits some of these same themes when speaking to the Zoramites in Alma 34. On that occasion he also echoes Abinadi, although not to the extent to which he does in Ammonihah. For example, Amulek states that the

After Amulek finishes speaking, Alma begins to further establish the points Amulek made. He likewise utilizes Abinadi's words while teaching the people of Ammonihah, echoing both Amulek and Abinadi in teaching that the wicked "shall be *as though there had been no redemption*" (Alma 12:18; compare Mosiah 16:5–6; Alma 11:41). Abinadi had taught that "this *mortal shall put on immortality, and this corruption shall put on incorruption, and shall be brought to stand before the bar of God, to be judged of him according to their works* whether they be good or whether they be evil" (Mosiah 16:10). Alma also utilizes these words, teaching that we will be "raised from this *mortality to a state of immortality,* and *being brought before the bar of God, to be judged according to our works*" (Alma 12:12). While the concepts of resurrection and judgment appear throughout scripture, these two chapters are the only places where these specific textual phrases are found.[10]

The example just cited compares Alma 12:12 with Mosiah 16:10. Additional textual similarities are found within this same cluster of scriptures, as illustrated in table 8.2.

Atonement brings "about the *bowels of mercy,* which overpowereth *justice,* and bringeth about means unto men that they may have faith unto repentance. And thus mercy can *satisfy the demands of justice*" (Alma 34:15–16). This is reminiscent of Abinadi's words that Christ would have "*bowels of mercy,* being filled with compassion towards the children of men; standing betwixt them and *justice;* having broken the bands of death, taken upon himself their iniquity and their transgressions, having redeemed them, and *satisfied the demands of justice*" (Mosiah 15:9).

10 The phrase "before the bar of God, to be" appears only in these two verses. The more generic phrase "before the bar of God" appears in two additional verses (Jacob 6:9 and Alma 5:22), and the word *bar* appears in twelve Book of Mormon verses. In addition, the words *mortal* and *immortal* appear together relatively infrequently in scripture (fourteen total verses in all scripture contain these two words).

Table 8.2. Parallel phrases between Abinadi and Alma

Abinadi	Alma
All mankind were *lost*; and behold, they would have been endlessly *lost* were it not that God redeemed his people from their *lost and fallen* state. . . . And *if* Christ *had not* risen from the dead, or have broken the bands of death that the grave should have no victory, and that death should have no sting, *there could have been no resurrection. But there is a* resurrection. (Mosiah 16:4, 7–8)	By [Adam's] fall, *all mankind* became a *lost and fallen* people. . . . Now, *if it had not* been for the plan of redemption, which was laid from the foundation of the world, *there could have been no resurrection* of the dead; *but there was a* plan of redemption laid. (Alma 12:22, 25)

The phrase "could have been no resurrection" appears only in these two passages.[11] The structure of "if . . . then . . . but . . ." also indicates intentional borrowing. Both Alma and Abinadi immediately negate their use of the phrase "could have been no resurrection" by testifying that God's plan has been put into effect. Thus, in form and text Alma utilizes Abinadi's words as part of his message to the people of Ammonihah.

Both Amulek and Alma incorporate multiple phrases from Abinadi while preaching in Ammonihah. Why do they do this? Is there a connection between Ammonihah and Noah's court? Or are they simply quoting one who stands at the head of the Nephite church's doctrinal position? While the text itself is silent on the issue, one potential clue stems from Zeezrom's question "Is the Son of God the very Eternal Father?" (Alma 11:38). Given Zeezrom's general rhetorical strategy of attempting to trap Amulek in his words, it is plausible that the particular issue of Christ being the Eternal Father was an important and controversial theological issue for some people

---

11 Note also that before the phrase "could have been no resurrection" occurs is the phrase "lost and fallen." This latter phrase, while perhaps sounding common, is used only three times in the Book of Mormon. Nephi₁ provides the other use (see 2 Nephi 25:17); however, he is talking about the gathering and scattering of Israel, not the effects of the Fall.

at that time. Perhaps Zeezrom was attempting to take Amulek down a path that could lead to the charge of blasphemy. If this were the case, it would make sense for Amulek and Alma to utilize Abinadi's words to rectify misconstrued meanings of Abinadi's teachings.

Another possible reason that Amulek and Alma referred to Abinadi was that they wanted to appeal to what for them might have been scriptural authority that they hoped would speak to the hearts of the people. Alma's father (Alma the Elder) was the founder of the Nephite church (see Mosiah 29:47). Very few words of his are recorded in the Book of Mormon; perhaps the only recent prophets that Amulek and Alma could reference were King Benjamin and Abinadi. A connected possibility is that Abinadi's words formed a significant part of Amulek and Alma's understanding of the principles they were teaching.

Alma's Use of Abinadi While Teaching Corianton

Corianton had at least three major issues that concerned him at the time his father counseled him. These concerns regarded the Resurrection (Alma 40:1), the plan of restoration (Alma 41:1), and the justice of God in punishing the sinner (Alma 42:1). As Alma provided doctrinal clarification to help his son, he frequently turned to the words of Abinadi. As described in detail in the following chapter, there are at least thirteen instances in which Alma appears to have utilized Abinadi's words when teaching Corianton. For example, phrases such as "carnal, sensual, devilish" or "stand as a testimony against you at the last day" appear only in those two pericopes within the Book of Mormon. Moreover, as we will see in the following chapter, most of Alma's use of Abinadi's words clusters around Corianton's specific concerns.

Mormon's Use of Abinadi's Words

As the editor of the Book of Mormon, Mormon clearly was aware of Abinadi's words and teachings. Indeed, Mormon's specific reference to Abinadi more than four hundred years after his death illustrates Abinadi's impressive influence (see Mormon 1:19). In this section I will demonstrate three specific instances in which Mormon uses Abinadi's words.

First, as Mormon summarizes Aaron's teachings to the father of King Lamoni, he states that Aaron "did expound unto him the scriptures from the creation of Adam . . . and also the plan of redemption, which was prepared from the foundation of the world, through Christ, . . . that he *breaketh the bands of death*, that *the grave shall have no victory*, and that *the sting of death should be swallowed up* in the hopes of glory" (Alma 22:13–14). This passage appears to be directly connected to Abinadi, who taught that "if Christ had not risen from the dead, or have *broken the bands of death* that the *grave should have no victory*, . . . there could have been no resurrection. But there is a resurrection, therefore the *grave hath no victory, and the sting of death is swallowed up* in Christ" (Mosiah 16:7–8).[12] In the Book of Mormon, the phrase "sting of death" appears only in three passages (these two and one other that will be discussed shortly).[13]

Why does Mormon use Abinadi's words when summarizing Aaron's teachings? It may be that Mormon is simply reflecting Aaron's actual teachings and that Aaron himself referred to Abinadi. Alternatively, perhaps Mormon uses a phrase that Abinadi said when preaching to King Noah to draw a contrast between the receptivity of Noah and the father of King Lamoni. Both kings received similar messages; the king of the Lamanites' acceptance of this prophetic word illustrates faith and humility that King Noah lacked.

Another possibility, admittedly speculative, is that Mormon is indirectly illustrating the significance of Abinadi's mission. In essence, the whole narrative of the Book of Mormon from Mosiah 12 forward hinges on Abinadi's words. Abinadi is the central figure in the narrative of Zeniff's people, and his words are instrumental in Alma the Elder's conversion. Every recordkeeper for the next three centuries is directly related to this convert of Abinadi. It is possible that the sons of Mosiah would not have gone on a mission to the

---

12 While key phrases in these passages appear in Isaiah 25:8 and 1 Corinthians 15:54–55, within the Book of Mormon the words *victory* and *death* appear together originally in the words of Abinadi and rarely thereafter. Abinadi uses these terms together in Mosiah 15:8 and Mosiah 16:7–8. Mormon uses them in Alma 22:14; 27:28; and Mormon 7:5. Outside Isaiah 25 and 1 Corinthians 15, these two words never appear together in any other passage of scripture.

13 The phrase "sting of death" also appears in 1 Corinthians 15:56.

Lamanites had their associate Alma's father not been converted by Abinadi. Thus, by using Abinadi's phraseology in describing Aaron's teachings, Mormon may be reminding us of the connection between Abinadi and the mission to the Lamanites.[14]

Another passage illustrating the extent to which Abinadi influenced Mormon's text is found in Abinadi's teaching that all people will "*stand before* the bar of *God, to be judged of* him according to *their works whether they be good or whether they be evil—if they be good, to the resurrection of endless life* and happiness; *and if they be evil, to the resurrection of* endless *damnation*" (Mosiah 16:10–11). Mormon uses these words almost verbatim as he records that all will "*stand before God, to be judged of their works, whether they be good or whether they be evil—if they be good, to the resurrection of everlasting life; and if they be evil, to the resurrection of damnation*" (3 Nephi 26:4–5). The sheer volume of related words in the parallel passages indicates intentional use by Mormon.

In this instance Mormon is paraphrasing the resurrected Jesus. Does this textual connection stem from Mormon or the Savior himself? This question cannot be answered with certainty. It is possible that Christ alluded to Abinadi as he expounded all scripture in one and that Mormon is reflecting this usage in his summary of Christ's words. If so, this would indicate a pattern on the part of Christ in referring to Abinadi's words.[15] If this is not the case, and Mormon is

---

14   Another indication that Mormon connects the sons of Mosiah with the labors of Abinadi is found in his use of Isaiah 52:7 to describe their work. Earlier, a priest had asked Abinadi about this passage, saying, "What meaneth the words which are written, and which have been taught by our fathers, saying: [begins quotation of Isaiah 52:7] 'How beautiful upon the mountains are the feet of him that bringeth good tidings; that publisheth peace; that bringeth good tidings of good; that publisheth salvation; that saith unto Zion, Thy God reigneth'" (Mosiah 12:20–21). Abinadi identifies Jesus Christ and those who testify of him as those whose feet are beautiful upon the mountains (see Mosiah 15:13–18). Mormon uses this same phraseology to describe the sons of Mosiah, saying, "They did publish peace; they did publish good tidings of good; and they did declare unto the people that the Lord reigneth" (Mosiah 27:37).

15   In the Book of Mormon, the phrase "light and the life of the world" is first spoken by Abinadi and later echoed by the Savior. The specific phrase "light

simply using these words of his own accord, it may indicate the extent to which Abinadi's words influenced Mormon's thoughts and writing.

The premise that Abinadi strongly influenced Mormon is also illustrated in Mormon's use of Abinadi's phraseology in his final words. Speaking to the remnant who would be spared, Mormon urged them to know that Christ had "gained the *victory over the grave*; and also in him is the *sting of death swallowed up*" (Mormon 7:5; compare Mosiah 16:8). Surely Mormon took seriously the prospect of writing his concluding comments in the book to which he had dedicated his life. Thus, Mormon's intense feelings about the importance of Abinadi's words may be shown through his use of Abinadi's phraseology in his final farewell. Although Abinadi's words represent a relatively small portion of the text of the Book of Mormon, these foregoing passages illustrate the influence Abinadi had on its chief editor.

Textual Connections between Abinadi and King Benjamin

In terms of textual influence, it may be that Abinadi's strongest influence was actually on King Benjamin. Both King Benjamin and Abinadi give extended discourses in the book of Mosiah. King Benjamin delivers his farewell address in Mosiah 2–5, and Abinadi testifies before King Noah's court in Mosiah 12–17. Although close in sequence, these sermons take place in two different locations: Benjamin's in the land of Zarahemla, and Abinadi's in the land of Nephi. John Sorenson estimates that these locations are 180 miles apart[16] and that traveling between them would take approximately twenty-two days—if one knew the way.[17]

It appears that there was no communication between these groups of Nephites. Amaleki, in reporting on a brother who went

---

and the life of the world" appears in Mosiah 16:9; 3 Nephi 9:18; 3 Nephi 11:11; and Doctrine and Covenants 12:9; 34:2; 39:2; and 45:7. The key words *light*, *life*, and *world* also appear in John 8:12 and Alma 38:9.

16   John L. Sorenson, *Mormon's Map* (Provo, UT: FARMS, 2000), 57.

17   Since they did not know the way, Ammon and the fifteen men who came with him took forty days to make the journey (see Mosiah 7:4). Given that the Lamanites also became lost in the same wilderness (see Mosiah 22:16), the terrain may have been difficult to navigate.

to the land of Nephi, said, "I have not since known concerning" him (Omni 1:30). Decades later King Mosiah "was desirous to know concerning the people who went up to dwell in the land of Lehi-Nephi, . . . for his people *had heard nothing from them* from the time they left the land of Zarahemla" (Mosiah 7:1).

Given the distance that separated the two groups of Nephites and the explicit reported lack of communication between them, it would seem unlikely that the discourses of King Benjamin and Abinadi were related. Furthermore, Mormon (in abridging and creating the text we have today) likely had access to written ancient versions of both speeches. Alma the Elder wrote down "all the words of Abinadi" (Mosiah 17:4) shortly after hearing them,[18] and King Benjamin "caused that the words which he spake should be written" (Mosiah 2:8). Because we are told that separate primary documents exist for each of the discourses, it seems less likely that in composing his abridgment Mormon would have altered the addresses to create textual similarities between them.[19]

Notwithstanding the foregoing, previous researchers have pointed to textual connections between these two speeches and wondered whether Benjamin and Abinadi had contact with each other. Lew Cramer, writing in the *Encyclopedia of Mormonism*, states, "Similarities between [Abinadi's] and Benjamin's words . . . could mean that [Abinadi] spent some time in Zarahemla with King Benjamin and his people," thus implying that Abinadi was influenced by Benjamin's speech.[20] But did Benjamin influence Abinadi, or was it the reverse? Or do they both draw on a similar text or prophetic voice? Before

---

18 Note that Alma the Elder recorded Abinadi's words (thus creating a source document for Mormon) before he returned to Zarahemla and gained access to King Benjamin's address.

19 As will be shown, there are a number of phrases that appear only in these two sections. It seems unlikely that Mormon would have modified these speeches, employing phraseology that was then never used elsewhere in the Book of Mormon.

20 Lew W. Cramer, "Abinadi," in *Encyclopedia of Mormonism*, ed. Daniel H. Ludlow (New York: Macmillan, 1992), 1:5. Cramer also suggests the possibility that Abinadi received "similar revelation" as King Benjamin "during this period."

discussing these questions, let us first establish the textual connections between the two sermons. Table 8.3 lists fourteen phrases that appear exclusively (or nearly so) in these two discourses.[21]

Table 8.3. Connections between the sermons of King Benjamin and Abinadi

Case #	Words from King Benjamin and his audience	Words from Abinadi and his audience	Allusion	Times exact phrase is used elsewhere in scripture
1	Mosiah 1:13; 2:29; 3:17; 3:20	Mosiah 13:28	And moreover, I say unto you	1 (Alma 5:47)
2	Mosiah 2:38; 3:19	Mosiah 16:5	Enemy to God	0
3	Mosiah 3:5; 4:2	Mosiah 13:34; 15:1; 7:27; 17:8	Come down . . . children of men	1 (Genesis 11:5)
4	Mosiah 3:8	Mosiah 15:2	He shall be called . . . Son of God	0 (1 John 3:1 is very similar)
5	Mosiah 3:12	Mosiah 15:27	Salvation cometh to none such	0
6	Mosiah 3:15	Mosiah 13:32	The law . . . except it were through . . .	0

---

21   For additional discussion of intertextual connections between some of these phrases and the New Testament, see Nicholas J. Frederick, "If Christ Had Not Come into the World," in *Abinadi: He Came among Them in Disguise*, ed. Shon D. Hopkin (Provo, UT: Religious Studies Center, Brigham Young University, 2018), 117–38.

7	Mosiah 3:17	Mosiah 16:13	Only in and through Christ	1 (Alma 38:9; 2 Nephi 10:24 is also similar)
8	Mosiah 3:20	Mosiah 16:1	Time shall come . . . every nation, kindred, tongue, and people	0
9	Mosiah 3:24	Mosiah 16:10	Judged . . . according to their works whether they be good or whether they be evil	1 (Alma 11:44)
10	Mosiah 3:24	Mosiah 17:10	Stand as a testimony against you	3 (2 Nephi 25:28; Alma 39:8; Ether 5:4; Doctrine and Covenants 98:27 is also similar)
11	Mosiah 3:25	Mosiah 16:11	And if they be evil . . . damnation	1 (3 Nephi 26:5; John 5:29; Alma 9:28; and Helaman 12:26 are similar)

12	Mosiah 4:6–7	Mosiah 15:19	Prepared from the foundation of the world	8 (Mosiah 18:13; Alma 12:30; 13:3, 5; 18:39; 22:13; 42:26; and Ether 3:14; Matthew 25:34; 1 Nephi 10:18; and 2 Nephi 9:18 are similar)
13	Mosiah 4:23	Mosiah 12:26	I say unto you, wo be unto	1 (Doctrine and Covenants 10:28)
14	Mosiah 4:30	Mosiah 13:10	But this much I tell you[22]	0

Not only are there multiple matching phrases, but they also often occur closely in sequence. For example, cases 3 and 4 above appear next to each other (compare Mosiah 3:5, 8 and 15:1–2), as do cases 9 and 11 (compare Mosiah 3:24–25 and 16:10–11). In addition, a high level of thematic coherence exists between the two speeches. Themes of fallen man being an enemy to God, the absolute necessity of Christ, the efficacy of the Atonement for ignorant sinners, the salvation of little children, judgment according to our works, and the damnation that awaits the evil all figure prominently in both discourses. These parallels are particularly concentrated in just a few verses in Mosiah 3 and 16. Table 8.4 illustrates how, when rearranged and slightly modified, selected phrases from Mosiah 3:17–25 closely resemble phrases from Mosiah 16:1–15.

---

22 These words (even when not used together as a phrase) appear together only in Mosiah 4:30 and 13:10.

Table 8.4. Selected phrases from Mosiah 3:17–25 and Mosiah 16:1–15

Benjamin's words	Abinadi's words
The natural man is an *enemy to God,* . . . [and] at the judgment day . . . *every man . . . shall be judged . . . according to his works, whether they be good, or whether they be evil. And if they be evil* . . . they have drunk *damnation* to their own souls. [But] *the time shall come when the knowledge of a Savior shall spread throughout every nation, kindred, tongue, and people* . . . [for] *salvation can come . . . only in and through* the name of *Christ, the Lord.*	He that persists in his own carnal nature . . . is . . . *an enemy to God* . . . [and all] *shall . . . be judged . . . according to their works whether they be good or whether they be evil* . . . *and if they be evil [they receive]* the resurrection of endless *damnation.* . . . [But] *the time shall come when . . . every nation, kindred, tongue, and people . . . shall see the salvation of the Lord . . . [for] only in and through Christ can ye be saved. . . . Redemption cometh through Christ the Lord.*

Based on the information in tables 8.3 and 8.4, it seems evident that these two sermons are related.[23] If we accept this premise, the natural question is "Who influenced whom?" While no explicit answers are found in the text, there are enough clues to at least rule out certain possibilities. Let us begin to answer this question by trying to ascertain which discourse came first in terms of chronology.

In light of the Nephite time line presented by Mormon, King Benjamin gave his address in about 124 BC (see Mosiah 6:4). In contrast, no explicit dating information is given about when Abinadi

---

23 While some of these connections are clearer than others, taken together they make a robust case for a relationship between the sermons. Many of these connections are stronger than they might initially appear. For example, Abinadi alludes to prophets who had said that "God himself should come down among the children of men, and take upon him the form of man, and go forth in mighty power upon the face of the earth" (Mosiah 13:34). This teaching was apparently so provocative that it led to his death, and it was cited almost verbatim by King Limhi (see Mosiah 7:27), leading us to believe that we are getting an actual account of Abinadi's words. This statement is very similar to King Benjamin's: "The Lord Omnipotent . . . shall come down from heaven among the children of men, and shall dwell in a tabernacle of clay, and shall go forth amongst men, working mighty miracles" (Mosiah 3:5).

spoke. Nevertheless, through contextual clues we can approximately determine this information. Alma the Elder died in 91 BC at the age of eighty-two (see Mosiah 29:45). Thus Alma the Elder was born in 173 BC. He was a "young man" at the trial of Abinadi (Mosiah 17:2). Unless the definition of "young man" is stretched to include one who is fifty years old, Abinadi clearly spoke before King Benjamin's address in 124 BC. If we assume "a young man" was about twenty years old, Abinadi spoke in 153 BC, approximately thirty years before King Benjamin.[24]

Accepting the premise that Abinadi spoke before King Benjamin eliminates the possibility that Abinadi heard Benjamin's address and used it as he spoke in King Noah's court. And it seems unlikely that Benjamin heard Abinadi's words and later used them in his speech, given that the people in Zarahemla had no knowledge of what had happened to Zeniff's descendants (see Mosiah 7:1–2).[25]

---

24 I gratefully acknowledge Heather Hardy for sharing this observation with me when she reviewed an earlier draft of this chapter. Another way to demonstrate that Abinadi spoke first is by looking at the time line of Limhi's people. Because Limhi's people arrived in Zarahemla between 121–120 BC and King Benjamin spoke in 124 BC, for King Benjamin to speak before Abinadi, all the events in Mosiah 17–22 would have had to have happened in less than three years—a very unlikely occurrence. For example, "Amulon began to exercise authority over Alma and his brethren, and began to persecute him, and cause that his children should persecute their children" (Mosiah 24:8). Amulon and his fellow priests left their Nephite wives and children behind when they fled with King Noah (see Mosiah 19:13; 20:3). However, after abducting the daughters of the Lamanites, they married and had children with their kidnapped brides (see Mosiah 23:33; 24:8; Alma 25:7). How much time would need to elapse before the children of Amulon would be capable of persecuting Alma the Elder's children? If we assume that Amulon's children had to be at least four years old to be able to persecute other children, a minimum of five years (and likely much more) would be needed between the kidnapping of the daughters of the Lamanites and Alma's captivity.

25 It is possible that in the two years between Abinadi's first and second appearance (see Mosiah 12:1), he went to the land of Zarahemla. Although he would not have heard King Benjamin's address at that time, perhaps he collaborated with "the holy prophets who were among his people" (Words of Mormon 1:16). While this idea cannot be completely ruled out, given

The possible influence of an angel

When we revisit the textual connections previously demonstrated, another possible explanation for the parallels emerges. Eleven of the fourteen textual connections (cases 1–11 in table 8.3) between the two discourses come not from King Benjamin's words but from the words of an angel who spoke to King Benjamin. In Mosiah 3:3 King Benjamin states, "And he [an angel] said unto me" (Mosiah 3:3) and commences a lengthy quote. While it is not entirely clear where the quotation ends, it seems most likely that it ends with Mosiah 3:27, given that Mosiah 4:1 says, "And now, it came to pass that when king Benjamin had made an end of speaking the words which had been delivered unto him by the angel of the Lord . . ."[26]

Because Mosiah 3:3–27 is a quotation from an angel, it is possible that the textual connections between the discourses of King Benjamin and Abinadi are the result of the same angel visiting both men (or different angels visiting each man but with similar messages). The strongest connections between King Benjamin's and Abinadi's discourses presented in table 8.3 and the allusions in table 8.4 occur when Abinadi's words are compared with Benjamin's quotation of an angel. This lessens the possibility that the connections stem from some common text, unless the angel was quoting unknown texts to both prophets.

The cluster of parallels surrounding the voice of the angel begs the question: Did the same angel who appeared to King Benjamin also appear to Abinadi? While we cannot know for certain, some have speculatively suggested another possibility—that Abinadi himself

---

the reported complete lack of communication between the two groups of Nephites, it seems unlikely that Abinadi's presence in the land of Zarahemla would have gone unnoticed.

26 In Mosiah 3:23 we read the phrase "And now I have spoken the words which the Lord God hath commanded me." It is possible that this signals the end of Benjamin's quotation of the angel (or they may be the words of the angel). However, even if the words in Mosiah 3:23 are King Benjamin's, he immediately begins another quotation (see Mosiah 3:24). Thus, either way the words in Mosiah 3:24–27 should not be attributed to Benjamin.

was the angel that appeared to King Benjamin.[27] While such an assertion must be extremely tentative, it is important to note that King Benjamin frequently refers to the angelic messenger (see Mosiah 3:2, 3; 4:1, 11). In addition, those in King Benjamin's audience specifically emphasize the angel's words, further highlighting his importance in King Benjamin's discourse (see Mosiah 5:5). In contrast, there is no mention of angels anywhere in the pericope surrounding Abinadi and those who heard his message, suggesting that an angelic messenger may not have played an important role in Abinadi's ministry. If Abinadi was in fact the angel who appeared to Benjamin, his words have an additional influence in the Book of Mormon through King Benjamin's important speech.

Therefore, What?

Abinadi's voice reverberates throughout the Book of Mormon. Amulek and Alma both utilize Abinadi's phraseology when teaching the people in Ammonihah. Alma clearly alludes to Abinadi when talking with his son Corianton, and Mormon also references Abinadi's words, including both lengthy and unique phrases. While we cannot establish that Abinadi directly influenced King Benjamin, there is an unmistakable textual connection between the two discourses, and Abinadi's speech clearly came first.

Abinadi's influence on the text of the Book of Mormon may be underestimated by some. As a pivotal prophet who spoke 450 years after Lehi left Jerusalem, he is responsible for the conversion of Alma the Elder. Alma the Elder and his posterity would keep the sacred records and guide the Church for the next 470 years. Abinadi, living chronologically halfway between Lehi and Mormon, thus radically shaped the second half of Nephite history. The textual connections I have described in this chapter illustrate instances in which multiple phrases from Abinadi appear in connection with specific later

---

27 Todd Parker offers this conclusion in "Abinadi: The Man and the Message (Part 1)" (Provo, UT: FARMS, 1996), 5, https://archive.interpreterfoundation .org/farms/pdf/preliminary_reports/Parker-Abinadi-The-Man-and-the-Message -part-1-and-The-Message-and-the-Martyr-Part-2-1996.pdf.

pericopes.[28] Abinadi's testimony of Christ affected generations and clearly had an important textual influence on later Book of Mormon individuals.

Abinadi's influence causes me to ponder Mormon's words about Abinadi's trial: "But *there was one* among them whose name was Alma. . . . He was a young man, and he believed the words which Abinadi had spoken" (Mosiah 17:2). The last Abinadi saw of Alma the Elder was him fleeing the court and King Noah sending guards to execute him. Abinadi may have died thinking his words had influenced only *one . . .* and that one had perished.

But Alma the Elder survived and went on to gather "four hundred and fifty souls" (Mosiah 18:35) from among the people. Eventually he became "the founder" of the church of the Nephites (Mosiah 23:16; 29:47). His son Alma, grandson Helaman, great-grandson Helaman, great-great grandson Nephi, and great-great-great grandson Nephi each in turn kept the plates. This last Nephi was present when Jesus Christ came and ministered to the Nephites. In other words, Abinadi's influence extended far beyond the "one" he was aware of.

The textual connections between Abinadi and later voices in the Book of Mormon speakers provide a literary reminder that there was more than "one" who listened to Abinadi's words. Seeing this big picture of Abinadi's influence reminds us that while at times our efforts may seem fruitless, we can influence generations unseen through our diligent efforts to teach others. Because there was one, literally millions were blessed.

In 2001, President James E. Faust shared the following story:

> Many years ago an elder who served a mission in the British Isles said at the end of his labors, "I think my mission has been a failure. I have labored all my days as a missionary here and I have only baptized one dirty little Irish kid. That is all I baptized."

---

28 In addition to these instances in which multiple textual connections appear in short succession, there are several phrases that appear to originate with Abinadi in the Book of Mormon that later appear throughout the text—for example, "vultures of the air" (Mosiah 12:2; compare Alma 2:38), "driven and scattered" (Mosiah 17:17; compare Alma 28:3; Mormon 5:20), and "filled with compassion towards [people]" (Mosiah 15:9; compare 3 Nephi 17:6; Doctrine and Covenants 101:9).

Years later, after his return to his home in Montana, he had a visitor come to his home who asked, "Are you the elder who served a mission in the British Isles in 1873?"

"Yes."

Then the man went on, "And do you remember having said that you thought your mission was a failure because you had only baptized one dirty little Irish kid?"

He said, "Yes."

The visitor put out his hand and said, "I would like to shake hands with you. My name is Charles A. Callis, of the Council of the Twelve of The Church of Jesus Christ of Latter-day Saints. I am that dirty little Irish kid that you baptized on your mission."

That little Irish boy came to a knowledge of his potential as a son of God. Elder Callis left a lasting legacy for his large family. Serving as a mission president for 25 years and in his apostolic ministry for 13 years, he blessed the lives of literally thousands.[29]

Sometimes we, like Abinadi, may reach only "the one," but we can have hope knowing that our influence may extend beyond what we know. On other occasions we might be "the one" to speak up in difficult circumstances. In a pivotal moment, Alma stood alone in believing the words of the Lord's prophets. We too may have opportunities to be the only one to stand for what is right—our decisions to do so can influence others in ways we could never predict.

---

29 James E. Faust, "Them That Honour Me I Will Honour," *Ensign*, May 2001, 46–47.

Chapter 9

Turning to Prophets: Similarities in the Words of Abinadi and Alma's Counsel to Corianton

Imagine your son is considering leaving the covenant path.[1] He has made some wrong choices and has doubts about the truthfulness of what he has been taught. Your son has agreed to listen to you share some thoughts with him, and this may be your last opportunity to persuade him to follow Jesus Christ. What words would you turn to as you prepare for this crucial conversation?

The prophet and father Alma faced a situation like this. His son Corianton had pursued a harlot while on a mission to the Zoramites and now had significant concerns with concepts such as the Resurrection, the plan of restoration, and the justice of God in condemning the sinner. As Alma responded to Corianton's concerns, he turned to the words of Abinadi. This makes intuitive sense; after all, his father had been converted by Abinadi and recorded his words (Mosiah 17:4). If you were trying to help your son, why not turn to the words of the prophet who helped your father? This is the story of a father who loves his son and is searching desperately for the best way to teach him life-changing doctrine.

---

1   This chapter is a revised version of John Hilton III, "Textual Similarities in the Words of Abinadi and Alma's Counsel to Corianton," *BYU Studies Quarterly* 51, no. 2 (2012): 39–60. Used with permission.

In this chapter we will examine a series of textual similarities between the words of Abinadi in Mosiah 12–16 and Alma's counsel to Corianton in Alma 39–42. These are particularly interesting texts to study because Alma's father wrote down Abinadi's words, and Mormon specifically tells us that the words in Alma 36–42 come from Alma's own record.

Altogether, at least thirteen phrases in Alma 39–42 appear to be connected to Abinadi. Many of these are used in the Book of Mormon only in these two instances. Standing alone, each of these examples may appear insignificant, but they collectively indicate the extent to which Abinadi influenced Alma's words. I will discuss these textual similarities in the order in which Alma alludes to them in the text. Table 9.1 summarizes these thirteen allusions and illustrates how relatively infrequently these allusions appear outside the teachings of Alma and Abinadi.

Table 9.1. Alma's use of Abinadi when speaking to Corianton (organized by Alma's references)

Case #	Alma's words	Abinadi's words	Allusion	Times exact phrase is used elsewhere in scripture[2]
1	Alma 39:8	Mosiah 17:10	Stand as a testimony against you at the last day	0
2	Alma 39:15–16	Mosiah 15:18	Tidings . . . salvation unto his people	0
3	Alma 40:2	Mosiah 16:10	Put on immortality, . . . put on incorruption	1 (1 Corinthians 15:53–54)

2 Information on how frequently certain variant phrases appear is included in a footnote for each individual case.

4	Alma 40:13	Mosiah 16:2	Gnashing of teeth	23 (but only once in the Book of Mormon)
5	Alma 40:13	Mosiah 15:26	They have no part	0 (but the shorter phrase "have no part" appears 9 times in the Old Testament and once in the New Testament)
6	Alma 40:15–17	Mosiah 15:21–26	First resurrection	9 (Revelation 20:5, 6; Mosiah 18:9; Doctrine and Covenants 45:54; 63:18; 76:64; 132:19 [twice], 26)
7	Alma 40:16–20; 41:2	Mosiah 15:21	The resurrection of Christ	3 (Acts 2:31; Helaman 14:17; 3 Nephi 6:20)
8	Alma 40:21	Mosiah 16:10	Brought to stand before God . . . be judged . . . according to their works	0
9	Alma 40:2–23	Mosiah 15:24, 26–27	Bringeth about the restoration	0 (but 2 Nephi 30:8 is nearly identical)
10	Alma 42:10	Mosiah 16:3	Carnal, sensual, and devilish	2 (Moses 5:13; 6:49)
11	Alma 42:11	Mosiah 15:19	It were not for the . . . redemption	0

| 12 | Alma 42:15 | Mosiah 15:9 | The demands of justice | 2 (Alma 34:16 [twice], and 2 Nephi 9:26 and Mosiah 2:38 are similar) |
| 13 | Alma 42:26 | Mosiah 15:19 | Prepared from the foundation of the world | 17 (Matthew 25:34; 1 Nephi 10:18; 2 Nephi 9:18; Mosiah 4:6, 7; 18:13; Alma 12:30; 13:3, 5, 7; 18:39; 22:13; Ether 3:14; 4:19; Doctrine and Covenants 128:5, 8; Moses 5:57) |

Textual Similarities between Specific Phrases

Case I: Stand as a testimony against you at the last day

When faced with the flames, Abinadi declared, "If ye slay me ye will shed innocent blood, and this shall also *stand as a testimony against you at the last day*" (Mosiah 17:10). Abinadi taught that serious sins could not be hidden and would have to be accounted for at Judgment Day. As Alma began to teach Corianton, he alluded to this phrase, saying, "Ye cannot hide your crimes from God; and except ye repent they will *stand as a testimony against you at the last day*" (Alma 39:8).[3] It may be that Alma alluded to Abinadi's words to help Corianton realize the seriousness of his situation. Perhaps Alma hoped

---

3 This connection of sins standing "as a testimony" against people "at the last day" occurs only in these two verses. Nephi uses the phrase "stand as a testimony against you" in 2 Nephi 25:28, and Moroni uses this same phrase in Ether 5:4. Both Nephi and Moroni refer to the words they wrote standing as a testimony against others. King Benjamin and Mormon both use similar phrases regarding the words they had spoken or written standing as a testimony at the last day (see Mosiah 3:24; Moroni 8:21). Abinadi and Alma are the only ones who speak of actions standing as a testimony against us.

that his son would recognize that just as Abinadi's murderers would be held accountable for their crimes, so too would Corianton.

Case 2: Tidings . . . salvation unto his people

Speaking to those in King Noah's court, Abinadi said, "O how beautiful upon the mountains are the feet of him that bringeth good *tidings*, that is the founder of peace, yea, even the Lord, who has redeemed his people; yea, him who has granted *salvation unto his people*" (Mosiah 15:18). Alma used a similar phrase when he counseled Corianton, saying, "[Christ] cometh to declare glad *tidings* of *salvation unto his people*" (Alma 39:15).[4]

The probability that Alma is directly alluding to Abinadi's words is strengthened by similar phrases that surround "salvation unto his people." In connection with those who bring "salvation unto his people," Abinadi talked of those who "[bring] good tidings" (Mosiah 15:18). Alma stated that Christ would come to "declare glad tidings" and told Corianton, "This was the ministry unto which ye were called, to *declare these glad tidings* unto this people" (Alma 39:15, 16).[5]

One of Abinadi's overarching messages in this section is the importance of those who "[bring] good tidings of salvation unto his people." It may be that Alma directly quoted or paraphrased these words to say in effect to Corianton, "You had the opportunity to be the person of whom Abinadi spoke, but you squandered it." Alma might also have used this statement to motivate Corianton, since he would again be "called of God to preach the word unto this people" (Alma 42:31).

---

4 The words *salvation, tidings,* and *people* appear together only in Mosiah 15:18 and Alma 39:15–16. The phrase "salvation unto his people" is used only these two times in the Book of Mormon. It also occurs in Luke 1:77. A similar phrase, "bring my people unto salvation," appears in 2 Nephi 3:15 and JST Genesis 50:33, raising the possibility that either Abinadi or Alma (or both) was drawing on one of these sources.

5 The connection to the "glad tidings" in these verses may be more connected to Abinadi's paraphrase of Isaiah 52:7 than to Alma's allusion to Abinadi; however, given the matching phrase "salvation unto his people," it may be that Alma was drawing on Abinadi's expansion of Isaiah. The phrase "salvation unto his people" collocates with *tidings* only in Alma 39:15 and Mosiah 15:18.

Case 3: Put on immortality, . . . put on incorruption

As Abinadi taught about the Resurrection, he explained, "Even *this mortal* shall *put on immortality*, and *this corruption* shall *put on incorruption*, and shall be brought to stand before the bar of God" (Mosiah 16:10). Alma told Corianton, "There is no resurrection—or, I would say, in other words, that *this mortal* does not *put on immortality*, *this corruption* does not *put on incorruption*—until after the coming of Christ" (Alma 40:2).[6]

Alma teaches Corianton about the Resurrection because he perceives Corianton is worried about this doctrine (see Alma 40:1). Alma would likely use Abinadi's words to address concerns about the Resurrection because Abinadi talked about *resurrection* more than any known prophet Alma could have turned to. Nephi and his father, Lehi, each used the word only once, and King Benjamin never used it. In contrast, Abinadi used *resurrection* sixteen times. Thus, if Alma wanted to turn to scripture to explain the Resurrection, Abinadi was his best source for teaching this grand doctrine.[7]

Case 4: Gnashing of teeth

After Abinadi explained that the day would come when all would confess before God (see Mosiah 16:1), he said, "Then shall *the wicked be cast out*, and they shall have cause to howl, and *weep, and wail, and gnash their teeth*; *and this because* they would not hearken unto the voice of the Lord" (Mosiah 16:2). Alma echoed these words, saying, "And then shall it come to pass, that the spirits of *the wicked* . . . [will] *be cast out* into outer darkness; there shall be *weeping, and wailing, and gnashing of teeth*, *and this because* of their own iniquity" (Alma 40:13).[8]

---

6   "Put on immortality" and "put on incorruption" appear together only in these two places in the Book of Mormon. The phrase "put on immortality" is also found in Enos 1:27 and Mormon 6:21, and the phrase "put on incorruption" is also found in 2 Nephi 9:7. A connection with "put on immortality" and "put on incorruption" is also shared with 1 Corinthians 15:53–54.

7   Alma could have turned to Jacob, who uses *resurrection* nine times.

8   The phrase "cast out" is fairly common in the Book of Mormon; however, all forms of teeth gnashing appear only three times therein. The third reference

Case 5: They have no part

Another connection between Alma 40:13 and the words of Abinadi occurs in the phrase *they have no part*. Abinadi, speaking of those who willfully choose evil over good, said that "*they . . . have no part* in the first resurrection" (Mosiah 15:26). Likewise, Alma said, "The spirits of the wicked, yea, who are evil—for behold, *they have no part* nor portion of the Spirit of the Lord; for behold, they chose evil works rather than good" (Alma 40:13).[9]

Thus, both prophets teach that those who rebel against God will *have no part* in some of the fruits of the Atonement. As Alma's conversation with Corianton progresses, it becomes apparent that Corianton is confused about why the wicked are not saved. As will be discussed, this confusion may have stemmed from Corianton's misunderstanding of Abinadi's words. Perhaps Alma used Abinadi's teachings to clarify and emphasize what Abinadi taught: that the wicked are not partakers of the same blessings as the righteous.

Case 6: First resurrection

Abinadi taught, "And there cometh a resurrection, even *a first resurrection*; yea, even *a resurrection of* those that *have been*, and *who are*, and *who shall be*, even until *the resurrection of Christ*—for so shall he be called" (Mosiah 15:21). The words italicized in this verse are all

---

is found in Alma 14:21. The phrases "cast out" and "gnashing of teeth" appear together in the Book of Mormon exclusively in these two verses (see also Matthew 8:12). References to teeth gnashing occur relatively frequently in other scriptural texts (five times in the Old Testament, nine times in the New Testament, six times in the Doctrine and Covenants, and twice in the Pearl of Great Price). It is possible that both Alma and Abinadi are drawing on an earlier text in their use of these words (e.g., Psalm 112:10).

9   The phrases "they have no part" and the shorter "have no part" are exclusive to Abinadi and Alma in the Book of Mormon. The phrase "have no part" appears nine times in the Old Testament and once in the New Testament. The shorter "no part" is used only two additional times in the Book of Mormon. It may be significant that these are the only two occurrences of "have no part" in the Book of Mormon, or it may be that rather than an intentional allusion, Alma is simply using words that are part of a pericope he has been recently studying.

phrases of two words or more that appear in the following statement from Alma: "And behold, again it hath been spoken, that there is *a first resurrection*, *a resurrection of* all those who *have been*, or *who are*, or *who shall be*, down to *the resurrection of Christ* from the dead" (Alma 40:16).[10] Even many of the nonitalicized words in these two verses show clear connections. Alma leaves no doubt that he is drawing on other words, stating, "It hath been spoken" (Alma 40:16; see also Alma 40:17, 22, 24). This statement provides additional credibility to the idea that Alma had a record of Abinadi's words and was so familiar with them that he could work them into his teachings.

Alma's uses of *first resurrection* follow his pattern of quoting from Abinadi to clarify doctrinal points. Abinadi had taught that those who kept the commandments would "come forth in the *first resurrection*," but those who "die in their sins . . . have no part in the *first resurrection*" (Mosiah 15:22, 26). While Abinadi's words may seem clear to modern readers, apparently some Nephites had trouble understanding the concept of the First Resurrection. Perhaps Corianton (and others generally) was confused about what was meant by the First Resurrection. Alma acknowledged that some believed the First Resurrection involved spirits going to paradise or darkness. He explained, "I admit it may be termed a resurrection, the raising of the spirit or the soul and their consignation to happiness or misery, according to the words which have been spoken. . . . Now we do not suppose that this *first resurrection*, which is spoken of in this manner, can be the resurrection of their souls and their consignation to happiness or misery. Ye cannot suppose that this is what it meaneth. Behold, I say unto you, Nay; but it meaneth the reuniting of the soul with the body, of those from the days of Adam down to the resurrection of Christ" (Alma 40:15–18). Thus Alma used Abinadi's words to clarify for Corianton the meaning of resurrection. This theme is further developed in the next section.

---

10   The phrase "first resurrection" appears ten times in the Book of Mormon: six times in the words of Abinadi, once in the words of Alma the Elder, and three times in the words of his son Alma. The phrase "first resurrection" also appears twice in Revelation 20:5–6 and six times in the Doctrine and Covenants.

Case 7: The resurrection of Christ

The allusion just mentioned, regarding the First Resurrection, relates to another connection between the texts: the phrase *the resurrection of Christ*.[11] Abinadi defines the First Resurrection as "a resurrection of those that have been, and who are, and who shall be, even until *the resurrection of Christ*" (Mosiah 15:21). Alma borrows this concept when he tells Corianton that the meaning of the First Resurrection is "the reuniting of the soul with the body, of those from the days of Adam down to *the resurrection of Christ*" (Alma 40:18).

In Alma 40:17 (the verse preceding the use of the phrase *the resurrection of Christ*), Alma clearly states that he is alluding to others' words, saying, "We do not suppose that this first resurrection, *which is spoken of in this manner*, can be the resurrection of the souls and their consignation to happiness or misery. Ye cannot suppose that this is what it meaneth." Then in Alma 40:18, Alma proceeds to re-state Mosiah 15:21. Thus Alma clarified Abinadi's words to alleviate Corianton's misunderstandings regarding the Resurrection.

Case 8: Brought to stand before God ... be judged ... according to their works

Abinadi taught that people would "*be brought to stand before* the bar of *God*, to *be judged* of him *according to their works* whether they be good or whether they be evil" (Mosiah 16:10). Similarly, Alma testified that there is a "time which is appointed of God that the dead shall come forth, and be reunited, both soul and body, and *be brought to stand before God*, and *be judged according to their works*" (Alma 40:21).[12]

---

11 This phrase appears nine times in the Book of Mormon and also in Acts 2:31. The phrase "the resurrection of Christ" is first used by Abinadi and later by Alma, Mormon, and Samuel the Lamanite. Each uses it one time, except for Alma, who uses it five times in Alma 40:16–20. Alma and Abinadi are also the only people to discuss the Resurrection of Christ in connection with the First Resurrection.

12 These phrases appear together only in the words of Abinadi and Alma. Nephi is the only other voice in the Book of Mormon to speak of people being "brought to stand before God" to be "judged" by their "works" (1 Nephi 15:33). He uses the phrase "to be judged of their works," a slight variant of

It may be that when Alma clarified Abinadi's teachings on the First Resurrection and the Resurrection of Christ, he wanted Corianton to see the connection between resurrection and judgment. The context of Alma 39–42 indicates that Corianton was confused about the principle of accountability, and Alma used Abinadi's words to illustrate how accountability relates to the concepts of resurrection, restoration, and the justice of God.

Case 9: Bringeth about the restoration

In speaking about the righteous and those who died in ignorance, Abinadi said, "And these are those who have part in the first resurrection. . . . And thus the Lord *bringeth about the restoration* of these; and they have a part in the first resurrection, or have eternal life, being redeemed by the Lord" (Mosiah 15:24). In contrast to the pleasant state of the righteous, Abinadi taught that "the Lord redeemeth none such that rebel against him and die in their sins" (Mosiah 15:26).

Similarly, in Alma 40:22–23 Alma told Corianton that after the Resurrection all would be judged, and this "*bringeth about the restoration* of those things of which has been spoken by the mouths of the prophets" (verse 22). Alma then spoke of the "awful death [that] cometh upon the wicked" (verse 26).[13] The surrounding context of resurrection and punishment of the wicked suggests Alma based his conversation with Corianton on these teachings from Abinadi.

Perhaps the most interesting connection between these verses is how Alma and Abinadi use the words *restoration* and *resurrection*.

---

the phrase used by Abinadi and Alma. The four-word phrase "brought to stand before" appears only seven times in scripture, exclusively in the Book of Mormon (see 1 Nephi 15:33; Mosiah 16:10; Alma 11:43; 12:8; 24:15; 40:21; Mormon 9:2). The four-word phrase "according to their works" and its variants are more common, appearing forty-one times in scripture: five times in the Old Testament, nine times in the New Testament, nineteen times in the Book of Mormon, and eight times in the Doctrine and Covenants.

13 The phrase "bringeth about the restoration" is used only by Abinadi and Alma. Nephi uses a nearly identical phrase ("bring about the restoration") in 2 Nephi 30:8; however, Nephi is clearly referring to the gathering of Israel.

There appears to be some confusion in Corianton's mind concerning the meaning of the word *restoration*, and Alma states that "some have wrested the scriptures, and have gone far astray because of this thing" (Alma 41:1). The concepts of restoration and resurrection appear together in the words of Jacob, Abinadi, Amulek, and Alma, and all four individuals use these words in ways that could be interpreted as being interchangeable.[14] This may have led to Corianton's confusion "concerning the restoration of which has been spoken" (Alma 41:1). Abinadi uses both *restoration* and *resurrection* in the context of those who die without knowing of Christ and teaches that those who die in ignorance will be restored to eternal life (see Mosiah 15:24).

Perhaps Corianton believed that those who feigned ignorance to God's commandments could "have a part in the first resurrection" (Mosiah 15:24). Or maybe he had tricked himself into believing in a universal restoration to good things, not realizing that while the Resurrection is universal, a restoration to good is not. To provide clarification, Alma states that after the Resurrection, all will "be brought to stand before God, and be judged according to their works. Yea, *this* [God's judgment at the last day] *bringeth about the restoration* of those things of which has been spoken by the mouths of the prophets" (Alma 40:21–22). It may be that Alma's use of the phrase "bringeth about the restoration" was intended to provide both an allusion and an amplification (continued throughout Alma 41) to Abinadi's words that would clarify a doctrinal misunderstanding about the meaning of the word *restoration*. The restoration spoken of by Alma and Abinadi is more than a universal resurrection. It also includes a restoration to the kind of being we were in mortality (see Alma 41:3–4).

Case 10: Carnal, sensual, devilish

Speaking of those who do not repent, Abinadi taught that "the devil has power over them; yea, even that old serpent that did beguile our first parents, which was the cause of their fall; which was the cause of all mankind becoming *carnal, sensual, devilish*" (Mosiah 16:3). Similarly,

---

14   See 2 Nephi 9:12; Mosiah 15:24; Alma 11:43; 40:23.

in discussing the effects of the Fall, Alma explained that humankind had "become *carnal, sensual, and devilish*" (Alma 42:10).[15]

The contexts surrounding these words are similar. In both instances, Alma and Abinadi teach about the Fall and point out that, because of God's redemption, these effects of the Fall can be overcome (discussed below). The fallen state of humankind may have been part of the reason why Corianton felt that it was unjust for God to condemn sinners (see Alma 42:1). Alma acknowledged the results of the Fall but went on to provide Corianton with hope as to how he could overcome these consequences.

Case II: Were it not for the redemption

Abinadi said, "For *were it not for the redemption* which he hath made for his people, . . . all mankind must have perished" (Mosiah 15:19). In Alma 42:11 Alma also employed a similar phrase to highlight the supreme importance of Christ in the plan of redemption. He said, "And now remember, my son, if *it were not for the* plan of *redemption*, (laying it aside) as soon as they were dead their souls were miserable, being cut off from the presence of the Lord."

While the exact wording is slightly different in the two passages,[16] in both cases Alma and Abinadi state that in the absence of God's plan for us, all humankind would perish. Christ provides hope for all humankind and makes it so all who desire to repent can do so. Thus Alma uses Abinadi's words to resolve Corianton's concern regarding the justice of God in condemning the sinner (see Alma 42:1).

---

15 The words *carnal, sensual,* and *devilish* appear together in the Book of Mormon only in the words of Alma and Abinadi. These words also appear together in Moses 5:13 and Moses 6:49. Thus, both Abinadi and Alma could potentially be referencing the brass plates. James 3:15 includes the phrase "earthly, sensual, devilish."

16 In a previous sermon, Alma had clearly quoted Abinadi's statement in Mosiah 15:19 while again substituting the phrase "plan of redemption" for the word *redemption*, increasing the possibility that Alma was alluding to Abinadi in this case. Compare Alma 12:25 with Mosiah 15:19.

Case 12: The demands of justice

Abinadi taught that Christ had "ascended into heaven, having the bowels of *mercy*; . . . having redeemed them, and satisfied *the demands of justice*" (Mosiah 15:9). Alma echoed this phrase in teaching Corianton that Christ "atoneth for the sins of the world, to bring about the plan of *mercy*, to appease *the demands of justice*" (Alma 42:15).[17]

Both Alma and Abinadi explain that Christ can exercise "mercy" and meet the "demands of justice" because of his atoning sacrifice. Once again, we see how Alma draws on the words of Abinadi to clarify Corianton's confusion (in this case regarding the justice of God). While God does require justice, he has also prepared a plan of mercy—mercy that can be extended to Corianton.

Case 13: Prepared from the foundation of the world

Abinadi taught of the "redemption" that Christ "hath made for his people, which was *prepared from the foundation of the world*" (Mosiah 15:19). Near the end of his conversation with Corianton, Alma said, "And thus God bringeth about his great and eternal purposes, which were *prepared from the foundation of the world*. And thus cometh about the salvation and the *redemption* of men, and also their destruction and misery" (Alma 42:26).[18] Although the phrase "from

---

17   The words *demand* and *justice* appear together only in the Book of Mormon. The specific phrase "demands of justice" is used only by Abinadi, Alma, and Amulek (see Alma 34:16). Variant phrases (e.g., "demands of his justice") appear in 2 Nephi 9:26 and Mosiah 2:38.

18   The exact phrase "prepared from the foundation of the world" appears eleven times in scripture (all in the Book of Mormon). It is used twice by King Benjamin (Mosiah 4:6–7), once by Abinadi (Mosiah 15:19), once by Alma the Elder (Mosiah 18:13), four times by Alma the Younger (Alma 12:30; 13:3, 5; 42:26), twice by Mormon (Alma 18:39; 22:13), and once by Jesus Christ (Ether 3:14). If we assume that Alma picked up the phrase from a previous prophet, the question is whether it was King Benjamin or Abinadi. While Alma undoubtedly studied the words of both, it may be more likely that Abinadi is the source of this phrase. This is based on two pieces of textual evidence. First is the flow of the phrase from Abinadi to Alma the Elder. If Alma the Elder is borrowing the phrase, it most likely came from Abinadi. While Alma might not have been alive when his father was quoted as using the phrase, the fact that it is one of only four phrases that Alma the Elder

the foundation of the world" is relatively common, it collocates with the word *redemption* only in the words of Abinadi and Alma or in connection with the sons of Mosiah (see Alma 18:39; 22:13). Thus it may be that Alma uses Abinadi's words to provide Corianton with encouragement. From the beginning, a plan had been put in place for Corianton and others to overcome the effects of the Fall, to be redeemed and stand in the presence of God.

Broader Themes

Stepping back to look at the larger picture reveals that Alma borrowed phrases clustered around specific themes from Abinadi. First, Alma makes two allusions to Abinadi that may have helped Corianton connect his ministry with Abinadi's (see Alma 39:8 [compare Mosiah 17:10] and Alma 39:15 [compare Mosiah 15:18]). All of Alma's remaining quotations from Abinadi relate to Corianton's major concerns—namely, the Resurrection, the plan of restoration, and the justice of God in punishing the sinner.

Three of Alma's allusions to Abinadi relate to resurrection. Phrases such as "this mortal does not put on immortality" (Alma 40:2; compare Mosiah 16:10), "first resurrection" (Alma 40:15; compare Mosiah 15:21), and "the resurrection of Christ" (Alma 40:16; compare Mosiah 15:21) directly point to the Resurrection.

Two of Alma's allusions concern the plan of restoration. Both Abinadi and Alma discuss how Christ "bringeth about the restoration" (Alma 40:22; compare Mosiah 15:24), and Alma explains

---

directly quotes from Abinadi may indicate it was one Alma would have noticed. A second piece of textual evidence is the connection between the word *redemption* and the phrase "prepared from the foundation of the world." Abinadi speaks of the "redemption" that Christ "hath made for his people, which was prepared from the foundation of the world" (Mosiah 15:19). Alma the Elder states that eternal life comes "through the redemption of Christ, whom he has prepared from the foundation of the world" (Mosiah 18:13). Three of the four times Alma uses "prepared from the foundation of the world," he uses the word *redemption* in connection with the phrase (Alma 12:30; 13:3; 42:26). In contrast, King Benjamin does not use the word *redemption* in connection with "prepared from the foundation of the world."

that restoration includes humankind being "brought to stand before" God and being "judged according to their works" (Alma 40:21; compare Mosiah 16:10).

The remaining six allusions address the issue of the justice of God in punishing the sinner. Alma and Abinadi are the only Book of Mormon prophets to speak of the wicked being "cast out" and "gnashing [their] teeth" (Alma 40:13; compare Mosiah 16:2). They alone say that the wicked who have become "carnal, sensual, and devilish" "have no part" in some of the fruits of the Atonement (Alma 42:10, 13; compare Mosiah 16:3; 15:26). They both teach that "were [it] not for the plan of redemption" that had been "prepared from the foundation of the world," "the demands of justice" would take effect at the Judgment Day (Alma 42:11 [compare Mosiah 15:19]; 42:26 [compare Mosiah 15:19]; 42:15 [compare Mosiah 15:9]).

In addition to common themes, most of Alma's quotations come from one section of Abinadi's words. Table 9.2 illustrates which passages from Abinadi were quoted by Alma as he spoke to Corianton.

Table 9.2. Alma's use of Abinadi when speaking to Corianton (organized by Abinadi's references)

Abinadi's words	Alma's words	Allusion
Mosiah 15:9	Alma 42:15	The demands of justice
Mosiah 15:18	Alma 39:15–16	Tidings . . . salvation unto his people
Mosiah 15:19	Alma 42:11	It were not for the . . . redemption
Mosiah 15:19	Alma 42:26	Prepared from the foundation of the world
Mosiah 15:21	Alma 40:16–20; 41:2	The resurrection of Christ
Mosiah 15:21–26	Alma 40:15–17	First resurrection
Mosiah 15:24	Alma 40:22	Bringeth about the restoration

Mosiah 15:26	Alma 40:13	They have no part
Mosiah 16:2	Alma 40:13	Gnashing of teeth
Mosiah 16:3	Alma 42:9–11	Carnal, sensual, and devilish
Mosiah 16:10	Alma 40:21	Brought to stand before God . . . be judged according to their works
Mosiah 16:10	Alma 40:2	Put on immortality, . . . put on incorruption
Mosiah 17:10	Alma 39:8	Stand as a testimony against you at the last day

As demonstrated in table 9.2, Alma's quotations from Abinadi come almost exclusively from the thirty-three verses from Mosiah 15:9 to Mosiah 16:10. The tight clustering of these passages makes it seem more plausible that Alma intentionally used a specific section of Abinadi's words when teaching Corianton.

Therefore, What?

If we assume that Alma intentionally used Abinadi's words, what implications does that have for us today? There are at least three important lessons that we can learn from this intertwining of their unique voices. First, family connections are important. Alma loved Corianton and wanted to teach him doctrine that would bring him to repentance.

It seems natural for him to turn to the prophetic words that once had this very effect on Corianton's grandfather—Alma the Elder. The family foundation of conversion to the gospel of Christ is Alma the Elder's transcription of Abinadi's teachings. Perhaps Corianton had heard his grandfather glowingly speak of Abinadi and was particularly interested in the words of one who had deeply impacted his family's heritage. Alma may have thought, "If the words of Abinadi sank deep into my father's soul and provoked a mighty change within his heart, what better words to share with his wayward grandson?"

Alma the Elder had long since passed away when Alma spoke to Corianton, but his legacy continued in the conversation as a mediating influence between Abinadi and Alma. Our faithful choices, including the records we keep of such choices, could have a lasting influence on our descendants who are yet unborn.

A second lesson is that Alma had clearly studied the scriptures and contemporary prophets. Whether we consider Abinadi as "scripture" to Alma or as a "recent prophet," we find a great example for modern readers. When Alma was faced with a very difficult situation, he turned to the words of scripture and recent prophets. Alma put forth significant effort to be so conversant with Abinadi's words that he could weave them into a conversation as though they were his own.

Third, Alma uses scripture to resolve concerns. In my mind's eye, I can see Alma poring over the words of his predecessors while trying to help assuage his son's doubts. It is significant that Alma's allusions to Abinadi cluster around the specific issues that troubled Corianton. As Alma sought to resolve his son's concerns, he trusted he could find answers in the scriptures. Do we do likewise?

Elder David A. Bednar shared an experience in which he was a new missionary. Along with other new missionaries, he was invited to a special fireside in the temple with President Harold B. Lee, then a member of the First Presidency. President Lee invited the missionaries to ask him questions on any gospel topic. Elder Bednar was amazed to watch President Lee answer each question by using the scriptures. Speaking of this experience, Elder Bednar wrote, "I knew I would never have the command of the scriptures that [President Lee] did, but then and there in the Salt Lake Temple I resolved to study and use the scriptures in my teaching and follow the example of President Lee. And that commitment as a new and inexperienced 19-year-old missionary has blessed my life in ways that cannot be counted or adequately described."[19]

As we face difficult challenges and strive to help others who are struggling, we can find answers in the scriptures and words of recent

---

19 David A. Bednar, "Because We Have Them before Our Eyes," *New Era*, April 2006, 4–5.

prophets. While every parent and every child is different, following Alma's example of (1) putting forth the effort to be familiar with prophetic words and (2) using them as we teach those we love can bring great blessings for parents and children alike. In addition, Alma shows the importance of seeking and following guidance from the Lord for each individual child. The Lord knew what Corianton needed to hear, and he gave Alma the voice to speak to him. God is the Eternal Father of my children, and he loves them even more than I do. This is a comforting truth for me as a parent. I can turn to him in prayer, search the scriptures, and then hopefully speak to my children in the way he knows they can hear.

Chapter 10

Fathers and Sons: Textual Connections between 2 Nephi 2 and Alma 42

Can two fathers, separated by hundreds of years, give the same words of wisdom to two very different sons? The answer is yes. As described in the previous chapter, Alma heavily drew on Abinadi's words of the life to come when speaking to his wayward son Corianton. In this chapter we will explore a different set of harmonizing voices by comparing Alma's words to his troubled son Corianton in Alma 42 with Lehi's words to his faithful son Jacob in 2 Nephi 2.

Both fathers loved the Lord and shared their testimonies, words of wisdom, and counsel with their sons. As his life drew to a close, Lehi gave a series of final speeches to his posterity. In 2 Nephi 2 he turned his attention to Jacob, after first addressing Jacob's older brothers. Similarly, Alma may have been approaching the end of his life[1] in Alma 36–42, when he took the time to speak with each of his sons. In Alma 39–42 he spoke to Corianton, after having first spoken to Corianton's older brothers.

The sons also shared some similarities. They both had fathers who were faithful patriarchs and prophets. In addition, both Jacob and Corianton are specifically mentioned as being ordained in

---

1 Although we do not have an actual death date for Alma (see Alma 45:17–19), the two instances of "farewell" in his addresses to his sons indicate that some sort of separation was about to take place (Alma 37:47; 38:15).

God's holy order. Jacob says he was "*ordained* after the manner of his *[God's] holy order*" (2 Nephi 6:2), while Mormon tells us that Corianton, along with others, "had been *ordained by the holy order of God*" (Alma 49:30).[2] These connections may be coincidental,[3] but they do prime us to look for similarities between 2 Nephi 2 and Alma 42. If we can assume that some version of 2 Nephi 2 was part of the canon with which Alma was familiar, it makes sense that Alma would turn to it when talking to Corianton because Lehi directly addressed the concern that plagued Corianton.[4]

---

2 Outside these verses, the words *holy*, *order*, and *ordain* appear together only in Alma 13:1, 6, 8, 10 and Doctrine and Covenants 77:11; 107:29.

3 Another potential connection between Lehi's and Alma's words is found in the word *great*, which appears six times in 2 Nephi 2 and four times in Alma 42. Three of the instances in Alma 42 are used to modify the word *plan*—Alma speaks of "the great plan of salvation" (verse 5), "the great plan of happiness" (verse 8), and "the great plan of mercy" (verse 31). He also speaks of the "great and eternal purposes of God." The word *great* appears nearly seven hundred times in the Book of Mormon, so Alma's use of it might not be related to Lehi's. Nevertheless, it is interesting to note that Lehi tells Jacob of "the greatness of God" (2 Nephi 2:2), the "great" importance to tell others about "the great Mediator" (verses 8, 27, 28), and "the punishment of the law at the great and last day" (verse 26).

4 Although Mormon was apparently not aware of the small plates when he began his record (see Words of Mormon 1:3), it is not clear at what point this record might have disappeared from the view of recordkeepers. It does seem that at some point in time, Nephite prophets may not have been fully aware of the material on the small plates. For example, Alma states, "And now we only wait to hear the joyful news declared unto us by the mouth of angels, of his [Christ's] coming; for the time cometh, we know not how soon. Would to God that it might be in my day; but let it be sooner or later, in it I will rejoice" (Alma 13:25). In contrast, Nephi was clear on the date of Christ's coming (see 1 Nephi 10:4; 19:8; and 2 Nephi 25:19). At the same time, Alma was somehow familiar enough with the words we have as 1 Nephi 1:8 that he was able to quote them to Helaman in Alma 36:22. Moreover, we know that Nephi "received a commandment that the ministry and the prophecies, the more plain and precious parts of them, should be written upon these plates; and that the things which were written should be kept for the instruction of [his] people, who should possess the land" (1 Nephi 19:3). Thus Nephi explicitly intended for the small plates to remain in circulation. Amaleki expressed his plan to do just that by giving the small plates to King

Corianton's Concern

Corianton's poor choices weren't Alma's only concern; Corianton also had doubts about key gospel doctrine. Alma explicitly states one of Corianton's concerns at the beginning of Alma 42, identifying it in two different ways: "And now, my son, I perceive there is somewhat more which doth worry your mind, which ye cannot understand—which is [1] concerning the justice of God in the punishment of the sinner; for ye do try to suppose that [2] it is injustice that the sinner should be consigned to a state of misery" (verse 1). Along with calling Corianton to repentance, Alma wanted to help his son find peace in Christ. At the forefront of our examination of connections between these chapters is the question "How might 2 Nephi 2 help one understand the justice of God in punishing a sinner?" Interestingly, with the exceptions of Alma 30 and 42, the word *punish* appears more times in 2 Nephi 2 than in any other chapter of the Book of Mormon, making it a likely candidate for Alma to employ when addressing this concern. Similarly, *misery* and its variants occur more frequently in 2 Nephi 2 than in any other chapter in scripture.[5] What father wouldn't use such a fitting resource at his disposal?

Ultimately, Alma's words to his son Corianton are full of doctrinal insights, due in part to Lehi's teachings to his own son generations before. In this chapter I will look at some of the key doctrines both fathers taught, as well as how they taught them. I will show that Alma employs 2 Nephi 2 in order to (1) expand Lehi's teachings on the Fall, (2) illustrate a series of oppositional statements demonstrating that punishment must exist in order for God to exist, (3) show how punishment has been "affixed," and (4) assert that people's ability to act ultimately gives them the freedom to choose what their rewards or consequences will be.

Benjamin (see Omni 1:25), and Benjamin passed on the records to Mosiah$_2$ (see Mosiah 1:16). Mosiah$_2$ in turn gave "all the records" in his possession to Alma (Mosiah 28:20). It seems reasonable that in the space of three generations, the small plates would not have been completely lost from view. In addition, although the logic is admittedly circular, the number of complex and convincing textual parallels discussed in this chapter indicate that Alma had access to some form of Lehi's words.

5   *Misery* and its variants occur eight times in 2 Nephi 2; the next highest number of occurrences is found in Alma 40 (four times).

Alma's Expansion of 2 Nephi 2:18–19, 21

After identifying and expressing Corianton's concern, Alma explicitly states that he will "explain this thing" to his son (Alma 42:2). Alma apparently first turns to the brass plates, quoting from what we have as Genesis 3:22–24. Table 10.1 provides a comparison between these two passages.

Table 10.1. A Comparison of Alma 42:2–3 and Genesis 3:22–24[6]

Alma 42:2–3[7]	Genesis 3:22–24
2 For behold, after *the Lord God sent our first parents forth from the garden of Eden, to till the ground, from whence he was taken—yea, he drove out the man, and he placed at the east end of the garden of Eden, cherubims, and a flaming sword which turned every way, to keep the tree of life—*	23 *Therefore the Lord God sent him forth from the garden of Eden, to till the ground from whence he was taken.*
	24 *So he drove out the man; and he placed at the east of the garden of Eden Cherubims, and a flaming sword which turned every way, to keep the way of the tree of life.*
3 Now, we see that *the man* had *became as God, knowing good and evil; and lest he* should *put forth his hand, and take also of the tree of life, and eat and live forever, that the Lord God placed cherubims and the flaming sword, that he should not partake of the fruit.*	22 And the Lord God said, *Behold, the man is become as one of us, to know good and evil: and* now, *lest he put forth his hand, and take also of the tree of life, and eat, and live for ever.*

Lehi had also evidently been reading from the same brass plates when he taught Jacob. He stated, "I, Lehi, *according to the things which I have read*, must needs suppose that an angel of God, *according to that which is written*, had fallen from heaven [Isaiah 14:12]. . . .

---

6   I acknowledge Ben McGuire's assistance in identifying this connection.

7   Alma 42:2–3, as quoted in this table, comes from Royal Skousen's *The Book of Mormon: The Earliest Text* (New Haven, CT: Yale University Press, 2009). This comparison shows even tighter connections than the current Book of Mormon—for example, "he was taken" (*Earliest Text*) versus "they were taken" (2013 text), or "cherubims" (*Earliest Text*) versus "cherubim" (2013 text).

Wherefore, he said unto Eve, yea, even that old serpent, who is the devil, who is the father of all lies, wherefore he said: Partake of the forbidden fruit, and ye shall not die, but ye shall be as God, knowing good and evil [Genesis 3:1–5]" (2 Nephi 2:17–18).

Lehi expands on what we have in Genesis, and Alma in turn expands on Lehi's teachings. Table 10.2 illustrates the connections between these expansions.

Table 10.2. A comparison of Alma 42:2–10 and 2 Nephi 2:18–19, 21[8]

Alma 42:2–10	2 Nephi 2:18–19, 21
2 *After* the Lord God sent *our first parents* forth from *the garden of Eden to till the ground*, from whence he was taken—*yea, he drove out the man*—and he placed at the east end of the garden of Eden cherubims. . .	19 And *after that Adam and Eve* had partaken of the forbidden fruit, *they were driven out* from *the garden of Eden to till the earth.* [See also Genesis 3:23.]
3 . . . *The man had became as God, knowing good and evil.* . . .	18 . . . *Ye shall be as God, knowing good and evil.* [See also Genesis 3:22.]
4 And thus we see that *there was a time granted unto man to repent, yea, a probationary time*, a time to repent and serve God.	21 *And the days of the children of men were prolonged*, according to the will of God, that they might *repent* while in the flesh. . . .
6 . . . *And man became lost* forever; *yea, they became fallen man.* . . .	21 . . . For he shewed unto *all men that they were lost* because of the transgression of their parents.
10 . . . *This probationary state became a state for them to prepare*; it became a preparatory state.	21 . . . *Wherefore, their state became a state of probation.* . . .

8   In this table the scriptural text comes from Skousen's *Earliest Text.* This comparison shows even tighter connections than the current Book of Mormon—for example, Alma 42:2 has "drove out" (*Earliest Text*) versus "drew out" (2013 text), compared with "driven out" (2 Nephi 2:19, *Earliest Text* and 2013 text). I also note that in these verses Alma also refers to other previous Nephite prophets. For example, compare Alma 42:6 and Mosiah 15:4.

Significantly, after naming Corianton's concern, the first thing Alma refers to is the Fall. While Lehi's discussion of the Fall takes place in the second half of 2 Nephi 2, Alma shifts this focus to the beginning of his discussion regarding the justice of God in punishing sinners. Why might this be the case? Some in Alma's society had misunderstood the Fall, and perhaps Corianton was among them. He might have subscribed to Korihor's words: "Ye say that this people is a guilty and a fallen people, because of the transgression of a parent. Behold, I say that a child is not guilty because of its parents" (Alma 30:25).

In a sense, one cannot fault Corianton if he feels God is unjust in having the descendants of Adam and Eve suffer the effects of the Fall—why should he be punished for his ancestors' mistakes? Alma answers this implicit question by explaining the concept of "a probationary time" (Alma 42:4). In doing so, he follows Lehi, who, as he taught Jacob about the Fall, explained that connected to the Fall was a space of time granted for people to repent. Lehi said, "The days of the children of men were prolonged, according to the will of God, that they might *repent* while in the flesh; wherefore, *their state became a state of probation*, and their *time* was lengthened. . . . *Behold, if Adam had* not transgressed he would not have fallen, but he would have remained in the garden of Eden" (2 Nephi 2:21–22). Drawing on Lehi's words, Alma says, "For *behold, if Adam had* put forth his hand immediately, and partaken of the tree of life, he would have lived forever, . . . having no space for repentance. . . . This *probationary state became a state* for them to prepare" (Alma 42:4–5, 10).[9]

These two passages share multiple textual connections. Both use the unique phrase "if Adam had"[10] to describe alternate scenarios surrounding the Fall. The phrase "state became a state" similarly appears only in 2 Nephi 2:21 and Alma 42:10. Alma follows Lehi's insight that a time of probation exists after the Fall and teaches (as did Lehi) that this time allows for repentance. Perhaps this was an

---

9   This time to repent was important because, as Alma later explains, "the plan of redemption could not be brought about, only on conditions of repentance of men in this probationary state" (Alma 42:13).

10 In scripture, the phrase "if Adam had," as well as the shorter "if Adam," appears only in these two verses.

effort to extend hope to Corianton so that he would know it was not too late.

Both fathers taught their sons about Jesus Christ. Shortly after Lehi taught about "a state of probation" (2 Nephi 2:21), he testified that "the Messiah cometh in the fulness of time, that he may redeem the children of men from the fall" (2 Nephi 2:26). Alma similarly connected Christ's Atonement with the probationary state, explaining, "The plan of mercy could not be brought about except an atonement should be made; therefore God himself atoneth for the sins of the world, to bring about the plan of mercy, to appease the demands of justice, that God might be a perfect, just God, and a merciful God also" (Alma 42:15). It may not be just for humans to suffer the effects of the Fall, but it is likewise not just for Christ's sufferings to take away these effects. In other words, any lack of justice received by humans because of the Fall is counterbalanced by an abundance of mercy received because of Christ's Atonement—a key concept for Corianton to understand.

Alma's intent was to point his son to Jesus Christ, the only source of real joy and salvation. Repentance was not easy, as Alma experienced long ago, but the alternative was a fate he hoped his son would avoid. So Alma taught plainly and boldly of repentance. The Savior's atoning sacrifice opens the possibility for both mercy and justice, predicated on repentance. Alma states that if it were not for "conditions of repentance . . . , mercy could not take effect" (Alma 42:13). However, he teaches that repentance does not exist in a vacuum: "*Repentance* could not come unto men except there were a *punishment*" (verse 16). Here Alma returns to the concern of the justice of God in punishing a sinner. This connection between repentance and punishment is crucial; but before we more carefully explore it, we must first examine it in the context of opposing forces and God ceasing to be God.

Opposition and God Ceasing to Be God

Lehi and Alma use a similar structure to discuss opposition and God ceasing to be God. Both Alma 42:11–23 and 2 Nephi 2:10–14 are organized as follows: (1) because of Christ, we can come into God's presence; (2) there is opposition; (3) if this opposition weren't in place, the justice of God would be destroyed; (4) a series of cause-and-effect statements; (5) a hypothetical statement that if these things weren't in place, God would cease to be God; and (6) a declaration that the hypothetical statement is not true—there is in fact a God. A closer textual examination of these passages is found in table 10.3.

Table 10.3. A textual comparison of Alma 42:11–23 and 2 Nephi 2:10–14

Alma 42:11–23	2 Nephi 2:10–14
If it were not for the plan of redemption, (laying it aside) as soon as they were dead their souls were miserable, being *cut off* from *the presence of the Lord*. . . .	Because of the intercession for all, all men *come unto God*; wherefore, they stand in *the presence of him* . . .
Therefore, according to justice, the plan of redemption *could not be brought about*, only on conditions of repentance of men in this probationary state . . . ; for except it were for these conditions, *mercy* could not take effect except it should *destroy* the work of *justice*. Now the work of *justice* could not be *destroyed*. . . .	For it must needs be, that there is an opposition in all things. If not so, . . . righteousness *could not be brought to pass*, neither wickedness, neither holiness nor misery. . . .
	. . . Wherefore, this thing must needs *destroy* the wisdom of God and his eternal purposes, and also the power, and the *mercy*, and the *justice* of God.
Now, how could a man repent except he should sin? *How could he sin if there was no law?* How could there be a law save there was a *punishment?* . . .	. . . *If ye shall say there is no law, ye shall also say there is no sin.* If ye shall say there is no sin, ye shall also say there is no righteousness. And if there be no righteousness there be no happiness. And if there be no righteousness nor happiness there be no *punishment* nor misery. And *if these things are not there is no God.* . . .
If there was no law given against sin men would not be afraid to sin. . . .	
. . . *If not so,* . . . *God would cease to be God.*	
But God ceaseth not to be God. . . .	. . . *For there is a God.* . . .

At the heart of both Lehi's and Alma's arguments is that without opposition, God would cease to be God. Lehi, teaching his obedient son, stated that a lack of opposition "must needs *destroy* . . . the *mercy* and the *justice* of God" (2 Nephi 2:12). It is interesting to note the parallel statement of Alma as he teaches his rebellious son: "*Mercy* could not take effect except it should *destroy* the work of *justice*" (Alma 42:13). Focusing on Corianton's concern about the "justice of God" in punishing the sinner, Alma emphasizes that God must have justice or he would not exist, providing at least a partial explanation of why God needs to exercise justice on unrepentant sinners and, hopefully, helping Corianton remove misplaced blame, anger, or rationalization.

Following Lehi's statement about the justice of God being destroyed, Lehi launches into a series of hypothetical statements: "If ye shall say there is no law, ye shall also say there is no sin. If ye shall say there is no sin, ye shall also say there is no righteousness. And if there be no righteousness there be no happiness. And if there be no righteousness nor happiness there be no punishment nor misery. And if these things are not there is no God" (2 Nephi 2:13). Lehi's chain of cause and effect can be diagrammed as follows:

No law	→	No sin	→	No righteousness	→	No happiness	→	No punishment or misery	→	No God

This type of extensive cause-and-effect logic appears in the Book of Mormon only in 2 Nephi 2 and Alma 42. Like Lehi, Alma connects law and sin, but before doing so he adds two important elements. This significant expansion of Lehi's teachings brings us back to a phrase discussed previously: "*Repentance* could not come unto men except there were a *punishment*" (Alma 42:16). As though going from repentance to punishment were too great a leap for Corianton (and perhaps some of us), Alma logically walks step-by-step through the connection between repentance and punishment. He states, "How could a man repent except he should sin? How could he sin if there was no law? How could there be a law save there was a punishment?" (Alma 42:17). Alma's connections could be diagrammed as follows:

Repentance requires sin	→	Sin requires law	→	Law requires punishment	→	Repentance requires punishment

Lehi touched on righteousness and happiness before connecting sin to punishment. In contrast, Alma goes directly from sin and law to punishment, perhaps to focus on the justice of God in punishing the sinner. Alma had previously taught that "according to justice, the plan of redemption could not be brought about, only on conditions of repentance of men . . . except it were for these conditions, mercy could not take effect except it should destroy the work of justice" (Alma 42:13). Therefore, the previous diagram could be expanded:

In order to not destroy justice, mercy requires repentance → Repentance requires sin → Sin requires law → Law requires punishment → In order to not destroy justice, mercy requires punishment

Mercy, a vital component in returning to live with God, requires punishment in order to not destroy the work of justice. Why is it just for God to punish sinners? Because without punishment there could be no repentance, and without repentance "mercy could not take effect except it should destroy the work of justice" (Alma 42:13). Justice would be destroyed without punishment, and if this happened, "God would cease to be God" (verse 23). Thus Alma points out that punishing a sinner is not a harsh mechanism; rather, it allows mercy, justice, and God himself to exist.

It is difficult to comprehend why it is that "if there be *no . . . punishment* . . . there is *no God*" (2 Nephi 2:13), but Alma reiterates this point: "The law inflicteth the *punishment; if not* so . . . *God would cease to be God*" (Alma 42:22). How does eliminating punishment eliminate God? Perhaps Corianton struggled to understand this as well. Let us explore this question by focusing on the word *affix* and its use in these two chapters.

The Punishment Which Is Affixed

Webster's 1828 dictionary defines *affix* as "to attach, unite, or connect with, as names affixed to ideas, or ideas affixed to things."[11] *Affix*

---

11   Noah Webster, *American Dictionary of the English Language* (New York: S. Converse, 1828), s.v. "affix," https://webstersdictionary1828.com/Dictionary /affix.

appears only six times in the Book of Mormon:[12] three in 2 Nephi 2 and three in Alma 42. In 2 Nephi 2:10 Lehi says, "Wherefore, *the ends of the law* which the Holy One hath *given*, unto the inflicting of the *punishment which is affixed, which punishment that is affixed* is in opposition to that of *the happiness which is affixed*, to answer the ends of the *atonement*." In other words, *law* is connected to *punishment*, and the *atonement* is connected to *happiness*.[13] Lehi does not explicitly say *who* has affixed law and punishment; Alma perhaps utilizes this ambiguity to allay Corianton's concern. In three separate instances, Alma speaks of *punishment* being *affixed* using the passive voice (as did Lehi):

- "Repentance could not come unto men except there were *a punishment*, which also was eternal as the life of the soul should be, *affixed* opposite to the plan of *happiness*, which was as eternal also as the life of the soul" (Alma 42:16).
- "Now, there was a *punishment affixed* and a just *law given*" (Alma 42:18).
- "But there is *a law given*, and *a punishment affixed*, and a repentance granted" (Alma 42:22).

The idea of punishment passively being affixed may be important to Alma's line of reasoning with Corianton. Corianton struggles to understand how it is just for God to punish the sinner, and Alma follows Lehi in showing that this punishment is connected with the law. The phrase "the punishment" appears only in 2 Nephi 2 and Alma 42, and even more significant are the similarities between the phrases "wherefore, the ends of *the law* which the Holy One has given, unto the *inflicting* of *the punishment*" (2 Nephi 2:10) and "*the law inflicteth the punishment*" (Alma 42:22).[14] While Lehi specifies that the law connected to punishment was given by the Holy One of Israel, Alma omits this detail. Perhaps by not identifying God as the one who

---

12 As well as two other times in all scripture (see Doctrine and Covenants 82:4; 135:7).

13 I am indebted to Sheila Taylor for pointing out this connection.

14 In scripture, the words *inflict* and *punish* appear together only in 2 Corinthians 2:6; 2 Nephi 2:10; Alma 42:22; and Doctrine and Covenants 134:10. *Law, inflict,* and *punish* collocate only in 2 Nephi 2:10 and Alma 42:22.

is (potentially) affixing the punishment, Alma in effect says, "Son, punishments and laws have been put in place. God is not arbitrarily being unfair—it is an inherent part of the system. These things are *affixed*, and if there were no punishment, there would be no God." Alma also points out that while certain laws are in place, one's destiny is not fixed. This brings us to the crucial point of acting and being acted upon, which is also emphasized by both Lehi and Alma.

Acting and Being Acted Upon

Partway through his words to Jacob, Lehi states that "God gave unto man that he should act for himself" (2 Nephi 2:16), but he later adds a caveat: "[Men] have become free forever, knowing good from evil; to act for themselves and not to be acted upon *save it be by the punishment of the law at the great and last day*" (verse 26). While we typically think of humans as being completely free to act, Lehi says there is an exception: the punishment of the law can act on us at the last day.[15]

Alma also makes a statement that could be construed as an instance in which humans are acted upon. He states, "Repentance, mercy claimeth; otherwise, justice claimeth the creature and executeth the law, and *the law inflicteth the punishment*" (Alma 42:22). Mercy and justice both *claim*,[16] which means "to ask or seek to obtain, by virtue of authority, right or supposed right; to challenge as a right; to demand as due."[17] Mercy claims repentance; otherwise justice makes its claim and executes the law, which leads to punishment. But sinners are not consigned to punishment. Alma teaches that "mercy claimeth the penitent, and mercy cometh because of the atonement" (Alma 42:23). Although mercy cannot *rob* justice, because of Jesus Christ it can *claim* those who repent—and repentance is a choice we can make.

---

15 It is interesting to note that in 2 Nephi 2:26 it isn't an individual (God) who acts but another force, "the law," that does the acting (although Alma 42:26 may suggest that it is God who is the controlling force).

16 *Mercy* and *claim* appear together in ten Book of Mormon verses and once in the Doctrine and Covenants but never in the Bible. In Mosiah 15:27 justice is spoken of as having a claim, and in Alma 42:22 justice claims.

17 Webster, *American Dictionary of the English Language*, s.v. "claim."

Ultimately, Lehi points out, we "are free to choose liberty and eternal life, through the great Mediator of all men, or to choose captivity and death, according to the captivity and power of the devil" (2 Nephi 2:27). Alma similarly states that we are free to choose which course we take: "Whosoever will come may come and partake of the waters of life freely; and whosoever will not come the same is not compelled to come; but in the last day it shall be restored unto him according to his deeds" (Alma 42:27).[18] In other words, Alma says, "Corianton, you have been worried about the justice of God in condemning the sinner, but you have misunderstood. God does not condemn sinners. People act for themselves; they are free. It is true that the law condemns sinners, but without punishment there could be no justice, and God would cease to exist. Ultimately, agency eliminates the argument that God is not just—because while the Fall allows the possibility of eternal death, Christ's Atonement grants the possibility of eternal life. It is not God (or your ancestors' decisions) who chooses your destiny. It all depends on your choices. So repent, and let mercy claim you."

Therefore, What?

I can imagine Alma asking Corianton at the end of his words something like this: "I've taught you these things; now, what will you choose to believe? What will you choose to do?" Alma must have wondered, "Will the doctrine I've taught help Corianton change?" We know that Corianton did in fact change. A few years after Corianton's conversation with Alma, we read that there was "great prosperity in the church because of [the diligent heed people] gave unto the word of God, which was declared unto them by Helaman, and Shiblon, and *Corianton*" (Alma 49:30). Corianton did in fact accept his father's invitation to "preach the word unto this people" (Alma 42:31).

Alma's use of Lehi's words to help Corianton reminds me of an oft-quoted statement from Elder Boyd K. Packer: "True doctrine, understood, changes attitudes and behavior. The study of the doctrines of the gospel will improve behavior quicker than a study of behavior will improve behavior. . . . That is why we stress so forcefully the study

---

18 Note again the passive voice: "It shall be restored unto him."

of the doctrines of the gospel."[19] Although Corianton has a behavioral problem, Alma does not spend very much of their conversation discussing behavior. Instead, he stresses gospel doctrine and testifies of truth.

On another occasion, Elder Packer taught:

> Most of the difficult questions we face in the Church right now . . . cannot be answered without some knowledge of the plan as a background.
>
> Alma said . . . : "God gave unto them *commandments, after* having made known unto them the *plan of redemption*" (Alma 12:32; emphasis added). Let me say that again: "God gave unto them commandments, *after* having made known unto them the plan of redemption." Now, let me say it again: "God gave unto them commandments, AFTER having made known unto them the plan of redemption."
>
> . . . If you are trying to give [your students or children] a "why," follow that pattern: "God gave unto them commandments, *after* having made known unto them the plan of redemption."[20]

God's plan of redemption was a core part of Alma's message to Corianton. As Alma spoke to Corianton, he taught doctrines such as Christ's Atonement, justice, mercy, and Resurrection. Alma provides a model of centering teaching not on the specific behavioral issue but rather on the doctrinal backdrop of God's plan for his children to return to his presence.

As described in the previous chapter, Alma was able to help Corianton by expounding on the words of previous prophets, which tells us something about the depth of Alma's scripture study. This same principle is seen in Alma's use of Lehi's words. The textual connections between Alma, Abinadi, and Lehi remind me that Alma must have spent a significant amount of personal time in the scriptures. His careful mining of scriptural text prepared him to know which sections would best help Corianton. We can do likewise as

---

19 Boyd K. Packer, "Little Children," *Ensign*, November 1986, 17.

20 Boyd K. Packer, "The Great Plan of Happiness" (address to religious educators at a symposium on the Doctrine and Covenants and Church history, Brigham Young University, August 10, 1993); emphasis in original.

we deeply study the scriptures, perhaps sometimes with the explicit intent of discerning how certain segments would address concerns others might have.

It is also interesting to identify places where Alma *does not* directly follow Lehi. For example, the words *mercy* and *repentance* each appear eleven times in Alma 42, in contrast to just twice each in 2 Nephi 2.[21] Perhaps part of the reason for this difference lies in the audience. Lehi's son Jacob had different needs than Corianton. Corianton was in a serious spiritual struggle, and Alma felt inspired to focus on both *mercy* and *repentance* in equal measure. The ability to personalize a message is also an important skill for parents and leaders to develop.

In addition, Alma's balanced use of *mercy* and *repentance* may be a helpful model for those assisting people struggling with serious sin. At times it may be tempting to focus only on God's mercy, which could inadvertently send a message that "whatever you do is OK, because God's mercy has you covered." On the other hand, a message solely concentrated on repentance might communicate, "If you don't get your act together, you're in big trouble." When teaching others (and pondering our own lives), we would do well to remember Alma's equal focus on repentance and mercy.

Just as Alma drew on Lehi's words, modern parents and teachers can turn to Alma, Lehi, and other prophets to teach the truths their loved ones need to hear today. These words speak of the power of agency and the sweetness of repentance. We can intertwine our own unique voices to testify to our children, or others who may need to hear it, that God is merciful and that when we choose him, we choose life.

---

21 In addition, the word *merciful* appears one time in Alma 42 and never in 2 Nephi 2.

Chapter 11
Samuel's Nephite Sources

We see him standing on a city wall with arrows whizzing by as he boldly testifies of Christ.[1] Samuel the Lamanite is a unique and powerful prophet in the Book of Mormon. Dennis Largey described him as "one of the most colorful figures in the Book of Mormon," stating that "few readers can forget the image of this fearless servant of God announcing the dramatic signs of Christ's birth and death, crying repentance from the walls of Zarahemla."[2]

The only Lamanite specifically cited by name as being a prophet, Samuel taught doctrine and prophesied to the Nephites in approximately 6 BC. He demonstrated extreme boldness; even after the Nephites "would not suffer that he should enter into the city . . . he went and got upon the wall thereof, and stretched forth his hand and cried with a loud voice, and prophesied unto the people whatsoever things the Lord put into his heart" (Helaman 13:4). Samuel's prophecies were specific and were remembered. For instance, Samuel

---

1   This chapter is a revised version of John Hilton III, Sunny Hendry Hafen, and Jaron Hansen, "Samuel and His Nephite Sources," *BYU Studies Quarterly* 56, no. 3 (2017): 115–39. Used with permission.

2   Dennis L. Largey, "Samuel the Lamanite," in *Book of Mormon Reference Companion*, ed. Dennis L. Largey (Salt Lake City: Deseret Book, 2003), 697.

provided a precise date of the Savior's coming, announcing that "five years more cometh, and behold, then cometh the Son of God" (Helaman 14:2).

His words were taken seriously; even unbelievers carefully monitored his prophecies to see if they would come to pass (see 3 Nephi 1:5). They were so important that the Savior instructed Nephi$_3$ to add their fulfillment to the official scriptural record (see 3 Nephi 23:7–13). Hundreds of years later, Mormon still referred to Samuel's words, indicating that they had been both written and remembered (see Mormon 1:19).

While many areas of Samuel the Lamanite's sermon have been explored, the intertextuality between his words and other scriptural sources has only begun to be unpacked. Quinten Barney identified a series of textual connections between Samuel the Lamanite's words and Christ's teachings in Matthew 23–24, speculating that the parallels between the texts could be attributed to Zenos.[3] As my colleague Shon Hopkin and I have described, Samuel the Lamanite utilizes a series of Old Testament phrases in unique ways.[4]

With respect to Samuel's Nephite sources, John W. Welch identified a key instance in which Samuel appears to reference the words of King Benjamin, as evidenced in table 11.1.[5]

---

3   See Quinten Barney, "Samuel the Lamanite, Christ, and Zenos: A Study of Intertextuality," *Interpreter: A Journal of Latter-day Saint Faith and Scholarship* 18 (2016): 159–70.

4   For example, Samuel the Lamanite uses the common Old Testament phrase "saith the Lord" more than any other Book of Mormon author. See Shon Hopkin and John Hilton III, "Samuel's Reliance on Biblical Language," *Journal of Book of Mormon Studies* 24, no. 1 (2015): 31–52.

5   See John W. Welch, "Textual Consistency," in *Reexploring the Book of Mormon*, ed. John W. Welch (Salt Lake City: Deseret Book; Provo, UT: FARMS, 1992), 21–23. Richard Dilworth Rust also hints at a possible allusion from Samuel to Zenos in *Feasting on the Word: The Literary Testimony of the Book of Mormon* (Salt Lake City: Deseret Book; Provo, UT: FARMS, 1997), 167.

Table 11.1. Samuel referencing King Benjamin

King Benjamin's Words	Samuel's Words
And he shall be called *Jesus Christ, the Son of God, the Father of heaven and of*[6] *earth, the Creator of all things from the beginning*; and his mother shall be called Mary. (Mosiah 3:8)	And also that ye might know of the coming of *Jesus Christ, the Son of God, the Father of heaven and of earth, the Creator of all things from the beginning*; and that ye might know of the signs of his coming, to the intent that ye might believe on his name. (Helaman 14:12)

The length and uniqueness of this connection argue for an intentional connection between the words of Samuel and King Benjamin. In this chapter, I will show that in addition to textual connections with the words of King Benjamin,[7] Samuel's teachings display important relationships with the words of Nephi, Jacob, Alma, Amulek, and Nephi$_2$, all of whom are sources that Samuel could have reasonably accessed.[8] I will discuss textual connections

---

6   The *of* in "of earth" has been omitted in later editions of the Book of Mormon but is present in Royal Skousen, ed., *The Book of Mormon: The Earliest Text* (New Haven, CT: Yale University Press, 2009).

7   Besides the example cited from Welch, consider the following potential textual connection between King Benjamin and Samuel. Benjamin taught, "Wo unto him who knoweth that *he rebelleth against God*! For salvation cometh to none such *except it be through repentance and faith on the Lord Jesus Christ*" (Mosiah 3:12). Speaking to a people who had "*rebelled against* [their] holy *God*" (Helaman 8:25), Samuel echoed Benjamin's words and prophesied, "Nothing can save this people *save it be repentance and faith on the Lord Jesus Christ*" (Helaman 13:6). Outside these two verses, the phrase "repentance and faith on the Lord Jesus Christ" appears only in Alma 37:33.

8   Some might wonder how it is that Samuel, a Lamanite, would have had the words of previous Nephite prophets. Approximately fifty years before Samuel preached in Zarahemla, "all those engravings which were in the possession of Helaman were written and sent forth among the children of men throughout all the land" (Alma 63:12). Such a sending forth of the prophetic word would surely have been made available to the many Lamanites who converted twenty years later (see Helaman 5). Indeed, while we do not have any record of Samuel's conversion, his sermon in Zarahemla was delivered

between Samuel and Nephite prophets by grouping them into two overarching themes that represent key ways Samuel uses the words of Nephite prophets.[9] First, I examine how Samuel uses those words to

---

twenty-five years after the miraculous preaching of Nephi$_2$ and his brother in the land of Nephi. Perhaps Samuel was one of Nephi$_2$'s converts from the prison in the land of Nephi (see Helaman 5:40–50). This possibility is suggested in Largey, "Samuel the Lamanite," 697. If that were the case, one can imagine that Nephi$_2$'s direct lineal connection to previous Book of Mormon recordkeepers would have only enhanced Samuel's access to and interest in these records, as well as the possibility that Samuel would have had ways of learning about the contemporary preaching of Nephi$_2$.

9   A third theme left unexplored in this chapter is how Samuel draws on the words of Nephite prophets in his teachings related to the plan of salvation. For example, Jacob told the Nephites, "*Ye are free to act for yourselves—to choose* the way of everlasting *death* or the way of eternal *life*" (2 Nephi 10:23). Samuel echoes these words, stating, "*Ye are free; ye are permitted to act for yourselves.* . . . [God] hath given unto you that ye might *choose life or death*" (Helaman 14:30–31). The phrase "ye are free" and the word *act* appear together only in these two verses. Across scripture, the words *choose, life,* and *death* appear only in six different verses. The fact that 2 Nephi 10:23 is closely related to 2 Nephi 2:26–27 raises the possibility that Samuel is actually drawing on Lehi's words rather than Jacob's in this instance. Samuel also appears to draw on Alma's teachings on spiritual death. One example of this pattern is found in the phrase "cut off from the presence of the Lord." This phrase appears eleven times in the Book of Mormon, typically in the context of sin leading to a loss of prosperity (see, e.g., 1 Nephi 2:21; 2 Nephi 5:20; Alma 50:20). Samuel and Alma each use this expression in a unique way, equating it with the spiritual death brought by the Fall. Alma says, "*The fall* had brought upon *all mankind a spiritual death as well as a temporal*" (Alma 42:9) and "Thus we see that *all mankind* were *fallen*, and they were in the grasp of justice; yea, the justice of God, which consigned them forever to be *cut off from his presence*" (Alma 42:14; see also verse 11). Samuel teaches, "For *all mankind*, by the *fall* of Adam *being cut off from the presence of the Lord*, are considered as *dead*, both as to things *temporal and to things spiritual*" (Helaman 14:16). In these verses, both Alma and Samuel speak of a universal separation from God by virtue of the Fall. Jacob also employs similar usage (see 2 Nephi 9:6). It is possible that Alma has drawn from Jacob (see also verses 11–12); however, additional textual similarities make it seem as though Alma, not Jacob, is Samuel's source in this instance. Other similar examples of intertextuality between Samuel and Alma are found in Alma 12:32 (compare Helaman 14:18); Alma 42:13, 23 (compare Helaman 14:11, 15, 17–18); Alma 41:3–4 (compare Helaman

directly indict the Nephites. Second, I will show how Samuel takes words regarding various members of the house of Israel and employs them to specifically refer to the Lamanites. Throughout this study, I consider Helaman 13–15 to consist of Samuel's actual words, or at least an approximation of those words as recorded by Nephi₂ or others who heard them. An alternative possibility is explored at the end of the chapter.

Theme 1: Samuel's Use of Nephite Prophecies to Indict the Nephites of His Day

As a Lamanite called to preach to the Nephites, Samuel found himself in a difficult position. While we do not know all the details concerning the relationship between the Nephites and Lamanites at this time, historically the Nephites had looked down on the Lamanites (see Jacob 3:5; Mosiah 10:10–17; Alma 26:23–24). Thus Samuel may have been looking for ways to bolster the rhetorical credibility of his message for an antagonistic audience. By appealing to the words of both ancient and contemporary Nephite prophets and leaders, Samuel strengthened his message and made his warnings even more ominous.

Samuel's use of Nephi to condemn the Nephites

As the eponymous ancestor of the Nephites, Nephi would be a primary person for Samuel to draw on when speaking to those in Zarahemla. Nephi had spoken stern words regarding his descendants and their situation during the time period of Christ's mortal ministry. While Nephi spoke of signs being given of Christ's birth, Samuel provides specific details about those signs (see 2 Nephi 26:3; Helaman 14:1–6, 20–28). Samuel also uses some of the same words as Nephi to describe these events. Prophesying of the signs of Christ's birth, death, and Resurrection, Nephi declared that at the time of their fulfillment, his descendants would "perish because *they cast out the prophets*, and the saints, *and stone them, and slay them*" (2 Nephi

---

14:30–31); and Alma 41:14 (compare Helaman 14:29). While these are interesting connections, this theme is not as pronounced as the other two and therefore is not discussed at length in this chapter.

26:3). Samuel makes it clear that that prophesied day had come.[10] Rather than speak in third person, as did Nephi, Samuel speaks in second person: "Yea, wo unto this people, because of this time which has arrived, that *ye do cast out the prophets*, and do mock them, *and cast stones at them, and do slay them*" (Helaman 13:24). Although Nephi was clearly speaking of the future, Samuel shifts Nephi's words from being about the future to being a time that "has arrived."

Speaking of this same general time period, Nephi had warned, "*The anger of the Lord* **shall be** *kindled against* **them**" (2 Nephi 26:6). Note that Nephi spoke in future tense and in third person in describing a later day and people. Samuel takes Nephi's words and again transforms the tense and directs the words toward his audience, saying, "*The anger of the Lord* **is already** *kindled against* **you**" (Helaman 13:30). This event that Nephi had prophesied has already occurred. Similarly, just as Nephi contemplated the future destruction of his people, stating that it would come because the Nephites "*choose* works of *darkness rather than light*" (2 Nephi 26:10), Samuel takes this phrase and again personalizes it for the Nephites of his day, directly asking them, "How long will ye *choose darkness rather than light*?" (Helaman 13:29).

Thus, in three instances within seven verses, Samuel takes a specific phrase used by Nephi to describe the time period of the Savior's birth and death and informs the Nephites that they are living in the day that Nephi foretold. Each of these connections is significant.[11]

---

10   While the Resurrection was still decades in the future, it was certainly much closer than it had been from Nephi's vantage point centuries earlier. While we do not have a record of prophets being killed during this time period (but see Helaman 13:24), 3 Nephi 7:14 indicates that such things did happen. Thus when Samuel says the time "has arrived," his wording suggests a bit of hyperbole since the time of the birth, death, and Resurrection of Christ had nearly arrived.

11   The exact phrase "cast out the prophets" appears only one time outside these two passages (see 3 Nephi 9:10). The phrase "choose . . . darkness rather than light" does not appear in any other verses in the Latter-day Saint scriptural canon, although the phrase "darkness rather than light" occurs in John 3:19. The phraseology of the "anger of the Lord" being "kindled against [you]" appears twelve times in the Old Testament and once in 2 Nephi 15:25 (which is similar to Isaiah 5:25).

Moreover, these unique phrases from 2 Nephi 26:3–10 cluster in Helaman 13:24–30. These proximal allusions suggest that Samuel is drawing on Nephi's six-hundred-year-old prophetic utterances to craft a forceful statement about the seriousness of the Nephites' present situation.

Samuel appears to use another phrase from Nephi: "All is well." While this might seem like a commonly used phrase, in the Book of Mormon it is surprisingly employed only by Nephi and Samuel.[12] Nephi had warned that Satan would attempt to "pacify [the people], and lull them away into carnal security, that they will say: *All is well* in Zion; yea, Zion prospereth, *all is well*—and thus the devil cheateth their souls. . . . Wo be unto him that crieth: *All is well!*" (2 Nephi 28:21, 25). While Nephi appears to have been specifically talking about latter-day readers (see 2 Nephi 28:1–3), Samuel attributes this same phrase to the Nephites of his day, accusing his listeners of not finding fault with false prophets who come among them and say that "*all is well*" (Helaman 13:28). The not-so-subtle implication to a Nephite audience would seem to be a stern reprimand—they themselves were articulating the very words of the devil that Nephi had warned against.[13]

Samuel's use of Alma and Amulek's preaching to condemn the Nephites

Samuel clearly utilizes words from Alma and Amulek's discourses in Ammonihah to condemn the Nephites. Let us first examine a series of connections between Samuel and Amulek, both of whom warn against the wickedness of their respective audiences and prophesy

---

12 Outside the Book of Mormon, this phrase appears in 2 Samuel 18:28 and 2 Kings 5:22.

13 It had been less than one hundred years since Nehor had preached a similar message to the Nephites by telling them that all men would receive eternal life. The Nephites who listened to Nehor "began to support him and give him money" (Alma 1:5), and Nehor began "to wear very costly apparel" (verse 6). Samuel may be telling the Nephites of his day that they respond to "all is well" messages in the same way: "Ye will give unto [a false prophet] of your gold, and of your silver, and ye will clothe him with costly apparel" (Helaman 13:28).

their destruction if they cast out the righteous. Both prophets accuse their listeners of being a "wicked and perverse generation," a phrase that appears only in these two pericopes.[14]

Amulek told the people of Ammonihah, "*If the time should come that this people should fall into transgression, they would be ripe for destruction. . . .* But it is by *the prayers of the righteous that ye are spared*; now therefore, if ye will *cast out the righteous from among you* then will not the Lord stay his hand" (Alma 10:19, 22). Samuel almost identically mirrors Amulek's words, saying to the inhabitants of Zarahemla, "It is for the *righteous' sake that [Zarahemla] is spared.* But behold, *the time cometh,* saith the Lord, that *when ye shall cast out the righteous from among you, then shall ye be ripe for destruction*" (Helaman 13:14). Both prophets teach that the people are spared because of the righteous who live among them but warn of what will happen when the righteous are cast out. Ominously, where Amulek's words were conditional, Samuel's are not. Amulek said, "*If* the time should come," while Samuel says, "The time cometh"—no *if.* Likewise, Amulek said, "*If* ye will cast out the righteous," but Samuel says, "*When* ye shall cast out the righteous."

Amulek specifically warned the people of Ammonihah that without repentance they would be "*smitten by famine, and by pestilence, and by the sword*" (Alma 10:23). Samuel echoes this warning, telling the people that the Lord had said he would visit them "*with the sword and with famine and with pestilence*" (Helaman 13:9). The clustering of these significant parallels adds credence to the notion that this is intentional intertextuality.[15]

Conceivably, Samuel's words could have been understood by his audience as a direct reminder of the people of Ammonihah's fate. Not only are Samuel's words thematically linked to Amulek's in terms of the prayers of the righteous protecting the people, Samuel also uses specific phrases such as "cast out the righteous" and

---

14 Besides the uniqueness of this specific phrase, the words *wicked, perverse,* and *generation* appear together only in Alma 9:8; 10:17, 25 and Helaman 13:29.

15 The words *sword, famine,* and *pestilence* appear together in only four Book of Mormon verses (see Alma 10:22, 23; Helaman 11:14; 13:19). These phrases do appear together in the Old Testament.

"smitten . . . with the sword and with famine and with pestilence"—phrases that appear rarely or never in other passages of scriptures.[16] Only seventy-five years had passed since the annihilation of the people of Ammonihah; the destruction of a city in one day had likely left a lasting impression on the people. Through his use of Amulek's words, Samuel reminds the Nephites of previous destruction that had been both prophesied and fulfilled. He thus implores the Nephites to learn from the past to change their future.

In addition to employing Amulek's words, Samuel utilizes Alma's rebuke to the people of Ammonihah. In Ammonihah, Alma preached, "*The Lamanites* shall be sent upon you; . . . and ye shall be visited with *utter destruction*; and it shall be according to the *fierce anger* of the Lord" (Alma 9:18). Samuel states that the Lord had said of the Nephites, "I will visit them in my *fierce anger*, and there shall be those of the fourth generation who shall live, *of your enemies*, to behold your *utter destruction*" (Helaman 13:10). These passages share both thematic and textual similarities. Alma warned the Nephites that if they did not repent, their perennial enemy (the Lamanites) would utterly destroy them because of the fierce anger of the Lord. Samuel echoes these themes; moreover, the phrases "utter destruction" and "fierce anger" appear together only in these two verses.[17]

Again, it seems clear that Samuel is using the words of Nephite prophets. Perhaps this is so that his heritage will not detract from his message. In fact, it may be significant that, unlike Alma, Samuel stops short of explicitly naming the Lamanites as those who will cause the Nephites' destruction. By employing the words of Nephite prophets who had taught a similar principle, Samuel may have been

---

16 The phrase "cast out the righteous" appears only in these two verses, and the words *smitten*, *sword*, *famine*, and *pestilence* appear only in two other scriptural passages outside these two (see Jeremiah 21:7; Ezekiel 6:11). In addition, the words *ripe* and *destruction* appear together in only eleven verses of scripture.

17 The phrase "fierce anger" appears eleven times in the Book of Mormon; three of those come from Isaiah quotations (see 2 Nephi 17:4; 23:9, 13), and four are spoken to the people of Ammonihah (see Alma 8:29; 9:12, 18; 10:23). Other verses that use this phrase are Mosiah 12:1; Alma 43:44; and Helaman 11:12.

trying to prevent his listeners from discounting his message as one coming from "the other."[18]

Samuel also appears to borrow some of Amulek's words to the Zoramites.[19] Amulek taught the Zoramites in Antionum, "Now is the time and the *day of your salvation. . . . Therefore, I beseech of you that ye do not procrastinate the day of your repentance until the end*" (Alma 34:31, 33). Samuel similarly speaks of the danger of procrastination; however, rather than providing a warning, he tells the Nephites it is too late for them to change: "But behold, *your days of probation are past*; ye have *procrastinated the day of your salvation until it is everlastingly too late*" (Helaman 13:38).[20]

Samuel thus both shifts and extends Amulek's statement forward into his own time and context. As he had done previously, he takes Amulek's warning plea ("do not procrastinate . . . until the end") and

---

18 Alternatively, it's possible that because most Lamanites were righteous (see Helaman 13:1), Samuel and the Nephites viewed the Gadianton robbers as representing the largest existential threat. Another example of Samuel employing Alma's words of condemnation to the people of Ammonihah may be found in Alma's statement that the Lord "would rather suffer that the Lamanites might destroy all his *people who are called the people of Nephi*, if it were possible that [the Nephites] could fall into sins and transgressions, after having had *so much light and so much knowledge given unto them* of the Lord their God; yea, after having been such a *highly favored people of the Lord*" (Alma 9:19–20). Similarly, Samuel said, "Wo unto this *people who are called the people of Nephi* except they shall repent, when they shall see *all these signs and wonders which shall be showed unto them*; for behold, they have been a *chosen people of the Lord*" (Helaman 15:3). While the phrase matches are not exact, they are thematically similar, and the phrase "called the people of Nephi" appears only in Jacob 1:2; Alma 9:19; Helaman 15:3; and 4 Nephi 1:43.

19 There is some evidence that the mission to the Zoramites had particular significance to the Lamanites. Aminadab appears to refer to the Zoramite mission as he encourages the Lamanites who had come to kill Nephi[2] to repent (see Helaman 5:41; Alma 31:32), and Lamanite action is connected with the Zoramite mission (see Alma 31:1–4; 35:8–10; 43:3–5).

20 The phrase "day of your salvation" is unique to Amulek and Samuel. The phrase "day of salvation" can be found in Isaiah 49:8; Luke 19:9; 2 Corinthians 6:2; 1 Nephi 21:8–9; and Alma 13:21. The word *procrastinate* appears only in Alma 13:27; 34:33, 35; and Helaman 13:38.

renders it past tense and unconditional ("ye have procrastinated . . . until it is . . . too late"). By transforming Amulek's statement, Samuel presents a portentous picture of what is to come for the Nephites.[21]

Samuel's use of Nephi₂'s words to condemn the Nephites

In addition to his reliance on the words of previous Nephite prophets, Samuel also used text similar to that of his contemporary among the Nephites, Nephi₂, whose key recorded prophecies occurred between 23 and 16 BC (see Helaman 7–11).[22] Perhaps more than any other prophet Samuel quotes, Nephi₂ may have been the most familiar to the Nephite people (since he was closest to their time); indeed, those who believed Samuel's words sought Nephi₂ for further teaching and baptism (see Helaman 16:1, 3). Not only were Nephi₂ and Samuel contemporaries in their prophetic missions, but Samuel may have seen direct connections between himself and Nephi₂. As he had done before, Samuel sought to establish credibility for his message specifically by utilizing the words of a Nephite prophet to rebuke the Nephites.

Nephi₂ had chastised the people, saying, "O ye fools, ye uncircumcised of heart, ye *blind*, and *ye stiffnecked people, do ye know how long the Lord your God will suffer you* that ye shall go on in this your way of sin?" (Helaman 9:21). Mirroring those words, Samuel warns, "*Ye stiffnecked people, how long will ye suppose that the Lord will suffer you? Yea, how long will ye suffer yourselves to be led by foolish and blind guides?*" (Helaman 13:29). While some of this may sound like generic language, across all scripture the phrase "ye stiffnecked people"

---

21 This is not to say that Samuel never holds out any hope for the Nephites; on occasion he indicates that destruction may be conditional for the Nephites (e.g., Helaman 14:19).

22 We read that "the seventy and seventh year began in peace; and the church did spread throughout the face of all the land; and the more part of the people, both the Nephites and the Lamanites, did belong to the church; and they did have exceedingly great peace in the land" (Helaman 11:21), which indicates that Nephi₂'s words could have reached the Lamanites. Therefore, it is plausible that Samuel had access to Nephi₂'s teachings.

appears only in these two passages,[23] and in the Book of Mormon the phrases "how long" and "suffer you" also appear together only in these two passages.[24]

Samuel also echoes Nephi$_2$'s words when he rebukes the people for their forgetfulness and pleads with them to repent and hearken to the Lord. Nephi$_2$ had said the following:

> *Ye will not hearken* unto the voice of the good shepherd. . . .
>
> *O, how could you have forgotten your God* in the very day that he has delivered you?
>
> . . . *Ye have set your hearts upon the riche*s and the vain things of this world, for the which ye do *murder*, and plunder, and steal, and bear false witness against your neighbor and *do all manner of iniquity*.
>
> *And for this cause wo shall come unto you* except ye shall repent. For if ye will not repent, behold, *this great city* . . . shall be taken away that ye shall have no place in [it]. (Helaman 7:18, 20–22)

Similarly, Samuel states:

> Behold ye, the people of *this great city*, . . . are cursed because of your riches, . . . because ye have *set your hearts upon them, and have not hearkened* unto the words of him who gave them unto you.
>
> *Ye do not remember the Lord your God in the things with which he hath blessed you, but ye do always remember your riches*; . . . your hearts . . . do swell with great pride, unto . . . *murders*, and *all manner of iniquities*.
>
> *For this cause* hath the Lord *God caused that a curse should come upon the land*. (Helaman 13:21–23)

While none of the matching phrases in these passages are particularly unique in and of themselves, the multiple relationships between these verses demonstrate a possible connection. Approximately twenty years had elapsed since Nephi$_2$ delivered these words from his garden tower. Samuel's use of similar words may be a textual way of indicating that while the Nephites briefly repented (see Helaman

---

23　The phrase "stiffnecked people" is more common, appearing six times in the Old Testament and fourteen times in the Book of Mormon.

24　These phrases also appear together in Matthew 17:17; Mark 9:19; and Luke 9:41.

11), they quickly returned to their former state. Moreover, as he did with Nephi's teachings, Samuel shifts Nephi$_2$'s words forward in time. While Nephi$_2$ had used the future tense when he stated, "Wo shall come unto you except ye repent," Samuel speaks in the past tense, saying that God "hath . . . [already] caused that a curse should come upon the land." The people have had sufficient time to repent; Samuel warns them that a point will come "when it is everlastingly too late" (Helaman 13:38).

Theme 2: Samuel's Use of Phrases about the House of Israel to Refer to the Lamanites

A second way in which Samuel utilizes the words of previous prophets is by employing their words to describe the Lamanites. Throughout Nephite history, Nephite prophets had spoken about various members of the house of Israel, including the Jews, the Nephites, and the Lamanites. Samuel takes words originally spoken about each of these groups and applies them specifically to the Lamanites, typically to show that the Lamanites are more righteous than the Nephites.

Samuel's use of Nephi's words to describe the Lamanites

In describing his people after their separation from the Lamanites, Nephi says they "*did observe to keep the judgments, and the statutes, and the commandments of the Lord according to the law of Moses*" (2 Nephi 5:10). Samuel takes these words (which were originally about Nephites) and applies them in his own context to describe the Lamanites: "I would that ye should behold that the more part of [the Lamanites] . . . *do observe to keep his commandments and his statutes and his judgments according to the law of Moses*" (Helaman 15:5). This lengthy use of nearly identical and unique phraseology[25]

---

[25] The key words *observe, commandments, judgments,* and *statutes,* coupled with the phrase "law of Moses," appear only in these two passages. As described by John W. Welch, connections between the words *statutes, commandments,* and *judgments* appear in 1 Kings 2:3 and likely appeared on the plates of brass. See John W. Welch, "*Statutes, Judgments, Ordinances,* and Commandments," in *Reexploring the Book of Mormon,* ed. John W. Welch (Salt Lake City: Deseret Book; Provo, UT: FARMS, 1992), 62–65. It is possible that

indicates intentional borrowing by Samuel. It seems that Samuel is poetically stating that the Lamanites of his time were just as righteous as Nephi's people were at the time of their separation from Laman and Lemuel. Samuel takes Nephi's words about people in the past and transforms them to describe the Lamanites of his day. The irony of this reversal derives from the fact that while Nephi's people once fled from the Lamanites so that they could safely live the law of Moses (see 2 Nephi 5:4–10), now the Lamanites set the example for the Nephites.[26]

This is not the only time Samuel shifts Nephi's words to make them specifically apply to the Lamanites. In another iteration of this pattern, Samuel applies Nephi's comparison of God to a shepherd specifically to the Lamanites. Nephi had taught that God "*numbereth* his *sheep*, and they know him; and there shall be one fold and one *shepherd*; and he shall feed his *sheep*, and in him they shall find pasture" (1 Nephi 22:25). Samuel makes it clear that the Lamanites too are within God's fold and will "be brought to the true knowledge, which is the knowledge of their Redeemer, and their great and true *shepherd*, and be *numbered* among *his sheep*" (Helaman 15:13).[27] By so doing, perhaps as a way of counteracting Nephite prejudice,

---

Samuel is thinking of other passages, such as Mosiah 6:6; Alma 8:17; 30:3; 58:40; or Helaman 3:20. However, given that the connection in 2 Nephi 5:10 and Helaman 15:5 is reinforced with the inclusion of the law of Moses, it seems Samuel intentionally draws on this particular passage.

26 While Mae Blanch does not discuss aspects of Samuel's intertextuality, she does suggest that Samuel's overall rhetoric regarding the Lamanites may have been "an effort to shame the Nephites into repenting." Mae Blanch, "Samuel the Lamanite," in *Studies in Scripture*, vol. 8, *Alma 30 to Moroni*, ed. Kent P. Jackson (Salt Lake City: Deseret Book, 1988), 121. This example of intertextuality could strengthen Blanch's claim.

27 Although this phraseology may seem common, outside these two verses the words *shepherd*, *number*, and *sheep* appear together only in 3 Nephi 16:3. While there are clear connections between John 10:16; 1 Nephi 22:25; and 3 Nephi 15:17, 21; 16:3, the verses in John and 3 Nephi do not speak of being numbered among the sheep as do 1 Nephi 22:25 and Helaman 15:13. Whereas Brant Gardner sees in these words "certain signs that Joseph was influenced by the New Testament," it is possible that this phrase stems from Nephi or other inspired sources. See Brant A. Gardner, *Second Witness: An-*

Samuel asserts that the gathering Nephi prophesied also applies to the Lamanites. As God's sheep, the Lamanites are here reaffirmed as a chosen people who are heirs to great promises. They are not defined by their past iniquities.

Samuel's use of Jacob's words to describe the Lamanites

Just as Samuel transforms some of Nephi's statements about other nations and applies them to the Lamanites, he does so with Jacob's teachings. Speaking of the Jews, Jacob said, "After they are *driven to and fro*, . . . they shall be *scattered, and smitten*, and hated; nevertheless, *the Lord will be merciful unto them*" (2 Nephi 6:11). Samuel applies these words to the Lamanites, saying, "Notwithstanding they [the Lamanites] shall be *driven to and fro* upon the face of the earth, and be hunted, and shall be *smitten and scattered* abroad, having no place for refuge, *the Lord shall be merciful unto them*" (Helaman 15:12). Samuel utilizes these unique phrases[28] to assert that the Lamanites are not secondary citizens but rather have a special part in God's plan. Their role is like that of the Jews—God's chosen people who still have marvelous promises extended to them. Samuel's words emphasize that the Lamanites too are part of God's covenant people and have the blessings that pertain to that covenant.

Samuel may be utilizing this same approach when he transforms Jacob's words about the descendants of the Nephites into a prophecy about the Lamanites. Jacob had taught, "Our children shall be *restored*, that they may come to that which will give them *the true knowledge of their Redeemer*" (2 Nephi 10:2). Samuel applies Jacob's words[29] to the Lamanites, referring to how many prophets have spoken "concerning the *restoration* of our brethren, the Lamanites, again . . . to *the*

---

alytical and Contextual Commentary on the Book of Mormon* (Salt Lake City: Greg Kofford Books, 2007), 5:208.

28 The phrase "scattered and smitten" appears only in these two verses; the word *driven* combined with the phrase "to and fro" appears only three times outside these two verses (see Job 13:25; Mosiah 17:17; 21:13).

29 It could be argued that Samuel refers to the words of Lehi or Nephi (see 1 Nephi 10:14; 2 Nephi 1:10). However, the phrase "true knowledge" appears only in 2 Nephi 10:2 and Helaman 15:13.

true knowledge, which is the knowledge *of their Redeemer*" (Helaman 15:11, 13). Thus Samuel uses Jacob's phrases to indicate that the Lamanites will receive blessings similar to those of the Nephites.

Several more of Jacob's phrases are later incorporated by Samuel, as illustrated in table 11.2.

Table 11.2. Samuel's use of Jacob's words about the Nephites

Jacob's words	Samuel's words
This people shall keep my commandments, *saith the Lord of Hosts*, or *cursed be the land for their sakes.* . . . I, the Lord, have seen the sorrow, and heard the mourning of the daughters of my people . . . *because of the wickedness and abominations* of their husbands. . . . I shall *visit them with a sore curse*, even unto destruction; for they shall not commit whoredoms, *like unto them of old*. . . . Behold, *ye have done greater iniquities than the Lamanites, our brethren.* (Jacob 2:29, 31, 33, 35)	Wo be unto all the cities which are in the land round about, which are possessed by the Nephites, *because of the wickedness and abominations* which are in them. And behold, a *curse shall come upon the land, saith the Lord of Hosts, because of the peoples' sake* who are upon the land, yea, *because of their wickedness and their abominations.* . . . Yea, wo unto this people, because of this time which has arrived, that ye . . . do all manner of *iniquity* unto them, *even as they did of old time.* . . . *Behold ye are worse than they.* (Helaman 13:16, 17, 24, 26)

There are multiple connection points between these two quotations. Both employ the relatively unique phrase "saith the Lord of Hosts"[30] to warn that "the land" will be "cursed" for the "people's sake because of the wickedness and abominations" of the people. In both cases Samuel and Jacob compare their listeners unfavorably to other nations. Jacob directly compares his Nephite listeners to the Lamanites; however, Samuel compares his listeners to those (presumably Nephites) of an earlier generation. Significantly, Samuel

---

30 This phrase is relatively rare in the Book of Mormon. Not including heavenly messengers or biblical authors quoted in the Book of Mormon, the only figures in the Book of Mormon who use this phrase are Nephi₁, Jacob, and Samuel the Lamanite. Shon Hopkin and John Hilton III discuss this phrase further in "Samuel's Reliance on Biblical Language" (see note 4).

uses Jacob's words to indicate that, as in Jacob's day, the Nephites are currently more wicked than the Lamanites. This message would undoubtedly have been difficult for Nephites to receive, particularly from a Lamanite. Perhaps Samuel felt that by using Jacob's words to deliver this news, he was in a sense shifting the responsibility for his ominous message to previous Nephite prophets.

Samuel's use of Nephi$_2$'s words to describe the Lamanites

When Nephi$_2$ stood on his tower, he specifically stated to his Nephite listeners, "*It shall be better for the Lamanites than for you except ye shall repent*" (Helaman 7:23). Samuel echoes this phrase, stating to the Nephites, "*It shall be better for them [the Lamanites] than for you except ye repent*" (Helaman 15:14). This relatively long phrase is unique in multiple ways. Across scripture, the phrase "it shall be better" appears in these two verses alone, and the words *better*, *except*, and *repent* also exclusively appear together in these two verses. It appears Samuel is specifically using this phrase from a contemporary prophet to emphasize the fact that, owing to Nephite wickedness, the Lamanites will ultimately receive a better result than will the Nephites.

Samuel's use of multiple prophets' words to describe the Lamanites

Perhaps Samuel's most significant instance of intertextuality describing the Lamanites is his use of the teachings of several previous prophets regarding the Lamanites. Unlike the previous examples, in which Samuel applies words that had been spoken about other groups to the Lamanites, in this instance he uses the words of previous prophets regarding the Lamanites. He explicitly refers to prophets (plural), speaking of the "time [that] shall come which hath been spoken of by our *fathers*, and *also by the prophet Zenos*, and *many other prophets*, concerning the restoration of our brethren, the Lamanites, again to the knowledge of the truth" (Helaman 15:11).

Throughout much of Nephite history, prophets had taught that while the Lamanites did not believe in Christ, they were in some respects more righteous than the Nephites, and the Lord would be merciful to them in latter days. This theme is first developed by Jacob, but King Benjamin, Alma, Nephi$_2$, and Samuel all repeat it. Samuel appears to combine unique phrases from each of these prophets, as illustrated in table 11.3.

Table 11.3. Samuel's use of multiple prophetic statements about the future of the Lamanites

Speaker	Quotation
Samuel	The time shall come which hath been spoken of by our fathers, and also by the prophet Zenos, and many other prophets, concerning the restoration of our brethren, the Lamanites, . . . in the latter times the *promises* of the Lord have been *extended to our brethren, the Lamanites*; . . . *the Lord shall be merciful unto them.* . . . And this is according to the prophecy, that *they shall again be brought to the true knowledge.* . . . *For behold had the mighty works been shown unto them which have been shown unto you*, yea, unto them who have *dwindled in unbelief because of the traditions of their fathers*, ye can see of yourselves that they never would again have *dwindled in unbelief.* (Helaman 15:11–13, 15)
Jacob	[God] *will be merciful unto them* [the Lamanites]; and one day they shall become a blessed people. . . . Their *unbelief* and their hatred towards you is *because of the iniquity of their fathers*; wherefore, how much better are you than they, in the sight of your great Creator? (Jacob 3:6–7)
King Benjamin	I say unto you, my sons, were it not for these things, . . . that even our fathers would have *dwindled in unbelief*, and we should have been like unto our brethren, the Lamanites, who know nothing concerning these things, or even do not believe them when they are taught them, *because of the traditions of their fathers.* (Mosiah 1:5)
Alma	*For there are many promises which are extended to the Lamanites*; for it *is because of the traditions of their fathers* that caused them to remain in their state of ignorance; *therefore the Lord will be merciful unto them* and prolong their existence in the land. And at some period of time *they will be brought to believe in his word.* (Alma 9:16–17)

> Nephi₂   For behold, they [the Lamanites] are more righteous than you, for they have not *sinned against that great knowledge which ye have received; therefore the Lord will be merciful unto them*; yea, he will lengthen out their days and increase their seed. (Helaman 7:24)

Samuel explicitly states he is aware of the teachings of previous prophets, and he evidently incorporates the text of multiple prophecies while crafting his own.[31] As he has done with the passages previously described in this study, Samuel uses the words of Nephite prophets to elevate the status of the Lamanites. While Samuel prophesies of the ultimate destruction of the Nephites, he emphasizes the latter-day restoration of the Lamanites. By using the words of Nephite prophets, he perhaps hopes that his listeners will be more receptive than they otherwise would be to words coming from a Lamanite.

Therefore, What?

Samuel the Lamanite has a penchant for quoting from previous Nephite prophets and leaders. His quotations cluster in areas where the Nephites are being indicted and the Lamanites are being praised. Throughout this chapter, I have assumed that Samuel's words in Helaman 13–15 are presented just as he said them, but it is possible that Mormon (or another redactor) reshaped Samuel's discourse to create or enhance these instances of intertextuality. After all, it would be very difficult for a contemporary listener in Zarahemla to precisely record Samuel's words as he spoke from the wall.

There are many theological motivations that might have led Mormon (or another redactor) to create these textual connections. It may be that he wanted to show that the Lord speaks the same

---

31 Because statements about the Lord being merciful to the Lamanites who have dwindled in unbelief appear throughout the Book of Mormon, it is difficult to know which specific prophecies Samuel refers to. However, his statement that "the promises of the Lord have been extended to our brethren, the Lamanites" appears to be directly related to Alma's words to the people of Ammonihah. The words *promise* and *extend* occur only in Alma 9:16, 24; 17:15; and Helaman 15:12. Other concepts, such as the Lord being merciful to the Lamanites, appear in multiple passages.

message to prophets from multiple nations (both Nephite and Lamanite). Perhaps he intended to emphasize the wickedness of the Nephites by creating a striking framework of comparisons, delivered by a Lamanite, that highlight the distinction between the two nations. These are powerful potential metamessages that we could gain by seeing intertextuality at the hands of later prophetic editing.

While Mormon or another redactor certainly could be the source of these connections, let us consider the possibility that they primarily originated with Samuel. Why would Samuel so frequently utilize the same words as his prophetic predecessors? Perhaps he felt the Nephites would be more receptive to the words of their ancestors. Alternatively, it may be Samuel felt insecure in his role as a Lamanite prophet and found strength by using the words of other prophets. Moroni₂ explicitly mentions his concerns regarding his weakness in writing, and Grant Hardy suggests that perhaps this is one reason why Moroni₂ may have borrowed so heavily from other prophets.[32] Perhaps a similar phenomenon occurred with Samuel.

Another intriguing possibility behind Samuel's frequent use of the words of previous prophets lies in a unique phrase used to describe Samuel's prophetic inspiration. In the scriptures there are only three instances in which God puts ideas or words *into* people's hearts; two of these concern Samuel.[33] After Samuel was rejected once by the Nephites, as he was "about to return to his own land . . . , the voice of the Lord came unto him, that he should return again, and *prophesy unto the people whatsoever things should come into his heart. . . .* Therefore he went and got upon the wall thereof, and stretched forth his hand and cried with a loud voice, and *prophesied unto the people whatsoever things the Lord put into his heart.* And he said unto them: Behold, I, Samuel, a Lamanite, do speak *the words of the Lord which he doth put into my heart*" (Helaman 13:2–5).[34]

---

32 See Hardy, *Understanding the Book of Mormon: A Reader's Guide* (New York: Oxford University Press, 2010), 266.

33 See Helaman 13:4–5. The other instance is in Nehemiah 7:5.

34 Christ emphasizes the fact that he was directing Samuel's words (see 3 Nephi 23:9–11).

In conjunction with this statement, Samuel uses the phrase "saith the Lord" more than any Nephite prophet.[35] Perhaps the precise "words" the Lord put into Samuel's heart were the words of previous prophets. While this could have happened simply through inspiration,[36] it is also possible that this came as a result of Samuel's intense study of the scriptures.[37] He can be seen as a role model of the Lord's injunction to "take [no] thought beforehand what ye shall say; but treasure up in your minds continually the words of life, and it shall be given you in the very hour that portion that shall be meted unto every man" (Doctrine and Covenants 84:85). It may be that Samuel had treasured up the prophetic word[38] and thus was able to be inspired to use these and other passages as he spoke to the Nephites. We can see Samuel as an outstanding example of one who followed this direction: "Lift up your voices unto this people; speak the thoughts that I shall put into your hearts, and you shall not be confounded before men; for it shall be given you in the very hour,

---

35 Samuel uses this phrase seventeen times, compared to fourteen instances by Nephi and ten by Jacob. The fact that Samuel employed the phrase more frequently than Nephi is particularly significant, given that Nephi's voice is heard much more frequently in the Book of Mormon than Samuel's.

36 Elder Jeffrey R. Holland has posited that similar scriptural language could be "another evidence that the Holy Ghost can reveal a truth in essentially the same words to more than one person." Jeffrey R. Holland, *Christ and the New Covenant: The Messianic Message of the Book of Mormon* (Salt Lake City: Deseret Book: 1997), 413.

37 This possibility is complicated by the significant probability that the Nephite language changed dramatically between the time of Nephi₁ and Samuel. Although all the engravings that were in Helaman's possession (which would have included the small plates) "were written and sent forth among the children of men throughout all the land" (Alma 63:12), it is not clear whether or how the language would have shifted over time.

38 If this is the case, Samuel's use of previous Nephite prophets' words may help us understand how much access people in the Book of Mormon had to prophetic word. The relatively lengthy allusions that Samuel the Lamanite makes to Nephi₁'s words indicate that at least parts of Nephi₁'s record were available to him. Similar statements could be made about Jacob, Alma, Amulek, and King Benjamin.

yea, in the very moment, what ye shall say" (Doctrine and Covenants 100:5–6).

Samuel is a model for modern-day parents and teachers who strive to be guided by God's Spirit in their teaching efforts. Elder David A. Bednar taught, "We have the obligation to study, treasure up, [and] ponder so that in the very moment we can be given that which is needful, or in the very moment connections will be created . . . that we have never noticed before."[39] Samuel's sermon on the wall of Zarahemla can inspire us to "treasure up in [our] minds continually the words of life" so that "it shall be given [us] in the very hour that portion that shall be meted unto every [person]" (Doctrine and Covenants 84:85).

---

39 "A Discussion with Elder David A. Bednar" (question-and-answer session at an S&I annual training broadcast, August 2, 2011), https://www.Churchof JesusChrist.org/broadcasts/archive/satellite-training-broadcast/2011/08.

Chapter 12

"Expound[ing] All the Scriptures in One": Christ's Use of Nephi's Words

Although Jesus is "the author and finisher of our faith" (Hebrews 12:2), he often uses the words of other authors when teaching. In the New Testament Jesus frequently quoted from the Old Testament;[1] he also quoted from Old Testament prophets when he spoke to the Nephites.[2] Because the premortal Christ spoke to Nephite prophets and Old Testament prophets, we can reasonably expect Christ to quote from both when he appears to Lehi's descendants. But while Christ explicitly mentions Moses, Isaiah, and Malachi as he speaks to the Lehites, the only previous Book of Mormon prophet he refers to by name is Samuel the Lamanite.

At the same time, Christ clearly alludes to the words of Micah, another Old Testament prophet, even though he does not explicitly

---

1   For examples, see Deuteronomy 8:3 (compare Matthew 4:4); Psalm 77:2 (compare Matthew 13:35); and Isaiah 61:1–2 (compare Luke 4:18–19). For a comprehensive examination of how Old Testament passages are used in the New Testament, see G. K. Beale and D. A. Carson, eds., *Commentary on the New Testament Use of the Old Testament* (Grand Rapids, MI: Baker Academic, 2007).

2   During his ministry among the Nephites, Jesus quoted from Old Testament prophets, including Micah (3 Nephi 20:17–19; 21:12–19), Moses (3 Nephi 20:23), Isaiah (3 Nephi 20:32–45; 21:29–22:17), and Malachi (3 Nephi 24–25).

tell us he does so. Could there likewise be textual connections between Christ's words and those of Book of Mormon prophets? Yes! In this chapter we will explore textual connections between the words of Nephi, the son of Lehi, and Jesus Christ as he appeared to the Nephites in 3 Nephi.[3] I will first identify these connections and then analyze them by theme.

Textual Connections between Christ and Nephi

When speaking in 3 Nephi, Jesus Christ makes several potential references to Nephi's words, summarized in table 12.1, which is organized sequentially by Christ's words in 3 Nephi.

Table 12.1. Textual connections between Christ's and Nephi's words[4]

Case #	Christ's words in 3 Nephi	Nephi's words	Allusion	Times exact phrase is used elsewhere in scripture
1	3 Nephi 9:8	2 Nephi 26:5	Depths of the earth . . . prophets . . . saints	0
2	3 Nephi 9:11	2 Nephi 26:3; 28:10	From the ground against them	1 (Doctrine and Covenants 136:36)

---

3   In this chapter I write as though Christ intentionally provided these allusions, perhaps for his Nephite audience or perhaps with an eye toward latter-day readers. It is also possible that Mormon, in his redaction of the Book of Mormon, created these allusions for his modern-day audience. If Mormon is responsible for the connections, it seems plausible that his reasons for doing so could have been the same as those I discuss as potentially being Christ's.

4   Words attributed to Nephi in this table include phrases in which Nephi is quoting the Lord or Jesus Christ.

3	3 Nephi 9:22	2 Nephi 26:24, 25	Laid down my life . . . come unto me [all] ye ends of the earth	0
4	3 Nephi 11:14	1 Nephi 11:33	Slain for the sins of the world	1 (Alma 30:26)
5	3 Nephi 11:40; 18:13	2 Nephi 28:28	Buildeth upon a sandy foundation	0
6	3 Nephi 15:15	2 Nephi 29:12	Other tribes . . . house of Israel . . . led away	0
7	3 Nephi 15:17, 21; 16:3	1 Nephi 22:25	One fold and one shepherd	1 (John 10:16)
8	3 Nephi 16:4	1 Nephi 15:13	Fulness of the Gentiles	2 (Romans 11:25; JS–H 1:41)
9	3 Nephi 16:10, 12; 20:28, 30	1 Nephi 10:14; 13:24; 15:13	Fulness of my gospel	18 (17 in the Doctrine and Covenants and once in JS–H 1:34)
10	3 Nephi 18:6	2 Nephi 32:6	Shall ye . . . observe to do	1 (Deuteronomy 8:1)
11	3 Nephi 18:10	2 Nephi 31:13, 14	Witness unto the Father that ye are willing to	0 (but see Alma 7:15 and Moroni 4:3)

12	3 Nephi 18:19, 21	2 Nephi 32:9	Always pray unto the Father . . . name	0
13	3 Nephi 18:22	2 Nephi 26:28	Not forbid/ none forbidden	1 (Acts 24:23)
14	3 Nephi 18:24; 27:21	2 Nephi 31:12	Which ye have seen me do	0
15	3 Nephi 18:32	2 Nephi 26:26	Cast him out of your synagogues, or . . . worship	0 (but see Alma 32:2, 5, 9, 12; 33:2)
16	3 Nephi 20:23	1 Nephi 22:20	A prophet shall the Lord your God raise up unto you	2 (Acts 3:22; 7:37)
17	3 Nephi 21:6	1 Nephi 15:17	Show . . . his power unto the Gentiles	0
18	3 Nephi 21:9	1 Nephi 14:7	A great and a marvelous work	0
19	3 Nephi 27:14	1 Nephi 11:33	Lifted up upon the cross	2 (Ether 4:1; Moses 7:55)
20	3 Nephi 27:14, 15	2 Nephi 26:24	Draw all men unto	1 (John 12:32)
21	3 Nephi 27:26	2 Nephi 29:11	Books which shall be written . . . world . . . judged	0 (but see Revelation 20:12; Doctrine and Covenants 128:6–7)

These twenty-one connections cluster around four themes: prophecies fulfilled, the sacrament, the Gentiles and the house of Israel, and the gospel of Jesus Christ. In the sections that follow, we will examine these linguistic links.

Theme 1: Prophecies Fulfilled (Cases 1–2, 16)

Two allusions center on prophecies Nephi made concerning events that would happen at the death of Christ. In 2 Nephi 26:3, speaking specifically of his people, Nephi explains that the day of Christ's death will be terrible for the wicked, who will perish "because they cast out *the prophets, and the saints* . . . ; wherefore the cry of *the blood of the saints* shall ascend up to God *from the ground against them*." Nephi also states that "they that kill *the prophets, and the saints, the depths of the earth* shall swallow them up" (verse 5).

As demonstrated in table 12.1, these phrases appear rarely in the rest of scripture; however, they are used repeatedly in 3 Nephi 9, as Nephi's words are fulfilled. While the Lehites sit in darkness, they hear Christ use these same distinct phrases: "The great city Moronihah have I covered with earth . . . that the blood of *the prophets and the saints* shall not come any more unto me against them" (3 Nephi 9:5). In verse 8 the Savior says he caused several cities to be "buried up in *the depths of the earth* . . . that the blood of *the prophets and the saints* should not come any more unto me against them." Christ also explains that he destroyed people so "that *the blood of the prophets and the saints* . . . might not cry unto me *from the ground against them*" (verse 11).

Nephi recorded that "the *fire* of the anger of the Lord" would come against the wicked at the time of Christ's death (2 Nephi 26:6). We see a literal fulfillment of this prophecy as Christ says, "That great city Jacobugath . . . have I caused to be burned with *fire* because of their sins and their wickedness . . . that *the blood of the prophets and the saints* should not come up unto me any more against them" (3 Nephi 9:9).

In addition to prophesying of destruction, Nephi also offers hope to his people. He writes, "*The righteous* . . . shall not perish. But the Son of Righteousness shall appear unto them; and *he shall heal them*, and they shall have peace with him" (2 Nephi 26:8–9). Similarly, after explaining the reasons for the catastrophic destruction,

Christ states, "O all ye that are spared because ye were more *righteous* than they, will ye not now return unto me . . . that *I may heal you?*" (3 Nephi 9:13).[5]

These tightly clustered phrases, combined with their rare use in scripture, indicate intentional allusions. Perhaps by using Nephi's words, Christ reminded the Nephites, as well as modern readers, that this destruction was a fulfillment of prophecy. He may also have been offering hope to the survivors that the peace in Christ, of which Nephi had also prophesied, would be extended to them.

One other textual connection related to fulfilled prophecy concerns a prophecy of Moses, referred to by both Nephi and Jesus Christ. Nephi writes, "And the Lord will surely prepare a way for his people, unto the fulfilling of the *words of Moses*, which he spake, saying: *A prophet shall the Lord your God raise up unto you, like unto me; him shall ye hear in all things whatsoever he shall say unto you. And it shall come to pass that all those who will not hear that prophet shall be cut off from among the people.* And now I, Nephi, declare unto you, that this prophet of whom Moses spake was the Holy One of Israel" (1 Nephi 22:20–21).

Christ utilizes these same words, saying, "Behold, I am he of whom *Moses spake*, saying: *A prophet shall the Lord your God raise up unto you* of your brethren, *like unto me; him shall ye hear in all things whatsoever he shall say unto you. And it shall come to pass that every soul who will not hear that prophet shall be cut off from among the people*" (3 Nephi 20:23).[6] Jesus Christ takes Nephi's words and shifts them forward in time, showing that the prophet referred to by both Moses and Nephi is now speaking to the people.

---

5   Compare also Malachi 4:2; 3 Nephi 25:2.

6   In 1 Nephi 22 and 3 Nephi 20, Moses's words have a stronger textual connection to Acts 3:22–23 than to Deuteronomy 18:18–19. However, the textual relationship between 1 Nephi 22:20–21 and 3 Nephi 20:23 is even tighter. See Brant A. Gardner, *Second Witness: Analytical and Contextual Commentary on the Book of Mormon* (Salt Lake City: Greg Kofford Books, 2007), vols. 1 and 5.

Theme 2: The Sacrament (Cases 10–12, 14)

A key theme in which we see the Savior develop Nephi's words involves a connection between his teachings on the sacrament and Nephi's words about baptism. Table 12.2 illustrates several textual similarities between 2 Nephi 31:13 and 3 Nephi 18:10–11.

Table 12.2. Textual similarities between 2 Nephi 31:13 and 3 Nephi 18:10–11

2 Nephi 31:13	3 Nephi 18:10–11
If ye shall follow the Son, with full purpose of heart, acting no hypocrisy and no deception before God, but with real intent, *repenting of your sins, witnessing unto the Father that ye are willing to* take upon you *the name of Christ, by baptism*—yea, by following your Lord and your Savior down into the water, according to his word, behold, *then shall ye receive the Holy Ghost.*	Blessed are ye for this thing which ye have done, for this is fulfilling my commandments, and this doth *witness unto the Father that ye are willing to* do that which I have commanded you. And this shall ye always do to those who *repent* and are *baptized in my name*; and ye shall do it in remembrance of my blood, which I have shed for you, that ye may *witness unto the Father* that ye do always remember me. And if ye do always remember me *ye shall have my Spirit* to be with you.

Nephi says that we witness that we "are willing to keep [Christ's] commandments" through baptism (2 Nephi 31:10, 14); by doing so, we witness "unto the Father that [we] are willing to take upon [us] the name of Christ" (verse 13). When Christ introduces the sacrament, he likewise states that it witnesses unto the Father a willingness to obey. Christ explicitly connects the ordinance with those who have been baptized in his name. This association, along with the textual connections of *witnessing unto the Father, willingness,* and *obedience,* creates a parallel between the ordinances of baptism and sacrament.

In the modern church setting, we readily see the association between the ordinances of baptism and the sacrament; however, when the sacrament was first initiated, Christ's followers may not have been aware of this relationship. Perhaps in introducing the sacrament, Christ employed language that Nephi had previously used regarding baptism. In doing so, Christ provided textual links to help listeners connect these two ordinances. The presence of other connections surrounding Nephi's words about baptism and Christ's about the sacrament enhances this possibility.

After teaching that baptism is necessary to enter the gate to the path that leads to eternal life (see 2 Nephi 31:17–18), Nephi states, "This is the doctrine of Christ, and there will be no more doctrine given until after he shall manifest himself unto you in the flesh. And when he shall manifest himself unto you in the flesh, *the things which he shall say unto you shall ye observe to do*" (2 Nephi 32:6). Thus Nephi opened up the possibility that Christ would provide additional ordinances when he would later appear. When Christ does manifest himself to the people in the flesh, he institutes the sacrament and echoes Nephi's phraseology: "Behold there shall one be ordained among you, and to him will I give power that he shall break bread and bless it and give it unto the people of my church, unto all those who shall believe and be baptized in my name. And this *shall ye always observe to do*" (3 Nephi 18:5–6). Christ's language may have intentionally echoed Nephi's, not to establish Christ's authority (which was already evident) but to signal a fulfillment of Nephi's words—that Christ was present in person, expanding on the ordinances that Nephi had previously explained.

Nephi states that Christ set the example[7] by being baptized: "It [Christ's baptism] showeth unto the children of men the straitness of the path, and the narrowness of the gate, by which they should enter, *he having set the example before them*" (2 Nephi 31:9). The Savior employs similar language after having instituted the sacrament, saying to his disciples, "And as I have prayed among you even so shall ye pray in my church, among my people who do repent and are baptized in my name. Behold I am the light; *I have set an example*

---

7   The word *example* is rare in scripture as it pertains to Christ (John 13:15; 1 Peter 2:21; and Mormon 7:10 are the only other references). Even more rare are the phrases "set an example" or "set the example," which, when used in conjunction with Christ, occur only in 2 Nephi 31 and 3 Nephi 18.

for you" (3 Nephi 18:16). While there are many ways of interpreting the reference to prayer in this passage, one is that of Christ praying over the sacrament.[8] This interpretation is plausible given that Christ was referring to prayers offered in church, and he had specifically linked such prayers with the sacrament (see 3 Nephi 18:5; compare 3 Nephi 18:16). Just as Nephi specifically says Christ set the example of baptism, Christ says he set an example in the sacrament, further linking those two ordinances.

This principle of Christ setting an example appears a second time. In 3 Nephi 18 Christ says *church* twice—in both cases he is speaking to his disciples and refers to the sacrament. Later, in 3 Nephi 27:21 he again refers to things that should take place in church. Context suggests that Christ was referring to the sacrament when he said, "Ye know the things that ye must do *in my church; for the works which ye have seen me do that shall ye also do; for that which ye have seen me do even that shall ye do.*" Similarly, Nephi recounted, "The voice of the Son came unto me, saying: He that is baptized in my name, to him will the Father give the Holy Ghost, like unto me; wherefore, follow me, and *do the things which ye have seen me do*" (2 Nephi 31:12). Again, this could be interpreted as Christ using Nephi's words to link baptism and the sacrament. It also may have reminded his earlier listeners (and us) that just as we follow Christ's example in being baptized, so too we follow his example in partaking of the sacrament.

Theme 3: Gentiles and the House of Israel (Cases 6–9, 17–18, 21)

Several of the textual connections between Christ and Nephi refer to various branches of the house of Israel, including "a remnant of the house of Israel."[9] Although this might seem like a topic consistently

---

8   Christ had just prayed over the sacrament, and in context he is specifically talking about prayers offered in church. A different possibility is that Christ is referencing his example of prayer in 3 Nephi 17.

9   This phrase appears in only four places in the Book of Mormon (title page; 1 Nephi 19:24; 2 Nephi 28:2; and 3 Nephi 20:10). Variant phrases using the words *remnant* and *Israel* (or *Jacob*) occur much more frequently throughout the Book of Mormon (as well as in the words of Isaiah).

discussed in the Book of Mormon, it is not. Themes regarding the Gentiles, as well as the gathering and scattering of Israel, are frequently mentioned by Nephi and Jacob, but after Jacob they essentially disappear until Christ appears to the Nephites.[10] Thus this overarching connection between Nephi and Christ is not only textual but thematic.

In 1 Nephi 22:25 Nephi taught that Jesus Christ "*gathereth* his children from the *four quarters of the earth*; and he *numbereth his sheep*, and they know him; and *there shall be one fold and one shepherd*." This passage has multiple parallels with Christ's following statement: "I have received a commandment of the Father that I shall go unto them, and that they shall hear my voice, and shall be *numbered among my sheep*, that *there may be one fold and one shepherd*; therefore I go to show myself unto them. . . . *I gather them in from the four quarters of the earth*" (3 Nephi 16:3, 5).[11]

In connection with the latter-day gathering, Nephi frequently spoke of the Gentiles. He wrote, "In the latter days, *when our seed shall have dwindled in unbelief*, . . . shall the fulness of the gospel of the Messiah come unto the Gentiles, and *from the Gentiles unto the remnant of our seed. . . . It* [the fulness of the gospel] *shall come by way of the Gentiles, that the Lord may show his power unto the Gentiles.*" (1 Nephi 15:13, 17).

Several of Nephi's phrases from this passage are restated by Christ as he speaks of the Book of Mormon coming "forth *from the Gentiles, unto your seed which shall dwindle in unbelief* because of iniquity; for thus it behooveth the Father that it [the Book of Mormon] *should come forth from the Gentiles, that he may show forth his power unto the Gentiles*" (3 Nephi 21:5–6).

As shown in the foregoing passages, records play a vital role in the latter-day gathering. This becomes even more apparent when Nephi quotes the Lord as saying, "For behold, I shall speak unto *the*

---

10 See Heather Hardy, "The Double Nature of God's Saving Work: The Plan of Salvation and Salvation History," in *The Things Which My Father Saw: Approaches to Lehi's Dream and Nephi's Vision*, ed. Daniel L. Belnap, Gaye Strathearn, and Stanley A. Johnson (Provo, UT: Religious Studies Center, Brigham Young University; Salt Lake City: Deseret Book, 2011).

11 The phrase "one fold and one shepherd" is also related to John 10:16 (see 3 Nephi 15:17, 21).

Jews and *they shall write it*; and I shall also speak unto the Nephites and *they shall write it*; and I shall also speak unto *the other tribes of the house of Israel*, which I have *led away*, and *they shall write it*; and I shall also speak unto all nations of the earth and *they shall write it*" (2 Nephi 29:12). Thus Nephi writes of his own record as well as that of the Jews and other tribes of Israel.

When personally visiting the Lehites, Christ mentions these same groups along with a reference to records, stating, "Neither at any time hath the Father given me commandment that I should tell unto them [the Jews] concerning *the other tribes of the house of Israel*, whom the Father hath *led away* out of the land" (3 Nephi 15:15). A few verses later the Savior says, "I command you that *ye shall write* these sayings . . . that my people at *Jerusalem* . . . and also of *the other tribes* . . . may be brought to a knowledge of me" (3 Nephi 16:4). At this point Christ continues to develop, both textually and thematically, ideas previously recorded by Nephi, who also emphasizes the role of the Gentiles with regard to the records. Table 12.3 highlights similarities in these two passages.

Table 12.3. Selected phraes from 2 Nephi 30:3–8 and 3 Nephi 16:4–5

2 Nephi 30:3–8	3 Nephi 16:4–5
After the book of which I have spoken shall come forth, and be *written unto the Gentiles*, . . . they shall carry them forth unto *the remnant of our seed*. . . . Wherefore, they shall be restored . . . *to the knowledge of Jesus Christ*. . . . The Jews which are scattered also shall begin to believe in Christ; and they shall begin to *gather* in upon the face of the land. . . . The Lord God shall *commence his work* among all nations . . . to bring about the restoration of *his people upon the earth*.	These sayings which ye shall write shall be kept and shall be *manifested unto the Gentiles*, that through the fulness of the Gentiles, *the remnant of their seed* [the Jews], who shall be scattered forth upon the face of the earth because of their unbelief, may be brought in, or may be brought *to a knowledge of me, their Redeemer*. And then will I *gather* them in from the four quarters of the earth; and then will *I fulfill the covenant* which the Father hath made unto all *the people of the house of Israel*.

Both Christ and Nephi state that after Lehi's seed dwindles in unbelief, a record of their ancestors will come forth to the Lehites through the Gentiles. Nephi further describes the role of the Gentiles in the gathering of Israel, saying that "*through the fulness of the Gentiles . . . in the latter days . . .* shall the *fulness of the gospel* of the Messiah come unto the Gentiles, and from the Gentiles unto *the remnant of our seed*" (1 Nephi 15:13). Christ uses similar language to describe the latter-day spreading of the gospel among the Jews. He states, "*Through the fulness of the Gentiles, the remnant of their* [the people at Jerusalem] *seed . . .* may be brought to a knowledge of me, their Redeemer . . . *in the latter day*" (3 Nephi 16:4, 7).

The gathering of Israel is sometimes referred to as a "marvelous work." Nephi quoted the Lamb of God as saying, "*I will work a great and a marvelous work among the children of men*" (1 Nephi 14:7). These words were echoed by Christ speaking to the Lehites: "For my sake shall the Father *work a work, which shall be a great and a marvelous work among them*" (3 Nephi 21:9).

Additional textual connections between Nephi and Jesus Christ surround the concept of *a marvelous work*. For example, Nephi quoted the Lord as saying that if the Gentiles "*repent and come unto me . . .* I shall proceed to do *a marvelous work among them*, that I may *remember my covenants . . .* , that I may set my hand again the second time to recover *my people, which are of the house of Israel*" (2 Nephi 28:32 –29:1).[12] Christ utilizes identical phrases to describe the Gentiles and the gathering of Israel, saying, "The *Gentiles . . .* may *repent and come unto me . . .* [and] be numbered among *my people*, O *house of Israel . . .* unto the *fulfilling* of the *covenant* which he hath made unto *the people who are of the house of Israel. . . .* For in that day . . . shall the Father work . . . *a marvelous work among them*" (3 Nephi 21:6–7, 9). Thus, both Nephi and Christ testify of the role of the Book of Mormon in inviting the Gentiles to come unto the Savior and discuss it in connection with covenants made to the house of Israel.

In the context of these verses, the Lord's people will be gathered in part because of sacred records. These records also relate to the final gathering that will occur at the Judgment Day. Nephi recorded the

---

12   Note that there is no chapter break in the 1830 edition.

Lord as saying, "For *out of the books which shall be written* I will *judge the world* . . . according to that which is *written*" (2 Nephi 29:11). Similarly, as Christ ended his ministry among the Nephites, he said, "*Out of the books which have been written, and which shall be written, shall this people be judged*" (3 Nephi 27:25). While Nephi spoke only in a future tense of "books which shall be written," Christ looked to the past ("books which have been written") as well as forward. It may be that Christ acknowledges that Nephi's book *has* been written and is part of the canon by which we will be judged.

Theme 4: The Gospel of Jesus Christ (Cases 3–5, 12–15, 19–20)

Noel B. Reynolds points out that the doctrine of Christ, including faith in Christ, repentance, baptism, the gift of the Holy Ghost, enduring to the end, and receiving eternal life, is comprehensively discussed in a unique way in three places in the Book of Mormon: 2 Nephi 31; 3 Nephi 11; and 3 Nephi 27.[13] This thematic coherence demonstrates an important relationship between the words of Nephi and Christ. In addition, several specific textual connections link the Savior's and Nephi's words regarding the gospel of Jesus Christ.

As Christ concluded defining his doctrine in 3 Nephi 11, he declared, "This is my doctrine. . . . Whoso shall declare *more* or *less* than this, and establish it for my doctrine, the same cometh of evil, and is not *built upon my rock*; but he *buildeth upon a sandy foundation*" (3 Nephi 11:39–40). Similarly, after concluding his administration of the sacrament among the Lehites, he said, "Whoso among you shall do *more* or *less* than these [things] are not *built upon my rock*, but are *built upon a sandy foundation*" (3 Nephi 18:13). Note that in both instances, doing *more* or *less* than the things Christ teaches causes us to build on a sandy foundation.

Christ's words expand those of Nephi, who had warned of a people who would say, "We have received, and we need no *more*!" (2 Nephi 28:27). In response to those who wanted *less* than what the Lord would give them, Nephi wrote, "He that is *built upon the rock*

---

13   See Noel B. Reynolds, "The Gospel of Jesus Christ as Taught by the Nephite Prophets," *BYU Studies* 31, no. 3 (1991): 31–50.

receiveth it with gladness; and he that is *built upon a sandy foundation* trembleth lest he shall fall" (verse 28).[14]

Another connection to the gospel of Christ is found in Nephi's teachings regarding baptism. Only Nephi and Jacob[15] teach about baptism specifically in the name of Christ before Christ's visit to the Americas.[16] Nephi writes, "And the Father said: *Repent ye, repent ye, and be baptized in the name of my Beloved Son*. . . . And also, the voice of the Son came unto me, saying: He that is *baptized in my name*, to him will the Father give the *Holy Ghost*, like unto me. . . . He that *endureth to the end*, the same shall be saved" (2 Nephi 31:11–12, 15). As discussed in chapter 5, while teaching the Lehites, Christ frequently talks about the importance of being baptized *in his name*. For example, Christ states, "Whoso *repenteth and is baptized in my name* shall be filled; and if he *endureth to the end*, behold, him will I hold guiltless. . . . Come unto me and be *baptized in my name*, that ye may be sanctified by *the reception of the Holy Ghost*, that ye may stand spotless before me at the last day" (3 Nephi 27:16, 20).

Related to baptism in the name of Christ is the principle of prayer in the name of Christ. Nephi and his nephew Enos are the only prophets who lived before Christ who explicitly mention praying in his name.[17] Moreover, Nephi is the only prophet to speak of praying *to the Father* in the name of Christ. He exhorts, "*Pray*

---

14   Although these passages resemble Matthew 7:24–27, the connections within the Book of Mormon are unique (e.g., the phrase "sandy foundation" appears only in 2 Nephi 28:28 and 3 Nephi 11:40; 18:13).

15   See 2 Nephi 9:23–24.

16   One possible exception is that Alma instructs the people to be "baptized in the name of the Lord" (Mosiah 18:10).

17   Jacob says, "Give thanks unto his holy name" (2 Nephi 9:52); King Benjamin says, "Calling on the name of the Lord daily" (Mosiah 4:11); Alma says to "call on his holy name" (Alma 13:28); and the Nephite army "call[s] on the name of their God" (3 Nephi 4:30). Although similar, these references are different from Nephi's direct instructions to "pray unto the Father in the name of Christ" (2 Nephi 32:9; compare Enos 1:15). While other Book of Mormon prophets teach about prayer, specific teachings about praying in Christ's name are not recorded again until after Christ's postmortal ministry among the Lehites.

always, and not faint; . . . *ye shall pray unto the Father in the name of Christ*" (2 Nephi 32:9; see 2 Nephi 33:12). Praying to the Father in the name of Christ is not explicitly mentioned after Enos until 3 Nephi, when Christ frequently admonishes the people to pray to the Father in his name. For example, he says, "Ye must *always pray unto the Father in my name*" (3 Nephi 18:19).

Another textual connection between the words of Nephi and the Savior that relates to the gospel of Jesus Christ concerns the universality of salvation. Nephi explains that the invitation to come unto Christ is extended to all, saying that Christ "*layeth down his own life. . . .* Wherefore, he commandeth none that they shall not partake of his salvation. . . . He saith: *Come unto me all ye ends of the earth,* buy milk and honey, without money and without price" (2 Nephi 26:24–25).

Similarly, as Christ addressed the Lehites sitting in darkness, he said, "Whoso repenteth and cometh unto me as a little child, him will I receive. . . . For such *I have laid down my life*, and have taken it up again; therefore repent, and *come unto me ye ends of the earth*, and be saved" (3 Nephi 9:22). Perhaps Christ alluded to Nephi's words to remind the Lehites that although they had suffered and were currently shrouded in darkness, these trials could still be turned into a blessing, as Christ does not do "anything save it be for the benefit of the world" (2 Nephi 26:24). He was aware of them, a principle that applies to us in our times of metaphorical darkness.

Nephi taught his people regarding Christ's inclusive nature. He writes, "Doth [Christ] cry unto any, saying: *Depart from me?* Behold, I say unto you, Nay. . . . Behold, hath he commanded any that they should *depart out of the synagogues, or out of the houses of worship?* Behold, I say unto you, Nay" (2 Nephi 26:25–26). Nephi then writes that "all men are privileged the one like unto the other, and *none are forbidden*" (verse 28).

Christ echoes these sentiments when he says, "And ye see that I have commanded that none of you should *go away*" (3 Nephi 18:25) and "Ye shall not *cast him out of your synagogues or your places of worship*" (verse 32). Christ also states, "Ye shall *not forbid any man* from coming unto you when ye shall meet together" (verse 22).

Three additional phrases related to the gospel of Jesus Christ are *slain for the sins of the world*, *lifted up upon the cross*, and *draw all men unto*. In vision Nephi saw Jesus Christ "slain for the sins of the world" (1 Nephi 11:33). The Savior uses these same words when he identifies himself to the Nephites, saying, "Arise and come forth unto me, that ye may thrust your hands into my side, and also that ye may feel the prints of the nails in my hands and in my feet, that ye may know that I . . . have been *slain for the sins of the world*" (3 Nephi 11:14).

In this same vision, Nephi saw the Son of God "lifted up upon the cross" (1 Nephi 11:33), and later, speaking of Christ's sacrifice, he taught that Christ died "that he may *draw all men unto him*" (2 Nephi 26:24). Christ echoes both phrases in 3 Nephi 27:14–15, saying, "And my Father sent me that I might be *lifted up upon the cross*; and after that I had been *lifted up upon the cross*, that I might *draw all men unto me*. . . . And for this cause have I been *lifted up*; therefore, according to the power of the Father *I will draw all men unto me*, that they may be judged according to their works."[18]

By providing these two connections, Christ demonstrates that Nephi's words have been fulfilled. Just as Nephi foretold that Christ would be "lifted up upon the cross and slain for the sins of the world," Christ states that he was "lifted up upon the cross" and "slain for the sins of the world." He reiterates that Nephi was correct—the purpose of the Savior's death was to draw all people to Christ.

Therefore, What?

When the phrases used by both Nephi and Christ are added together, there are approximately 150 words recorded by Nephi that are echoed by Christ.[19] While this is certainly not as many words

---

18 As noted in table 12.1, the phrase "draw all men unto" appears in John 12:32, as does the phrase "lifted up." Yet closer textual matches are found in 1 Nephi 11:33 and 2 Nephi 26:24, as discussed. These two verses, although not closely connected in the Book of Mormon, come together in the words of Christ in 3 Nephi.

19 In addition to the passages discussed in this chapter, there are other textual connections between Nephi and Jesus Christ. For example, at the end of his discussion of Christ's doctrine, Nephi writes, "This is the . . . true doctrine

as Christ quoted from Isaiah or Malachi, it is more than he quotes from Micah or Moses. If in fact Christ is intentionally drawing on Nephi, this could expand our understanding of the extent to which Christ honors the statements of prophets in scripture. The first words he said when he appeared to the Lehites were "Behold, I am Jesus Christ, *whom the prophets* testified shall come into the world" (3 Nephi 11:10), emphasizing his association with the prophets. Indeed, after inviting the people to individually witness the tokens of his Crucifixion, the Savior called forward Nephi₃, the current prophet. Perhaps Christ's allusions to Nephi are another way Christ supports and vindicates prophetic words—by using the exact same language as Nephi did. In the Doctrine and Covenants Christ said, "Whether by mine own voice or by the voice of my servants, *it is the same*" (Doctrine and Covenants 1:38). The precise links between some of Christ's words and those of Nephi could indicate a deeper meaning behind the phrase "it is the same."

The textual connections between Nephi and Christ surrounding baptism and the sacrament make it clear that Christ has set the example for us to follow. In chapter 5 I wrote of how understanding Christ's emphasis on baptism can help us see its importance; the same principle—shown in textual connections between Nephi and Christ surrounding the sacrament—reminds us of the importance of regularly partaking of the sacrament. It is not simply a weekly ritual —in partaking, we are literally following his example. Although it may be tempting to do more (or less) than Christ's clear teachings in 3 Nephi 11 and 18, the Savior and Nephi warn that this is not the right course of action. Instead, we can joyfully focus on doing what Christ *has* taught.

As described above, topics surrounding the Gentiles and gathering Israel are frequently mentioned by Nephi and Jacob but drop out of the record until Christ appears to the Nephites. In other words,

---

of the Father, and of the Son, and of the Holy Ghost" (2 Nephi 31:21). Jesus uses similar phraseology when telling the Lehites that people should be baptized "in the name of the Father, and of the Son, and of the Holy Ghost" (3 Nephi 11:25). Both Nephi and Jesus Christ endorse "the words of Isaiah" (2 Nephi 11:2; 3 Nephi 23:1) and speak of a time when the prophecies of "Isaiah shall be fulfilled" (2 Nephi 25:7; 3 Nephi 16:17).

prophets such as Abinadi, King Benjamin, Mosiah, Alma, Helaman, and Nephi₂ do not appear to have emphasized these topics. Joseph M. Spencer suggests that this change came as Abinadi focused more on personal salvation, whereas Nephi focused more on the salvation of peoples.[20] While both are important topics, my experience suggests that modern readers typically focus on personal application of scripture, akin to the personal applications made by Abinadi, Alma, and others, perhaps because the salvation of peoples seems less relevant to our own lives.

Christ's multiple allusions to Nephi's words regarding the Gentiles and the house of Israel remind us that in addition to the importance of personal salvation, we must also attend to the salvation of groups of peoples. For me, this is a reminder that while we go to church to seek personal spiritual fulfillment, that is not the only reason to attend sacrament meetings. Each Sunday a portion of Israel is literally being gathered; beyond our own personal interests in attending church, we have a part to play in the modern-day gathering. This fact can motivate us to actively participate in church services even at times when they might not feel as personally beneficial as we would hope. In addition, thinking about the importance of groups of people can reframe the way we think about church. Rather than attending church and thinking, "What is in this for me?" we can instead say, "How can I encourage more people to be here, and how can I help those who are here connect with Jesus Christ?"

The textual connections presented in this chapter add meaning to the phrase "Jesus . . . expounded all the scriptures in one" (3 Nephi 23:14) and provide us with increased motivation to truly "feast upon the words of Christ" (2 Nephi 32:3). While speaking to the Lehites, Jesus Christ weaves together words from Isaiah, Malachi, Micah, Moses, Nephi, and others.[21] Robert Millet says, "What a tribute

---

20   See Joseph M. Spencer, *An Other Testament: On Typology* (Salem, OR: Salt Press, 2012), 141–69.

21   Much more work remains to be done in identifying Nephite prophets quoted by Jesus Christ. As one example, consider Jacob's words: "While his arm of mercy is extended towards you in the light of the day, harden not your hearts" (Jacob 6:5). During a time when it was pitch black, Jesus Christ said, "Mine arm of mercy is extended towards you" (3 Nephi 9:14). It is possible

to scripture that the master of scripture should command us to be involved in scripture—that he should quote the scriptures, that he should expound upon them. It also provides a pretty strong recommendation as to how we as we meet together as Latter-day Saints ought to conduct the meetings of the church. We should look for occasions to teach, to quote, to paraphrase holy writ."[22]

One other lesson can be gleaned from the fact that many of the instances I have discussed in this chapter come not directly from Jesus Christ quoting Nephi, but rather from Jesus referring to statements Nephi had made when he (Nephi) was quoting Deity.[23] One possible reason why Christ may have provided these allusions to his Lehite audience was to illustrate the principle that prophets literally speak God's words. By speaking to the Lehites in the exact same language he used with their ancestors some six hundred years previously, Christ could be powerfully illustrating that he "is the same yesterday, today, and forever," speaking "the same words unto one nation like unto another" (2 Nephi 29:8–9). This can motivate us to pay careful attention to the prophetic words—both from ancient scripture and from living prophets, seers, and revelators.

---

that Christ refers to Jacob's words, suggesting to the Lehites that although the light of day has disappeared, Christ's arm of mercy continues to be extended (compare also Mosiah 16:12; Alma 5:33).

22 Robert L. Millet, personal communication, June 16, 2023.

23 The phrases the "depths of the earth," "come unto me ye ends of the earth," "the other tribes of the house of Israel," "witness unto the Father that ye are willing to," "which ye have seen me do," "[work] a great and [a] marvelous work among," and "out of the books which shall be written" are all instances when Jesus is quoting Nephi quoting Deity.

Conclusion

In the introduction of this book, I quoted Elder Neal A. Maxwell as saying, "The [Book of Mormon] is like a vast mansion with gardens, towers, courtyards, and wings. There are rooms yet to be entered, with flaming fireplaces waiting to warm us. The rooms glimpsed so far contain further furnishings and rich detail yet to be savored."[1]

This volume has provided a glimpse into the corner of the room devoted to how individual Book of Mormon voices distinctively speak and harmonize with others. Multiple connections remain to be explored. What unique speaking patterns can we find in the words of the Lord? Do individual speakers quote the Lord in different ways? How are Lehi's words employed throughout the Book of Mormon? As Christ ministers in Bountiful, does he refer to the words of Book of Mormon prophets besides Nephi? What can we learn from studying the voices of minor speakers like Zeniff? Why are there so many connections between the voices of Ammon and Alma?[2] These and

---

1   Neal A. Maxwell, *Not My Will, but Thine* (Salt Lake City: Bookcraft, 1988), 33.

2   Alma and Ammon are the only Book of Mormon speakers to use phrases such as "this is my joy" (Alma 29:9; 26:37), "behold the marvelous light of God" (Mosiah 27:29; Alma 26:3), "his great mercy" (Alma 38:7; 26:20), "sing redeeming love" (Alma 5:9; 26:13), "do not boast" (Alma 38:11;

many other questions can begin to be answered as we carefully examine the Book of Mormon with the lens of unique voices.

More than forty years ago, Noel B. Reynolds wrote: "There are at least two distinct reasons to examine the literary structure of the Book of Mormon. For those who recognize the Book of Mormon as sacred scripture, such a study can enhance their appreciation of its teachings. For others, a literary analysis provides a subtle test of the skeptical hypothesis that this book is a unique product of early nineteenth-century American folk culture."[3] My hope is that our exploration of the voices in the Book of Mormon has both enhanced your appreciation for prophetic teachings and strengthened your testimony that the Book of Mormon is the ancient record Joseph Smith testified it was.

Research about unique phrases and speech patterns in the Book of Mormon, as intellectually interesting as it is, is not an end in itself. For me, reading with the lenses of "Who is speaking?" and "Who is this speaker drawing on?" have helped me find many lessons that I might have otherwise missed. They have illuminated key doctrine and principles, such as the reality of hell and the blessings of baptism. They have motivated me to strive to emulate the Book of Mormon authors who carefully read scripture and have shown me that as I teach others, I should draw on scriptural teachings.

In the introduction I posed two questions to consider in our exploration of the voices in the Book of Mormon: What insights might we gain from examining distinctive voices found in the book? And what meaning can studying unique voices of the past lend to our lives today?

I hope our study of some of the voices in the Book of Mormon—both in how they are unique and in how they harmonize with others—has led you to deeper insights that will enrich your testimony

---

26:11), and "wanderers in a strange land" (Alma 13:23; 26:36). More work is needed to further examine the significance of these textual connections.

3   Noel B. Reynolds, "Nephi's Outline," in *Book of Mormon Authorship: New Light on Ancient Origins*, ed. Noel B. Reynolds, Religious Studies Monograph Series 7 (Provo, UT: FARMS, 1982), 54.

of the Savior and your life. This is the purpose of all scripture—to lead us to Jesus Christ.

Nephi taught that "the Lord God giveth light unto the understanding; for he speaketh unto men according to their language; unto their understanding" (2 Nephi 31:3). Perhaps this is why we have the records of so many different prophets with their own unique stories, focus, and delivery: it allows more ways for the Lord to speak to us in a language we might understand. Perhaps Jacob's anxiety resonates with some, while Alma's care for our souls may be the message others need to hear. There are 149 individuals or groups who are portrayed as speaking in the Book of Mormon. When you close the pages of this book, I hope you will pick up your Book of Mormon and continue the study of these voices. What are they saying? Whom are they saying it to? To what previous words do they allude? And why does it matter?

Throughout this book, at the end of each chapter has been a section called "Therefore, What?" It is a powerful phrase meaning "OK, I understand, so now what?" It implies action on our part, taking a step beyond what's been given. So, now that you have read this entire book, tables and all, I ask, "Therefore, what?" What does it mean to you? What will you do with what you've learned and felt?

You have heard their voices. And now, therefore, what?

Appendix A
Alphabetized List of Speakers

A cry throughout the land of the Jaredites (Ether 14:18)

Aaron

Abinadi

Abinadom

Ahaz

Akish

Alma₁

Alma

Amaleki

Amalekite, an (Alma 21:5–6, 8)

Amalickiah

Amaron

Aminadab

Ammaron

Ammon₁

Ammon₂

Ammon₂ and his brethren

Ammoron

Amulek

Angel (quoted in 2 Nephi 6)

Angel to Alma

Angel to Amulek

Angel to King Benjamin

Angel to Laman₁ and Lemuel

Angel to many people

Angel to Nephi

Angel to Samuel the Lamanite

Angels quoting the Lord

Antionah

Brethren in the land of Zarahemla

Brother of Jared₁

Chemish

Chief judge of Ammonihah

Daughter of Jared₂

Daughters of Ishmael

Devil, the

Disciples

Elders and priests

Enos

Ether

Father, the

Father of Lamoni

Five men sent from the garden of Nephi₂

Gid

Giddianhi

Giddonah

Gideon

Gidgiddoni

Helaman$_2$

Helaman$_3$

Isaiah

Jacob

Jacob (Israel)

Jared$_1$

Jared$_2$

Jarom

Jesus Christ

John the Baptist

Joseph (in Egypt)

Joshua

Judges who belonged to the band of Gadianton

King Anti-Nephi-Lehi

King Benjamin

King Lamoni

King Mosiah

King Noah

King of the Lamanites in Mosiah 20

Korihor

Laban

Lachoneus

Laman$_1$

Laman$_1$ and Lemuel

Laman$_4$

Lamanite guards

Learned, the

Lehi$_1$

Limhi

Lord, the

Lord of the vineyard

Malachi

Many of the people of Ammonihah

Mormon

Moroni$_1$

Moroni$_1$'s soldier

Moroni$_2$

Moses

Multitude at the prison

Multitude listening to King Benjamin

Nephi

Nephi$_2$

Nephi$_2$ and Lehi$_2$

Nephi's brethren

Nephite army that conquers Zemnarihah

Nephites who make a covenant

Nine Nephite disciples

Omni

One foremost among the poor Zoramites

Other Lamanites in Lamoni's house

Others who were at Nephi$_2$'s trial

Pahoran

People, the

People at the garden of Nephi$_2$

People gathered at the burial of Cezoram

People gathered at the judgment seat of Cezoram

People of Alma$_1$

People of Ammonihah

People of King Noah

People of Limhi

People of Moronihah lamenting destruction

People of Mosiah

People of Zarahemla lamenting destruction

People pleading because of the war

People speaking to Gidgiddoni

People who harden their hearts against prophecies

People who reject Samuel the Lamanite's message

People who watched Jesus pray

Priest of King Noah

Priests of King Noah

Prophets who publish good tidings

Samuel the Lamanite

Sariah

Seraph$_1$

Seraph$_2$

Servant (vineyard)

Servant of Helaman$_3$

Servant of King Lamoni

Servants of Amalickiah

Servants of King Lamoni

Servants of the father of Lamoni

Sherem

Some who said the time was past for Christ's birth

Sons of Mosiah

Spies from the Nephite armies

Spirit, the

Stripling soldiers

Syria, Ephraim, and the son of Remaliah

Unidentified person

Unknown prophet

Unknown prophet quoted by Moroni

Unlearned, the

Voice of the people in Alma 27

Wife of Lamoni

Zeezrom

Zeniff

Zenock

Zenos

Zerahemnah

Zeram, Amnor, Manti, and Limher

Zoramites

Appendix B
List of Speakers in Order of Appearance

Moroni$_2$
Nephi
Lehi$_1$
The Lord
Laban
Angel to Laman$_1$ and Lemuel
Laman$_1$ and Lemuel
The Spirit
Sariah
John the Baptist
Angel to Nephi
Jesus Christ
Nephi's brethren
Daughters of Ishmael
Laman$_1$
Zenos
Isaiah
The Father
Unknown prophet

Moses
The devil
Joseph (in Egypt)
Jacob
Angel (quoted in 2 Nephi 6)
Seraph$_1$
Seraph$_2$
Unidentified person
Syria, Ephraim, and the son of Remaliah
Ahaz
The unlearned
The learned
Lord of the vineyard
Servant (vineyard)
Sherem
Enos
Jarom
Omni

Amaron
Chemish
Abinadom
Amaleki
Mormon
King Benjamin
Angel to King Benjamin
Multitude listening to King Benjamin
Limhi
Ammon$_1$
Zeniff
Abinadi
King Noah
People of King Noah
Priests of King Noah
Priest of King Noah
Prophets who publish good tidings

Alma$_1$

People of Alma$_1$

People of Limhi

King of the Lamanites in Mosiah 20

Gideon

King Mosiah

Angel to Alma

Alma

People of Mosiah

Zeram, Amnor, Manti, and Limher

People of Ammonihah

Amulek

Angel to Amulek

Angel to many people

Angels quoting the Lord

Zeezrom

Antionah

Chief judge of Ammonihah

Many of the people of Ammonihah

Ammon$_2$

Servants of King Lamoni

King Lamoni

Servant of King Lamoni

Wife of Lamoni

Other Lamanites in Lamoni's house

Father of Lamoni

An Amalekite (Alma 21:5–6, 8)

Aaron

Servants of the father of Lamoni

King Anti-Nephi-Lehi

Brethren in the land of Zarahemla

Ammon$_2$ and his brethren

Voice of the people in Alma 27

Joshua

Korihor

Giddonah

Zoramites

One foremost among the poor Zoramites

Zenock

Moroni$_1$

Zerahemnah

Moroni$_1$'s soldier

Helaman$_2$

Nephites who make a covenant

Jacob (Israel)

Servants of Amalickiah

Amalickiah

Ammoron

Laman$_4$

Lamanite guards

Stripling soldiers

Gid

Spies from the Nephite armies

Pahoran

Servant of Helaman$_3$

Helaman$_3$

Nephi$_2$ and Lehi$_2$

Multitude at the prison

Aminadab

Nephi$_2$

Judges who belonged to the band of Gadianton

People at the garden of Nephi$_2$

Five men sent from the garden of Nephi$_2$

People gathered at the judgment seat of Cezoram

People gathered at the burial of Cezoram

Others who were at Nephi$_2$'s trial

People pleading because of the war

Samuel the Lamanite

Angel to Samuel the Lamanite

People who reject Samuel the Lamanite's message

People who harden their hearts against prophecies

Some who said the
time was past for
Christ's birth

Giddianhi

Lachoneus

People speaking
to Gidgiddoni

Gidgiddoni

Nephite army that
conquers Zemnarihah

People of Zarahemla
lamenting destruction

People of Moronihah
lamenting destruction

The people

People who watched
Jesus pray

Disciples

Malachi

Nine Nephite disciples

Ammaron

Moroni$_2$

Unknown prophet
quoted by Moroni

Jared$_1$

Brother of Jared$_1$

Daughter of Jared$_2$

Akish

Jared$_2$

A cry throughout the
land of the Jaredites
(Ether 14:18)

Ether

Elders and priests

Appendix C
Speakers Organized from the Greatest to Least Amount of Words

Mormon

Nephi

Alma

Moroni$_2$

Jesus Christ

The Lord

Jacob

Isaiah

Helaman$_2$

Lehi$_1$

King Benjamin

Amulek

Samuel the Lamanite

Moroni$_1$

Abinadi

Lord of the vineyard

Ammon$_2$

Nephi$_2$

Angel to Nephi

Zeniff

The Father

Limhi

King Mosiah

Enos

Amaleki

Angel to King Benjamin

Pahoran

Jarom

Korihor

King Anti-Nephi-Lehi

Alma$_1$

Father of Lamoni

Zenos

King Lamoni

The Spirit

Nephi's brethren

Giddianhi

Brother of Jared$_1$

Helaman$_3$

Gideon

Angel to Alma

Ammoron

Judges who belonged to the band of Gadianton

Multitude listening to King Benjamin

People who harden their hearts against prophecies

People of King Noah

Sherem

People of Ammonihah

Zoramites

Gid

Zeezrom

Ammon$_1$

Aaron

Voice of the people in Alma 27

Elders and priests

Joseph (in Egypt)

Servant (vineyard)

King Noah

Omni

Five men sent from the garden of Nephi$_2$

Angel to many people

Wife of Lamoni

An Amalekite (Alma 21:5–6, 8)

Amaron

Unknown prophet

Jared$_1$

Laman$_1$

Daughter of Jared$_2$

Ammaron

Servants of King Lamoni

Zerahemnah

Chief judge of Ammonihah

Moses

Nephite army that conquers Zemnarihah

Abinadom

Zeram, Amnor, Manti, and Limher

Brethren in the land of Zarahemla

The devil

People at the garden of Nephi$_2$

Angel to Amulek

Antionah

Giddonah

People who watched Jesus pray

Disciples

Sariah

Malachi

Jacob (Israel)

Gidgiddoni

One foremost among the poor Zoramites

Chemish

Nephites who make a covenant

Lamanite guards

Stripling soldiers

Aminadab

Laman$_4$

Others who were at Nephi$_2$'s trial

Angel to Laman$_1$ and Lemuel

People of Moronihah lamenting destruction

Servants of Amalickiah

People who reject Samuel the Lamanite's message

Moroni$_1$'s soldier

People pleading because of the war

Sons of Mosiah

Ether

John the Baptist

People of Limhi

Daughters of Ishmael

Laman$_1$ and Lemuel

Nine Nephite disciples

King of the Lamanites in Mosiah 20

Nephi$_2$ and Lehi$_2$

Many of the people of Ammonihah

Multitude at the prison

Syria, Ephraim, and the son of Remaliah

People of Zarahemla lamenting destruction

Lachoneus

People speaking to Gidgiddoni

Akish

People gathered at the burial of Cezoram

Spies from the Nephite armies

Angels quoting the Lord

Other Lamanites in Lamoni's house

Servants of the father of Lamoni

Some who said the time was past for Christ's birth

Zenock

Angel (quoted in
2 Nephi 6)

People gathered at
the judgment seat
of Cezoram

Jared$_2$

Priests of King Noah

The unlearned

Amalickiah

Priest of King Noah

Seraph$_1$

Seraph$_2$

A cry throughout the
land of the Jaredites
(Ether 14:18)

Ammon$_2$ and
his brethren

People of Mosiah

The learned

Angel to Samuel
the Lamanite

Ahaz

Laban

The people

Joshua

Servant of King
Lamoni

People of Alma$_1$

Servant of Helaman$_3$

Unidentified person

Prophets who pub-
lish good tidings

Unknown prophet
quoted by Moroni

Appendix D (Digital)
Speaker Chronology

Appendix D details who is speaking in any given Book of Mormon passage. You can find this digital appendix at https://johnhiltoniii .com/voicesinthebookofmormon.

Index

Aaron, 158–59
Abinadi, 63–65, 80–81
    influence on Book of Mormon,
        151–53, 168–70
    martyrdom of, 64
    quotations used by, 78–79
    quoted by Mormon, 157–60
    references to Deity, 70–71
    references to names, 71–73
    seemingly insignificant words used
        by, 74–78
    textual connection between Alma
        and, 119, 157, 171–88
    textual connections between Amu-
        lek and Alma and, 153–57
    textual connections between King
        Benjamin and, 160–68
    theologically significant words used
        by, 65–68
    use of term *resurrection*, 54–55
abyss, darkest, 124–25
accountability, 180
acting, and being acted upon, 200–201
affix, 198–99
again, Abinadi's use of term, 76
agency, 200–201, 208n9

Allington, Daniel, 31n18
"All is well," 211
Allred, Philip, 46–47
allusions. *See also* intertextuality
    criteria for determining, 109–12
    potential, in Book of Mormon, 20
Alma 42, textual connections between
    2 Nephi 2 and, 189–203
Alma the Elder
    and Alma's counsel to Corianton,
        186–87
    and Alma's quoting of Abinadi,
        183n18, 186–87
    birth and death years of, 166
    captivity of, 56–58
    as founder of Nephite church, 157
    heeds divine counsel, 62
    and influence of Abinadi, 64,
        151–52, 158–59, 168, 169
Alma the Younger, 41–43, 60–62
    and intertextuality in Book of Mor-
        mon, 20, 115, 116–17, 124–25
    as major speaker in Book of Mor-
        mon, 15, 41
    pattern of asking questions, 58–60

Index

Alma the Younger (*continued*)
    Samuel's use of, to condemn Nephites, 211–15
    seemingly insignificant words used by, 43–46
    similarities in words of Abinadi and, 153–57, 171–88
    textual connection between Abinadi and, 119
    textual connections between Lehi and, 189–203
    theologically significant words used by, 46–58
    word cloud of, 4*f*
Amaleki, 160–61
Aminadab, 214n19
Ammon, 124–25
Ammonihah, 153–57, 212–13
Amulek, 115–16, 153–57, 211–15
Amulon, 56–57, 166n24
and again, Abinadi's use of term, 76
Andersen, Neil L., 101
angel
    appears to Alma the Younger, 42, 49, 56, 58
    and textual connections between King Benjamin and Abinadi, 167–68
angels to the devil, 33
anger of the Lord, 210, 213, 231
Antionum, 214
anxiety, 27
Arnold, Marilyn, 27
Atonement
    Abinadi's teachings on, 66–67
    and Abinadi's use of negatives, 78
    justice satisfied through, 134, 142
    mercy and justice and, 154n9, 183, 195, 199
    and plan of salvation, 195
    textual connections between Jesus and Nephi on, 231
awful guilt, 34
awful monster, 38

Balla, Peter, 107
"bands of death," 154
baptism
    invitations to, 91–92
    of Jesus Christ, 234–35
    Nephites' confusion regarding, 82n13
    textual connections between Jesus and Nephi on, 233–35, 240, 243
baptize, Jesus's use of term, 87–93, 100
"baptized unto repentance," 89–91
Barney, Quinten, 206
Barthes, Roland, 105
Bassist, Larry, 8
Bednar, David A., 23–24, 187, 226
"before the bar of God," 155n10, 179
behavior, role of doctrine in changing, 201–2
behold, 74
beliefs, Alma's direct questions about, 59–60
beloved brethren, 35–36
Benjamin, King
    and intertextuality in Book of Mormon, 115, 116–17, 127
    textual connections between Abinadi and, 160–68
    textual connections between Jacob and, 136–43
    textual connections between Samuel the Lamanite and, 206–7
Benson, Ezra Taft, 128
Bible, intertextuality between Book of Mormon and, 112–14. *See also* New Testament; Old Testament
blood of the saints, 125–26
Blumell, Lincoln, 109
body, Alma's use of term, 50–51
bondage, 56–58, 64
Book of Mormon. *See also* intertextuality; major speakers in the Book of Mormon

alphabetized list of speakers in, 251–53
assigning of unclear voices in, 18–22
authorship of, 23–24
author's study of voices in, 10–13
benefit of unique voices in, 248–49
close exploration of, 22
and gathering of Israel, 236–38
intertextuality and translation of, 122–23, 136
intertextuality between Bible and, 112–14
Jesus Christ as main character of, 83–84
literary analysis of, 248
as multiauthored work, 9–10, 22
possibility of creating distinct voices in, 8–9
proportional use of words in, 17–18
punctuation added to, 58n21
quotations in, 11–14
small plates, 190n4
speaker chronology in, 263
speakers in order of appearance in, 255–57
speakers organized from greatest to least amount of words in, 259–61
unique voices and translation of, 7–8
unique voices and truthfulness of, 3–4
using different lenses in study of, 128
Voices in the Book of Mormon Database, 15–17
wordprints and authorship of, 6–7
brass plates, 118–19, 192–93
brethren, beloved, 35–36
Brown, S. Kent, 41n1
Bushman, Richard, 11–12

Callis, Charles A., 169–70
"Can ye . . . ?," 60

captivity, remembering, 56–58, 64
carnal, 181–82
children, teaching, 150
Church, name of Nephite, 95
Church of Jesus Christ of Latter-day Saints, The, name of, 95–96
clarifying clauses, 76
commandments, 98
condescension of God, 36
connecting clauses, 75–76
content words, 9
Corianton
    Alma's counsel to, 53–54, 56
    and textual connections between Abinadi and Alma, 157, 171–88
    and textual connections between Lehi and Alma, 189–203
covenants, 99
Cowdery, Oliver, 136n7
Cramer, Lew, 161
cross
    "lifted up upon the," 242
    term used by Jacob, 36

darkest abyss, 124–25
"day of your salvation," 214n20
death
    Abinadi's use of term, 66, 68
    "bands of," 154
    of Jesus Christ, 231, 242
    physical and spiritual, 38, 208n9
death and hell, 38, 134
Deity. *See also* God; Jesus Christ; Lord
    Abinadi's and Nephi$_2$'s references to, 70–71
    Jacob's references to, 29–32
    labeling voices of, in Book of Mormon, 18–19
deliverance, 56–58
destroy/destruction
    Abinadi's use of term, 69
    of Ammonihah, 212–13
    Nephi$_2$'s use of term, 69
    of Nephites, 210, 213, 214–15

Index

destroy/destruction (*continued*)
 textual connections between Jesus
 and Nephi on, 231–32
devil
 angels to the, 33
 and Fall, 181–82
 and parallels between Nephi and
 Jacob, 134
 and secret combinations, 147
 yielding to enticings of, 141
devilish, 181–82
divine counsel, heeding, 62
doctrine, role in changing behavior,
 201–2
doctrine of Christ, textual connections
 between Jesus and Nephi on,
 239–42
Dutsch, Dorota M., 8

Emerson, Ralph Waldo, 105
endless torment, 32–33, 134, 140
enduring to the end, 140–41
enticings, 141
example, Jesus Christ as setting,
 234–35, 243
except, 68–69
Eyring, Henry B., 150
Ezias, 72

Fall
 Alma's teachings on plan of salvation and, 53
 spiritual death as effect of, 208n9
 textual connections between Alma
 and Abinadi on, 181–82
 textual connections between Lehi
 and Alma on, 192–95
Farrer, Austin, 22–23
Father, Jesus's use of term, 96–99, 101
Faust, James E., 169–70
Feast of Tabernacles, 113
Fields, Paul, 8
fierce anger, 213
fire and brimstone, 32–33, 134, 140
First Resurrection, 177–78, 179

foundation, 239–40
Frederick, Nicholas J., 120–21

Gadianton robbers, 214n18
Gardner, Brant, 21, 143, 218n27
"garments, that I might rid my,"
 126–27
Gentiles, textual connections between
 Jesus and Nephi on, 235–39,
 243–44
Girdlestone, Robert Baker, 109
God
 Abinadi's and Nephi$_2$'s references
 to, 70–71
 and affixing of punishment,
 199–200
 anger of, 210, 213
 "before the bar of," 155n10, 179
 calling on, in Christ's name, 95
 condescension of, 36
 counseling with, 36–37
 cut off from presence of, 208n9
 Jacob's references to, 29–32
 Jesus's use of term *Father*, 96–99,
 101
 labeling voice of, in Book of Mormon, 18–19
 Nephi versus Jacob's use of term,
 30–32
 opposition and, ceasing to be God,
 195–98
 "pleasing word of," 39
 power of, 146–47
 puts words/ideas into people's
 hearts, 224–26
 quoted by Jesus, 98–99
 remembering, 140
 "saith the Father," 98–99
 as shepherd, 218–19
 trusting, 122–23
 unity of Jesus Christ and, 99, 101,
 153
Godhead, 84. *See also* Deity; God; Jesus
 Christ; Lord
Good Shepherd, 71

gospel of Christ, textual connections
between Jesus and Nephi on,
239–42
great
Abinadi's and Nephi$_2$'s use of term,
76–77
and textual connections between
Lehi and Alma, 190n3
Green, Deidre Nicole, 26, 36
guilt, awful, 34

happiness, 140–41
Hardy, Grant, 9–10, 60–61, 114,
117–18, 124n38, 152, 224
"have no part," 177
Hays, Richard B., 110–11, 124n39,
128
heart, words/ideas put into people's,
224–26
Helam, 56–58
Helaman$_2$, 15, 60–61, 115–16
hell, 37–39, 134
Hilton, John, 6–7
Hilton, Joseph, 30
Holland, Jeffrey R., xiii, 101, 121n34,
225n36
Holy Ghost / Holy Spirit
promptings of, 62
revelations of, 225n36
yielding to enticings of, 141
Holy One of Israel, 29–30
Hopkin, Shon, 10–13, 206
hypothetical statements, 19–20

immortality, putting on, 176
incorruption, putting on, 176
in fine, 135
intertextuality, 105–9, 127–29. *See
also* Abinadi; Alma the Younger;
Jacob; Samuel the Lamanite
allusions based on given criteria,
124–27
between Book of Mormon and
Bible, 112–14

criteria for determining allusions,
109–12, 128
examples of, in Book of Mormon,
114–18
guiding principles for finding allusions, 123–24
identifying, in Book of Mormon,
128–29
textual connections between Jesus
and Nephi, 228–45
textual connections between Lehi
and Alma, 189–203
unique considerations of, in Book
of Mormon, 118–23
Isaiah, 74, 138
Israel/Israelites
and intertextual connections between Old and New Testaments,
107
and Samuel's references to Lamanites, 217–23
textual connections between Jesus
and Nephi on, 235–39, 243–44

Jacob, 25–28, 39–40
cases of textual echoes from,
132–48
distinctive phrases of, 32–37
intertextuality between Bible and,
112–14
and intertextuality in Book of Mormon, 126–27
references to Deity, 29–32
Samuel's use of, to describe Lamanites, 219–21
and textual connections between
Lehi and Alma, 189–203
textual legacy of, 131, 149–50
unique phrases of, 37–39
use of term *spirit*, 51
words used by, 4f, 27–29
Jesus Christ
Abinadi's and Nephi$_2$'s references
to, 70–71
and Abinadi's use of negatives, 78

Jesus Christ (*continued*)
   baptism in name of, 240
   baptism of, 234–35
   coming unto, 241
   connection between *baptize* and, 91
   death of, 231, 242
   and intertextuality in Book of Mormon, 125–26
   Jacob's references to, 29–32
   and Lord's speaking patterns, 84–86
   as main character of Book of Mormon, 83–84
   Moses's prophecy concerning, 232
   name of, 142, 240–41
   praying in name of, 240–41
   quotes from Old Testament, 227–28
   Resurrection of, 179
   salvation and redemption through, 62, 67
   Samuel the Lamanite prophesies of coming of, 205–6
   as shepherd, 236
   signs of birth, death, and Resurrection of, 209–10
   as source of power of resurrection, 35
   speaking of, 100–101
   textual connections between Nephi and, 228–45
   unity of God and, 99, 101, 153
   use of term *baptize*, 87–93, 100
   use of term *Father*, 96–99, 101
   use of term *name*, 93–96, 100
   voice of, in Book of Mormon, 18–19, 83–84, 99–102
   word cloud of, 5f
Jews. *See* Israel/Israelites
Johnson, Jana, 10–13
judgment. *See also* punish/punishment
   Alma and Amulek quote Abinadi's teachings on, 154–55
   Mormon quotes Abinadi's teachings on, 159–60
   and resurrection, 145–46, 154–55, 179–80
   similarities between Alma's and Abinadi's teachings on, 179–82
   textual connections between Alma and Abinadi on, 174–75
   textual connections between Jesus and Nephi on, 238–39
   and textual connections between Lehi and Alma, 191
justice, 134, 142, 154n9, 183, 185, 191, 195, 197–99, 200. *See also* judgment; punish/punishment

Keller, Roger, 9
Korihor, 49, 194
Kristeva, Julia, 106

Lamanites, 217–23
Lamoni, King, father of, 158
Largey, Dennis, 205
last day, standing as testimony at, 174–75
law, punishment as affixed to, 198–200
law of Moses, 67, 74
law of witnesses, 136
Lee, Harold B., 187
Lehi, 189–203
"lifted up upon the cross," 242
"light and the life of the world," 159n15
"light of God, marvelous," 124–25
Limhi, 166n24
log-likelihood (LL), 31–32, 44n3
Lord. *See also* Deity; God; Jesus Christ
   Abinadi's quoting of, 79
   anger of, 210, 213, 231
   Nephi versus Jacob's use of term, 30–32
   "saith the Lord," 225
   "saith the Lord of Hosts," 220
   speaking patterns of, 84–86
Lord of Hosts, 220

major speakers in the Book of Mormon, 14–15
  use of questions, 59*t*
  use of term *baptize*, 87–88*t*
  use of term *Father*, 97*t*
  use of term *name*, 94*t*
  use of term *plan*, 52*t*
  use of term *resurrection*, 55*t*
  use of terms *now* and *yea*, 44–45*t*
  use of term *soul(s)*, 47–48*t*
manna, 107
"marvelous light of God," 124–25
"marvelous work," 238
Maxwell, Neal A., xiii–xiv, 247
McKay, David O., 106
mercy, 154n9, 183, 195, 197–99, 200, 203, 221–23. *See also* judgment; punish/punishment
Meribah, 113
merism, 135
Messiah, name of, 142. *See also* Jesus Christ
Millet, Robert, 244–45
miracles, 146–47
misery, 191
missionary efforts, future impact of, 64, 151–52, 158–59, 168, 169–70
monster, awful, 38
more or less, 239
Mormon, 11–12, 15, 157–60
Moroni$_1$, 10n15, 117–18, 143–48
Moroni$_2$, 224
mortality, 194–95
Moses, 74, 232
Mosiah, sons of, 159n14
Mulekites, 143
"My soul delighteth," 50

name(s)
  Abinadi's and Nephi$_2$'s references to, 71–73
  baptism in Christ's, 240
  Jesus's use of term, 93–96, 100
  Jesus's use of term *baptize* and, 88–89

of Messiah, 142
  prayer in Christ's, 240–41
natural man, 141
negatives, Abinadi's and Nephi$_2$'s use of, 77–78
Nehor, 211n13
Nelson, Russell M., 62, 96n23, 128
Nephi, land of, 160–61
Nephi$_1$
  accuracy of record of, 13
  as major speaker in Book of Mormon, 15
  phrases unique to, 50
  Samuel's use of, to condemn Nephites, 209–11
  Samuel's use of, to describe Lamanites, 217–19
  textual connections between Jacob and, 132–36
  textual connections between Jesus and, 228–45
  use of terms *Lord* and *God*, 30–32
  words of Alma versus, 45n4
Nephi$_2$, 63, 64–65, 80–81
  quotations used by, 78–79
  references to Deity, 70–71
  references to names, 71–73
  Samuel's use of, to condemn Nephites, 215–17
  Samuel's use of, to describe Lamanites, 221
  Samuel the Lamanite as possible convert of, 208n8
  seemingly insignificant words used by, 74–78
  theologically significant words used by, 65–66*t*, 68–70
Nephite language, 225n37
Nephite prophets, Samuel's use of, to describe Lamanites, 221–23
Nephites. *See also* Samuel the Lamanite
  confusion of, regarding baptism, 82n13
  future destruction of, 210, 213, 214–15

Nephites (*continued*)
  unification of Mulekites and, 143
New Testament
  intertextual connections between
    Old Testament and, 106–8, 111
  intertextual parallels between Book
    of Mormon and, 120–22
  Jesus's use of term *baptize* in, 92–93
Nibley, Hugh, 22
Noah, King, 64, 73, 151–52
no part, 177
now, 43–46

O, Abinadi's and Nephi₂'s use of term,
    77
Oaks, Dallin H., xiii n6
obedience, 233
Old Testament
  intertextual connections between
    New Testament and, 106–8, 111
  Jesus Christ quotes from, 227–28
  as source for phrases of Samuel the
    Lamanite, 206
opposition, textual connections between
    Lehi and Alma on, 195–98

Packer, Boyd K., xiii, 201–2
paradise of God, 148
parallelomania, 109–10
Paul, 107–8, 111, 127
pierce, 27–28
plan
  term used by Alma, 51–54
  textual connections between Lehi's
    and Alma's use of term, 190n3
plan of salvation / plan of redemption
  Alma's teachings on, 51–54, 61
  Mormon quotes Abinadi's teachings
    on, 158
  and resurrection, 156
  similarities between Alma's and
    Abinadi's teachings on, 182,
    183–85
  and textual connections between
    Lehi and Alma, 190n3, 195, 202

and textual connections between
    Samuel and Nephite prophets,
    208n9
Platt, Jennifer Brinkerhoff, 10–13
pleasing bar of God, 39, 117, 148
pleasing word of God, 39, 40
poor, 145. *See also* riches
power of the resurrection, 35
prayer(s)
  in Jesus's name, 95
  and Jesus's use of term *Father*, 98
  sacrament, 234–35
"prepared from the foundation of the
    world," 183–84
pride, 133–34
promptings, spiritual, 62
prophetic counsel, heeding, 62, 245
prophetic fulfillment, textual connec-
    tions between Jesus and Nephi
    on, 231–32
prophets
  cast out, 210
  Samuel's use of, to describe Lama-
    nites, 221–23
proportional use of words, 17–18
Psalm 95, 112–14
punctuation, added to Book of Mor-
    mon, 58n21
punish/punishment, 185, 191, 194,
    195, 197–200, 201. *See also*
    judgment; justice

questions, Alma's pattern of asking,
    58–60
quotations
  in Book of Mormon, 11–14
  used by Abinadi and Nephi₂, 78–79

Rasband, Ronald A., 101
recordkeeping, 60–61, 62, 236–38
redemption, 61–62, 66, 68, 183–84.
    See also plan of salvation / plan
    of redemption
remembrance, 56–58, 140
repentance

Abinadi calls Nephites to, 64
"baptized unto," 89–91
and dying in sins, 148
of Gentiles, 238
intense phrasing and stirring people
up to, 34
Nephi$_2$'s use of term, 68–69
and parallels between Jacob and
Benjamin, 139–41
and punishment as affixed, 199
textual connections between Lehi
and Alma on, 195, 197, 200,
203
and textual connections between
Samuel and Amulek, 214–15
restoration, Alma's and Abinadi's teachings on, 180–81, 184–85
resurrection
and Abinadi's use of negatives, 78
Abinadi's use of term, 66, 67, 74
Alma's allusions to statements on,
20
Alma's use of term, 50–51, 54–56
of Christ, 179
and judgment, 145–46, 154–55,
179–80
and plan of salvation, 156
"power of the," 35
similarities between Alma's and
Abinadi's teachings on, 184
textual connections between Alma
and Abinadi on, 176, 177–79
and textual connections between
Samuel and Nephi, 209–10
Reynolds, Noel B., 119n32, 239, 248
riches, 133–34, 145
rock, building foundation on, 239–40
Roper, Matt, 8

sacrament, 233–35, 243
sacrifice, 150
saints, blood of the, 125–26
"saith the Father," 98–99
"saith the Lord" / "saith the Lord of
Hosts," 220, 225

salvation. *See also* plan of salvation /
plan of redemption
Abinadi's use of term, 66, 67
"day of your," 214n20
textual connections between Alma
and Abinadi on, 175, 183–84
textual connections between Jesus
and Nephi on, 241, 244
Samuel the Lamanite, 205–9, 223–26
applies words spoken about Israel to
Lamanites, 217–23
Old Testament phrases used by, 206
textual connections between King
Benjamin and, 206–7
textual connections between Nephite prophets and, 207–17
sandy foundation, 239–40
Satan. *See* devil
scripture
finding answers in, 187–88, 202–3
Jesus expounds upon, 244–45
studying and treasuring up, 226
2 Nephi, distinctive phrases of Jacob
in, 32–37
2 Nephi 2, textual connections between
Alma 42 and, 189–203
2 Nephi 9
Benjamin's allusions to, 136–43
Nephi's allusions to, 132–36
2 Nephi 28, and Jacob's textual legacy,
132–36
secret combinations, 147, 214n18
sensual, 181–82
shame, 36
shepherd
God as, 218–19
Jesus Christ as, 236
sins
dying in, 148
and judgment, 174–75
Skousen, Royal, 38n33, 39n34, 134n5
"slain for the sins of the world," 242
small plates, 190n4
Smith, Joseph, 9, 22, 23–24, 136n7
sons of Mosiah, 159n14

Sorenson, John L., 160
soul(s), 47–51
Spencer, Joseph M., 120–21, 244
spirits, 50–51
spiritual death, 38, 208n9
spiritual promptings, 62
state, 46–47
"statements that may not have been said," 20–22
stylometry, 5–9
suicide, 101

Tanner, John S., 26–27, 28, 149
teeth, gnashing of, 176
testify, 70
testimony, standing as, at last day, 174–75
"that I might rid my garments," 126–27
3 Nephi 11, 88
Thomas, Catherine, 113
Thucydides, 13
tidings, 175
torment, endless, 32–33, 134, 140
trust, in God, 122–23

Uchtdorf, Dieter F., 106
Unabomber, 5–6
unity, of God and Jesus Christ, 99, 101, 153

verily, 86
Voices in the Book of Mormon Database, 15–17, 30

Warner, C. Terry, 26
wealth, 133–34, 145
Welch, John W., 10, 29, 115n26, 116–17, 143, 206
welfare of others' souls, 49–50
white, Moroni's and Jacob's use of term, 145
witnesses, law of, 136
wo, 69, 135, 140
word clouds, 4–5

word of God, "pleasing," 39
wordprints, 5–7
Wright, Randal, 10–13

yea, 43–46
yielding, 141

Zarahemla, 160–61. *See also* Samuel the Lamanite
Zedekiah, 72–73
Zeezrom, 115, 116, 153, 156–57
Zoramites, 214

About the Author

John Hilton III is a professor of religious education at Brigham Young University. He has a master's degree from Harvard and a PhD from Brigham Young University, both in education. John has published several books, including *Considering the Cross: How Calvary Connects Us with Christ*. He is also the author of the video course and podcast *Seeking Jesus*. John and his wife, Lani, have six children. John loves teaching, reading, spending time with his family, doing humanitarian work, snowboarding, and practicing magic tricks.